The Diplomacy of Detente
THE KISSINGER ERA

The Diplomacy of Detente
THE KISSINGER ERA

Coral Bell

St. Martin's Press
NEW YORK

© Coral Bell 1977

All rights reserved. For information, write:
St. Martin's Press, Inc., 175 Fifth Avenue, New York, N.Y. 10010
Printed in Great Britain
Library of Congress Catalog Card Number: 77-82634
ISBN: 0-312-21122-8
First published in the United States of America in 1977

LIBRARY
The University of Texas
At San Antonio

Contents

	Foreword	vii
CHAPTER 1	The Nature and Provenance of Detente	1
CHAPTER 2	Kissinger: The Policy-Maker as Theorist	20
CHAPTER 3	Kissinger: The Theorist as Policy-Maker	37
CHAPTER 4	Strategic Doctrine and Arms Control: The Nature of Stability	54
CHAPTER 5	The Middle East War: Some Rather Loud Signalling	80
CHAPTER 6	Europe: Security and Identity	98
CHAPTER 7	South East Asia: A Means of Disengagement	120
CHAPTER 8	Cyprus: The Scope for Local Intransigence	138
CHAPTER 9	Portugal and Southern Africa: Setback and Rebound	156
CHAPTER 10	Australia: The Range of Middle-Power Manoeuvre	184
CHAPTER 11	The Enemies and Sceptics of Detente	201
CHAPTER 12	A Balance of Ambivalences	223
	Notes	251
	Bibliography	269
	Index	271

Foreword

Most of the books about detente are concerned to analyse American–Soviet relations, especially their impact on German and East European affairs and on arms control. A few have considered the American detente with China, and its impact on Japan. This book differs from both groups: it is a first tentative effort to put together an account of detente as an American foreign policy concept deployed in relationships with both China and the Soviet Union: that is, to see detente as a diplomatic strategy for a triangular power balance.

It is essentially focused on the policies of Dr Kissinger from 1969 to 1977, but with a brief sketch in the first chapter of those strands in the evolution of detente before 1969 that seemed to me to influence events after that date, and a few reflections on the early weeks of the Carter administration. I am very conscious that there is a great deal more to be written about American policy-making in this field in the 1963–8 period, and about developments in the European allies of the U.S.A. I am also apologetically conscious that only my fellow-Australians will think it warranted to include a chapter on Australian policy in a study of detente diplomacy, but one of my objectives has been to illustrate how widespread the fringe-effects of detente have been, and policy processes in Canberra seemed to provide a case study of more than Australian interest.

I have dealt with the German *Ostpolitik* only occasionally and incidentally, not from any lack of consciousness of its vital importance to the American policy of detente, but because it is the one aspect of this entire confluence of policies that already has quite a substantial literature of its own. For the same sort of reason I have touched only lightly on arms control. There are already several excellent studies of SALT, and I therefore felt it justifiable to look rather at less explored aspects of the way in which detente has influenced the conduct of international politics. In particular I have been interested in its influence on crisis-management in areas where its effect has not as yet been much considered, such as Cyprus, or in which its long-term influence has been much argued over, such as the Middle East.

This is necessarily an interim and partial account of a very complex historical process, whose ultimate interpretation will require longer and later books. They cannot be written yet because the documents are not yet available, the memoirs are not yet written, and many of the policy-makers are still busy making policy. Thus one can at the moment put together only a 'trial balance' of the debits and credits of detente as a diplomatic strategy. The draft of this book was completed during the early months of 1977, when it seemed that the Republican administrations of the previous eight years were due for a first reassessment, as the new policy-makers started to make their foreign-policy choices. Only time can prove how well the decisions of 1969–77 served the nation and the general peace. I believe that history's verdict on detente, the central diplomatic strategy of that time, will redress any damage done to it during the 1976 U.S. electoral debate.

Aside from published sources, the material in this book is derived mostly from interviews in Washington and London. My thanks are particularly due to the Woodrow Wilson International Center for Scholars in Washington, the Royal Institute of International Affairs and the International Institute for Strategic Studies in London, and the Australian National University in Canberra, for much kind help, and to the British Committee on International Theory, whose members listened patiently to many of these chapters in draft, and supplied comment from their great knowledge and experience. The deficiencies and misinterpretations that remain are entirely my own.

Coral Bell
June 1977

CHAPTER 1

The Nature and Provenance of Detente

Who gained by detente? To construct an answer to that question one must look at the meanings or functions of detente as they appeared to the policy-makers who used the concept. And since this book is concerned primarily with American policy, it is appropriate to start with an American definition: detente is a mode of management of adversary power. The phrase is adapted from a statement of Dr Kissinger's,[1] but it seems to me one that might be used in moments of candour by the other two main groups of policy-makers with whom we shall be concerned, the Soviet and Chinese leaderships. Arguments will be advanced in due course to sustain the proposition that the management of adversary power has been the main preoccupation of those who determine the nature of the policy, not only in Washington, Moscow and Peking, but in the other capitals that have used or responded to it.

The power of one's adversaries, or potential adversaries, and the modes of living with or offsetting that power at endurable cost and risk to one's own society are, of course, the necessary constant preoccupations of foreign offices and defence departments everywhere. Looking at the post-war period as a whole, one may say that for most of the quarter-century after 1945, the dominant mode or strategy of managing adversary relations in the central balance was cold war. Since 1969 it has been detente. The difference between the two is that detente supposes a conscious and deliberate *reduction* of tensions in the central balance (or in a local balance, as in the South African area of the concept) whereas cold war assumes a conscious *maintenance* of tensions at a relatively high level. The choice of a level of tension in relations with the chief adversary powers (or indeed in other relationships) is not, of course, wholly a matter of detached intellectual calculation for the dominant policy-maker. If it takes two to make a quarrel, it also takes two (or in this case, I shall presently argue, three or more) to maintain a detente. But comparing Dr Kissinger, as the intellectual strategist of the detente, with Mr Dulles, as the intellectual strategist of the fully developed Cold War, one is struck by the fact that moral feeling is in both cases as important as intellectual calculation in the formulation of policy.

Other people than the policy-makers we have so far been considering have had notions of detente, of course, and their concepts in many cases have been at odds with the way I have defined it. Indeed, detente has been a widely misunderstood idea, and that proved to be its major political weakness. But the misunderstandings were not surprising, since the word until recently was only to be found in the dusty traditional vocabulary of the diplomatic historian,[2] and some acquaintance with recent diplomatic history is necessary for an understanding of its evolution and limitations. 'A high-falutin' word,' Mr George Wallace complained during the 1976 U.S. presidential primaries, 'why don't they just say gettin' together?' Most people would probably be with him in the assumption that 'gettin' together' – the increased frequency of summit meetings between East and West – was the main sign of detente. But that phenomenon is related to the actuality of detente the way the whistle of a train is related to the locomotive itself. It may be how people are alerted to what is passing, but it does not tell one much about the weight or direction of the traffic.

Words are political acts for high policy-makers, and ambiguities are among their necessary weapons. So one should not expect academic precision about the nature of detente from all of those who use the concept. In particular, Chinese official spokesmen do not employ the word for the change in their own relationship with the United States; they reserve it for the

Soviet–American relationship, and usually attack it even more fiercely than right-wing American analysts as a Soviet trick under whose cover the Russians are plotting world hegemony. Nevertheless, since there is no other word that conveys the required meaning of reduction of tensions, we must continue to use it to describe the change in relations between Washington and Peking after 1969, as well as the change in relations between Washington and Moscow. In fact, on the literal meaning (reduction of tension), the detente with China was a more notable achievement than the detente with the Soviet Union, in the simple sense that the level of tension with China had been far higher in the previous seven years than that with the Soviet Union. The parallelism in the two processes, as far as Washington was concerned, is a point of considerable importance, for I propose to look at detente as *an American diplomatic strategy consciously deployed within a triangular power balance, vis-à-vis both China and the Soviet Union*. It is this basing of the relationship on the triangular balance that in my view distinguishes the successful detente after 1969 – Dr Kissinger's detente – from the less successful efforts at detente in the period from 1963, or indeed from 1953.

Detente pursued exclusively vis-à-vis the Soviet Union would have had quite a different meaning and function from detente pursued simultaneously and in parallel with that country and China. Detente pursued exclusively with *China*, leaving the relationship with the Soviet Union at the stage it had reached by 1969, would again have had a different meaning, and in my view a far more dangerous and unpredictable one than its advocates have understood. A detente strategy that balanced the two relationships had the desired effect, I shall argue, of maximizing American options, leverage and diplomatic mobility. It had not been yet possible, at the moment of writing, to make the relationships with the two communist powers formally symmetrical because of American domestic political obstacles, especially during the election year, to full normalization of diplomatic relations with China. But even with this handicap the triangular balance was proving viable enough.

The use of the word strategy is not intended to be in any way pejorative, or to imply that there is no moral content to the notion of detente, whether employed by American policy-makers, or Russians, or Chinese, or any others who have employed it. A strategy is by definition a means to an end, but both means and ends in political life are subject to moral judgement. In the three cases mentioned, the ends of policy – the objectives that the three sets of decision-makers have had in mind – obviously differed very widely, and it may be asked whether a single strategic concept, detente, could be used to promote objectives so much at variance. But a situation directly analogous to this is accepted without difficulty in military contests. A given strategy – the joining of battle or the avoidance of battle, a retreat, a siege, a campaign of attrition – may be equally useful to either party to the conflict. The skill of the governing mind will be shown by the choice of the battlefield and the use of the strategy. Ideology determines objectives; calculation determines strategies. But moral judgements, as I said, are applicable to both.

The question of whether the adoption of a strategy of detente must be construed as a dereliction of ideological duty has been a controversial one within all three of the chief decision-making elites involved. Mr Brezhnev was clearly addressing himself to the Soviet argument on this point in his report to the Party Congress in the Soviet Union in February 1976:

> Detente does not in the slightest abolish, nor can it alter, the laws of the class struggle.... We make no secret of the fact that we see detente as the way to create more favourable conditions for peaceful socialist and Communist construction ... As for the ultra-leftist assertions that peaceful co-existence is freezing the socio-political *status quo*, our answer is this: every revolution is above all a natural result of the given society's internal development.[3]

The 'ultra leftists' who were asserting unfavourable views on Mr Brezhnev's conduct of detente have obviously had equivalents in both China and the United States: persons who rejected the decision-maker's choice of strategy on ideological grounds. Their views will be considered in more detail in a later chapter.

But one point connected with this question has had so determining an effect on the whole shape of the triangular relationship with which we shall be concerned that it must be stated at the beginning of the analysis. It accounted for the fact that there had been, up to the time of writing (a few months after Mao Tse-tung's death) no third side to the triangle, so to speak: no detente between China and the Soviet Union. The Chinese, in accordance with a Maoist analysis, which will be looked at presently, chose to make a detente with the *less* dangerous, as Mao and Chou saw it, of China's two potent adversaries, the United States, against the *more* dangerous, the Soviet Union. The Russians, on the contrary, chose detente with the *more* dangerous of their two potential adversaries, the United States, for various reasons including the hope of economic benefit. The United States, more pragmatic and ideologically flexible than either (at least while Dr Kissinger was the chief intellectual formulator of policy), made a detente with both. And it was this situation – that it alone had a rapprochement with both potential adversaries – that gave the United States a flexibility and capacity for diplomatic manoeuvre superior to either China's or the Soviet Union's. The succession crisis in China, which was perhaps not yet over at the time of writing, had as yet not produced any indication that the new leadership would change this situation.

Defining detente as a diplomatic strategy may, I hope, help to underline the essential point that it does not in any way imply an end to the contest for diplomatic influence, only a mode of making the contest less dangerous, moving it back from the nuclear brink and giving it possibly a more creative orientation. Detente should certainly not be mistaken for peace. Peace is an objective; detente is a diplomatic mode or strategy by which that objective (or others) may be sought. On the other hand, it should not be mistaken for appeasement either. Appeasement was a policy that disregarded the balance of power in pursuit of the supposed requirements of justice to the German national interest. Detente was quite the contrary: a policy or strategy that grew out of careful and subtle calculation of power balances. It has a strong moral component, in my view, but it can certainly not be accused of neglecting power calculations, and those on which it is based will be explored in more detail presently.

If, as I have argued, detente may be seen as a strategy for the management of adversary power for all three of the main groups of policy-makers with whom we shall be concerned – Americans, Chinese and Russians – can it be seen, over any length of time, as a *successful* strategy from the point of view of the national interests of each of them? Will not one or other of the three political elites decide in due course that it is not paying off for their particular society, and that they would be better served by a reversion to some other strategy, such as cold war? The short answer is that this is certainly quite possible, and that therefore the detente has to live by a carefully even-handed sharing out of benefits. (The belief that there was disadvantage rather than benefit to the American national interest was of course the gravamen of the charges against detente in the 1976 U.S. presidential campaign.) But the possibility of an even-handed and satisfactory distribution of benefits from the point of view of all three groups of policy-makers is enhanced by one vitally important and seldom adequately considered aspect of detente. The three Powers seek and obtain their 'pay-offs' in different fields: the Russians mainly in economic benefits, the Chinese in improvement of their strategic position, and the Americans in increased diplomatic leverage, flexibility and power of manoeuvre, and reduction of their burdens in maintenance of the status quo. So it is not, as the mathematicians say, a zero-sum game. Gains for any of the three parties do not have to be equated with losses to the other two.

Let us now look at the evolution of the concept up to 1969, since it is only in the light of that history that the changes after 1969 can be understood.

Detente first emerged as an articulate Western aspiration (not yet a policy or a strategy) at the coldest moment of the Cold War years, about the time of Stalin's death, and with Mr Dulles conducting the affairs of the West. The initial spokesman of the idea of detente was one who, like Dr Kissinger, was considerably steeped in balance of power theory and nineteenth-century political history: Winston Churchill. At the time, though he was still Prime Minister, his reputation was rather under a cloud from the supposition that his great age and a minor stroke had diminished his acuity of judgement. Yet in retrospect his intellectual grasp of the phase that the post-war balance of power had reached in the early 1950s appears much more perceptive than that of his younger colleagues.

The Churchillian initiative towards detente with the Russians was developed most thoroughly from early 1953 to the summer of 1955, though in fact in his first speech after his return to power, at the Guildhall in November 1951, he remarked (gazing at the figures of the twin ancient giants, Gog and Magog, which adorn the hall) that his main purpose was to keep the giants of his own age from colliding.[4] And earlier yet, in a speech in 1948, he had begun to suggest that diplomatic accommodation with the Russians was not impossible. He got very little response to these early efforts: as someone on the Opposition benches said, the Prime Minister's main trouble was that he was trying to ignite a lot of wet flannel around him. But he returned with renewed optimism to the idea in the first Commons debate on foreign policy after Stalin's death, clearly feeling some intellectual curiosity about the new men in the Kremlin: 'It would be a mistake', he said, 'to assume that nothing could be settled with Russia until everything was settled'; the problem of reconciling the security of Russia with the freedom and safety of Western Europe was not insoluble. A few months later, again at the Guildhall, he observed that 'Many people think that the best we can do is get used to the Cold War, like eels are said to get used to skinning', but the policy of Her Majesty's government was 'peace through strength, together – and mark this – with any contacts, formal or informal, which may be thought to be helpful'.

From early 1954 this drive for some easier *modus vivendi* with the Russians was pursued with a new passion as the Prime

Minister absorbed intellectually the information beginning to be available about the results of American nuclear weapons tests. Again his historical imagination was more responsive than that of younger men: he said at one point that this information filled his mind 'out of all comparison with anything else'. But again he got very little response: indeed in June 1954 he was so exasperated by the failure of his efforts to persuade Eisenhower and Dulles of the necessity of an attempt at detente with Russia that at one point – apparently while he was on the ship bringing him home from America – he proposed to Mr Malenkov, then the Russian Prime Minister, a private meeting 'in a friendly fashion, without agendas, with the sole purpose of trying to find a sensible way of living side-by-side in an atmosphere of growing trust, ease and happiness'.

This seems to have been the only instance, in twenty-two years' evolution towards detente, of the chief British decision-maker proposing a course of action disliked by the chief American decision-makers of the time, and it did not get far. The rest of the Cabinet appears to have sat upon the Prime Minister and induced him to abandon the proposal, a development that rather irritated the Russians.[5] But no other Western statesmen could be got to endorse it: certainly not Dulles in Washington or Adenauer in Germany, and the French prime ministers of the period were totally absorbed in the approaching end of the French involvement in Vietnam.

The only favourable response was in fact from the other side of the hill: from the new collective leadership in Russia. At this point the Soviet government was still in a phase of trauma and readjustment, recovering from Stalin's last years and his death. Relations between the members of the collective leadership were fluid and competitive. Malenkov's position as Prime Minister did not indicate a true ascendancy over his colleagues, but Khrushchev's rise to pre-eminence was only tentatively foreshadowed. Probably the definition I have suggested of detente as a strategy for the management of adversary power will be more readily accepted as it concerns Russian decision-makers than as it concerns Americans. (One might indeed argue that

Dr Kissinger adopted the other side's strategy to America's better advantage.) Certainly in the Russian case it has the longer pedigree, dating back to Lenin's time, though in the earlier period it appears as the doctrine of 'peaceful coexistence'. There are perhaps differences between the two strategic concepts, but these differences appear to me to stem rather from the situation in which they are applied than from the basic substance of the idea itself.

Russian policy-makers from Lenin's time onward have certainly always been conscious of the potential economic advantages of better relationships with the West, even when, as up to 1956, this consciousness was combined with an official doctrine of the inevitability of war. In the Soviet economy, as in others, there is an inescapable competition between the demand for resources imposed by defence requirements and the allocation of resources to consumption and investment. This competition is much more acute in the Soviet than the Western case, because of the low productivity of the Soviet economy, especially in agriculture. Detente eases the problem, on the one hand by making defence demands less urgent, and on the other by opening prospects of the importation of Western goods and technologies, and the possibility of 'import-led growth' in the economy. Even the kinds of economic goods required as between the Lenin and Brezhnev periods do not seem to have changed very much: on the one hand food-stuffs, on the other hand advanced Western technologies, whether machine-tools in the earlier phase or computers and such in the later.

Malenkov began his drive towards detente just after Stalin's death, when the relationship between the members of the initial collegiate leadership was still quite ambiguous. Beria, one of the original triumvirate, was executed within a few months. The sense of vulnerability induced by domestic political disarray or uncertainty was clearly to be seen in Soviet diplomacy. In fact one may argue that this period saw the only substantial sacrifice of a Soviet territorial position in the pursuit of detente, in the Austrian State Treaty of 1955, which was a sort of price paid for the first 'summit' meeting in Geneva in 1955. If this marked the point of the greatest Soviet sense of the necessity of making concessions, one might argue that the West should then have tried more far-reaching initiatives. But Mr Dulles could not be persuaded of the usefulness of detente as a strategy for the West, and besides at this time the world power balance remained bilateral, so the outcome then would have been quite different from what it actually was in 1969.

However, if we look at Khrushchev's detente drive in 1959, we may say that the emergence of the triangular balance is foreshadowed in it, for his sense of vulnerability clearly arose less from domestic factors than from the Soviet relationship with China. The Middle East crises of the summer of 1958 (Iraq, Lebanon and Jordan) had precipitated sharp differences over strategy between the Soviet and Chinese leadership. The Quemoy–Matsu crisis of September further embittered these differences. The Russians were beginning to show consciousness of how very awkward and difficult an ally China could be, one who might push them towards a nuclear confrontation with the Americans while they knew themselves to be still vastly weaker in nuclear strike-forces. Moreover, this awkward ally was already developing an independent nuclear capacity, thanks originally to Russian help, and could conceivably one day use it to 'trigger' a nuclear exchange, if the alliance were maintained. These were the circumstances in which Mr Khrushchev made his journey to America, the 'spirit of Camp David' was generated, and the Russians unilaterally denounced their agreement on atomic aid to the Chinese.

When we come to Brezhnev's time, no doubt the Chinese preoccupation remained still a strong factor in the Russian wish for better relations with America, and was greatly reinforced by Dr Kissinger's demonstration in 1971 that an American–China rapprochement was possible.[6] But there is also a reversion to the Leninist hopes of economic development with Western aid: some of the proposals of 1922 seem direct ancestors to the contemporary projects for the development of Siberian oil and gas. These Leninist antecedents are a major asset in the maintenance of the policy by the Soviet Union.

The Nature and Provenance of Detente

Detente has encouraged the growth of Soviet trade as much or more with the West Europeans as with the Americans. However, if the value of detente for the Russians were *purely* economic, one might expect that the cultivation of the E.E.C. countries as a possible source of both capital and advanced technologies would be of as much importance to them as the cultivation of the relationship with the United States. That this has not been so, because of other strategic components in the whole concept, is illustrated by the differing Soviet approaches to France and Germany.

De Gaulle's preoccupation with the possible uses of detente (a main strand of his foreign policy from 1964 to 1968) provides an episode rich in historical irony: a classic piece of *realpolitik*, except that the power calculations seem to have been based on the world of his youth, fifty years earlier. Like any traditional French nationalist before the First World War, he saw Russia (a name and concept he preferred to that of the Soviet Union) as the natural and predestined ally of France in the containment of German power. The cultivation of detente by France with Russia could revive not only this historically established complementarity of interests, but also a new one, even more vital to the Russians: the 'containment' of American power in the world balance. De Gaulle's personal resentment of the Americans must be traced to the snubbings he received during the Second World War from Roosevelt and Cordell Hull, and he extended it to the British as American fellow-travellers and thus no true Europeans. He often spoke as if 'the Anglo-Saxons' were a single enemy, determined to cheat France of the destiny he must construct for her. But though he was more able to block British enterprises than American (as in the vetoes on E.E.C. membership), Britain was a relatively marginal element in the balance of power he had in mind – a quadrilateral whose centres would be Washington, Moscow, Peking and Paris. In order that Paris should speak with equal resonance to the other three, it must obviously be the leader of an 'anti-hegemonial alliance' and the hegemony against which this must be formulated must inevitably be that of the United States. (China later and rather more successfully also claimed to speak as the leader of an antihegemonial alliance, but in her case the hegemony resisted is nominally that of both super-powers, and no detente with the Soviet Union is required.)

De Gaulle was perhaps influenced in this notion by Maurras, who had put forward a somewhat fanciful picture of France's attraction for a 'league of lesser powers':

> We would need neither to seek friends nor to invite them: the secondary states would be driven in our direction by the force of circumstances: we would see them flock to us. It is up to us, then, to be wise enough and show ourselves vigorous enough to inspire confidence to appear as effective protectors ... This 'league of lesser peoples' could entrust us with its military command, and the policy which the kings of France always followed – of blocking the creation of any world-wide monarchy or the excessive growth of this or that coalition – would again triumphantly shine forth from Paris, more skilfully than Prussia or Piedmont, by an adroit use of friends, protégés and newly liberated peoples trained and strengthened by our help.[7]

This notion of France as the leader of a world anti-hegemonial alliance directed against the United States had little resemblance to the actual situation, in which the French had only recently and reluctantly divested themselves of an Empire. The Chinese version of the role, directed against both super-powers, has at least a base in revolutionary sentiment and a sort of anti-white solidarity which has considerable appeal in the Third World. For the Russians, a condominium shared with America had many attractions, but one shared with France seems to have struck Soviet leaders as pointless. Besides, de Gaulle's Chinese policy was an irritant, and his capacity for exerting leverage within Nato was seriously diminished by the decision to quit the integrated command. Another of the difficulties in his efforts at rapprochement with Russia lay in an inconsistency between the identity he proclaimed for the West European powers (which in effect rather came down to the notion of a train of attendant sovereigns for France's *roi soleil*) and the alternate concept which was necessary to serve the notion of a general European reconciliation, that of 'Europe to the Urals'. This was a clumsily back-handed way of bidding for Russian favour, since the Urals cannot be a political boundary of any sort without a great truncation of the Soviet Union. The implication of the phrase almost appeared to echo the Chinese hints that the Soviet Union is in Asia only as a successful European imperialist power, clinging to the ill-gotten gains of past centuries. De Gaulle, like Kissinger, perceived the importance of the Soviet leaders' preoccupation with China but was much more heavy-handed in dwelling upon it. 'Doubtless Soviet Russia, although having helped Communism become established in China, realizes that nothing can happen to prevent it from having to reckon with the yellow multitude which is China – numberless and wretchedly poor, indestructible and ambitious.'[8]

The phase of American policy that began with the 1965 involvement in Vietnam increased both the incentives and the apparent opportunities for a detente between France and Russia. It increased the incentives because de Gaulle was always irritated by the intrusion of 'the Anglo-Saxons' into ex-French colonial areas, whether in the Middle East, Africa or South East Asia, since they inevitably undermined the French linguistic and cultural legacy, and he was bound to see the American involvement in Vietnam in that light. Further, the prospective worsening of American-Russian relations with the beginning of American bombing of North Vietnam about the time of Mr Kosygin's visit to Hanoi early in 1965 appeared to offer an irresistible opportunity. De Gaulle's declaration of independence of Nato, shortly after this episode, makes large claims for the French move:

> The reappearance of a nation whose hands are free, as we have again become, obviously modifies the world interplay which, since Yalta, seemed to be limited to two partners.[9]

In the course of a Kremlin banquet in his honour during his 1966 visit to the Soviet Union, he put his bid candidly: 'an entente between hitherto antagonistic states is, to the French, above all a European problem ... Until the time when all of Europe reaches the point of finding together the ways and means leading to these essential goals, everything, in our view, commits France and the Soviet Union to do so between themselves right now.'[10] But the limit of France's ability to deliver was made apparent a few months later when Mr Kosygin paid a return visit to Paris and could not obtain French recognition of East Germany. De Gaulle had recognized the Oder–Neisse line soon after his return to office, and had offended the government in Bonn on a number of other points, but he could not venture as far as the Russians wished without destroying the relationship with West Germany, which was the essential foundation of his ability to remain intransigent with other Western powers.

The *événements* of May 1968, which weakened de Gaulle's domestic standing, and the Russian invasion of Czechoslovakia in the same year, may be taken as marking the end of the Gaullist bid to use detente as an instrument of French rivalry with America. In some ways one may say that his was theoretically the 'best offer' the Russians received, since de Gaulle had spoken of not only detente but entente, real co-operation in manipulating the balance of power, a real interest in modifying or ending the existing Western alliance. And that has been a notion or a possibility that the other Western practitioners of detente policies have regarded as the danger most carefully to be avoided. But the Russians could never be persuaded that a special relationship with France would deliver anything as useful as what might be hoped vis-à-vis either the United States or Germany, and this was clearly a realistic calculation. De Gaulle's situation with the Russians was rather that of the heir of a great and proud family in reduced circumstances, still valiantly trading in the fortunes that his interlocutors knew to have been lost long ago. As late as the 1975 visit of President Giscard d'Estaing to Moscow, the evidence appeared to show that the Russians continued to regard the importance of France to the detente as relatively low.

That was certainly not their view of the role of the Federal German Republic in this matter. Brandt's *Ostpolitik* and *Deutschlandpolitik* were most vital components from every conceivable point of view in the way things went after 1969, though Erhart and Kiesinger in the intervening years had already done a good deal to soften the original German stance of the Adenauer era. The essence of the Adenauer policies had been that detente must flow from German reunification rather than the other way round, and that reunification could only be contemplated from the 'position of strength' inherent in Germany's integration into the Western alliance, along with a total American commitment to that alliance and an intransigent resolve against Soviet diplomatic blandishments. Even Mr Dulles did not fully meet Dr Adenauer's requirements in this last respect. During the Berlin crisis of 1958-9, just before Mr Dulles's death, quite sharp differences of opinion developed between them as to the right way of meeting Soviet tactics. Dr Adenauer had no difficulty in resisting apparent prospects of reunification, as in the Soviet note of March 1952, regarding them as mere snares and delusions if they carried any hint of neutralization or Western disengagement on the Central Front.

The Brandt *Ostpolitik* reversed most of these assumptions. Reunification, if it arrives at all, will be a consequence of detente. In the meantime, the earlier West German claim to provide the sole legitimate spokesman and representation of the German people must be tacitly abandoned. The formula of 'two states in one nation' was found, to allow acquiescence in the existing reality of the German Democratic Republic. Reunification became a matter of self-determination for the East Germans. The frontiers created for Germany by the Second World War were in essence accepted. All these concessions by West Germany were the real basis for the territorial stabilization of Europe that was given a ceremonial if not a legal form in the Helsinki declaration of 1975. These developments, however, belong to the period after 1969, and will be discussed later.

The reason why 1969 was the year that determined the shape of the detente was not only the emergence of Brandt and Kissinger as policy-makers in Germany and America, but, even more, the sharp deterioration in relations between China and the Soviet Union. The Sino-Soviet crisis of early 1969 seems to have been for each a turning-point towards real apprehension of major war with the other. It dominated the period from

March to September 1969, was marked by substantial hostilities in the border areas, and allegedly included a 'practice dry run' by Russian aircraft, miming a strike at Chinese cities. Intentionally or not, the Russians signalled to the Chinese that they were contemplating preventive war, perhaps including nuclear strike, against China. Their signals were so deliberate, clumsy and obvious that it is difficult not to believe that they were stage thunder, a Russian effort to frighten the Chinese decision-makers into a more compliant attitude. The signals included, for instance, letters to communist parties in the West that seemed to be asking for advance approval of a strike against China. (I was shown a copy of the letter addressed to the Australian Communist party, pro-Russian wing, which seemed at the time to be readily available to any interested enquirer.) The Russians apparently offered, via the military attachés in Washington and Moscow, at least a clear hint if not an actual bid for American acquiescence or collusion in such a strike. They were firmly snubbed by the American policy-makers concerned, and knowledge of the bid and the snub were, naturally, conveyed to the Chinese government.

It might seem that these Russian moves were so crashingly ostentatious that they would inevitably have been regarded as mere bluff, not true indications of military intentions. Yet the Chinese appear to have taken them seriously, and no doubt they had evidence not available in the West of the level of Russian preparations for military action. The Russian preoccupation with China even emerged at the SALT negotiations:

> A stunning glimpse of Moscow's Chinaphobia was provided: on learning of plans for some 'provocative' action or attack the two sides – the United States and the Soviet Union – would take joint steps to prevent it, or, if too late, joint retaliatory action to punish the guilty party. The Soviets, in effect, were proposing no less than a super-power alliance against other nuclear powers. Although clearly aimed at China the proposal risked arousing Nato, whose membership includes two other nuclear powers – Britain and France. The Soviets never would explain exactly what might constitute provocative actions. Washington rejected the idea immediately and just as swiftly, informed the other Nato governments lest they hear of it through another channel and conclude that, as they had feared, SALT really did foreshadow a great power axis, or condominium.[11]

It is thus clear that the Chinese leadership, by 1969, believed it had good reason for elevating the Soviet Union to the status of China's most dangerous adversary, despite any remaining ideological consanguity, if indeed the latter was still conceded to exist. There was in existence a Maoist text for an analogous conflict, the 1941 essay *On Policy*,[12] written in the context of the war with Japan and the necessary tactical alliances with the Kuomintang and the Americans. The application of Maoist strategic analysis yields prescriptions for policy that are strikingly like those of traditional *realpolitik*, the principle involved in both cases being that of the balance of power. (The traditional Chinese phrase 'using barbarians to check barbarians' also appears to apply.) Having in Maoist practice distinguished the order of priority among your enemies (with the Soviet Union in this case being awarded the palm), you are then able to make temporary and tactical alliances with the subsidiary enemies. The parallel with 1941 is clear: Japan was then for the time being the chief enemy, so alliance with the Kuomintang and the Americans was in order. The order of priorities established in 1969 clearly put the Soviet Union at the head of the list of enemies, and as of early 1977 there had been no sign of that assumption undergoing change; if anything it appeared reinforced. Nor had there been even the most nominal progress towards detente between the two communist powers in the intervening period. Whether this obduracy of ill-will had its origins in the territorial disputes between the two powers, or in the ideological ones, or in Mao's long and resentful memory of Russian injury to Chinese interests, cannot really be known with any certainty by the Western world. The Russians were speaking in 1977 as if they expected the conflict to persist for the indefinite future, whereas a few years earlier they had spoken as if it might end with Mao's death.

The attitude of the Chinese leadership did not of course imply any assumption of true Western benevolence towards China, or disregard of future possibilities of Soviet–American collusion. The relation between Russia and America is defined as both contention and collusion. 'Contention is absolute and protracted, whereas collusion is relative and temporary.' The Chinese have, with the development of the American–Soviet detente, become intent upon impressing visiting Europeans with the view that the danger from Russia is primarily towards themselves: that the Soviet revisionists were 'making a feint to the East while attacking in the West', and stepping up their expansion in 'the Mediterranean, the Indian Ocean and every place their hands can reach'.[13] This argument that Russian hostility towards China represents a mere *ruse de guerre* was obviously of tactical and diplomatic convenience in the circumstances (quaintly, it was the same argument as was originally put forward by very far right-wing Westerners), but the actual solid indications of Chinese fear of Russian nuclear strike (which took the form, for instance, of underground shelters in Peking and other cities) were too real for the apprehensions of 1969 to be doubted, and though they had at times appeared to diminish, their dominance over other preoccupations remained very marked as late as 1977.

On the Soviet side also, early 1969 represented a period of alarmed endeavour towards offsetting the strategic dangers that might stem from the Sino-Soviet conflict. The revival of efforts towards a European Security Conference began in March 1969, at the height of the border hostilities with China. By the December 1969 meeting of Nato the Russians had made it clear that they were no longer seriously trying to exclude American forces from Europe. Rumours of the beginning of the American approaches to China, via first France and then Pakistan, would probably have reached Moscow by then. The Soviet proposals for 'collective security' in Asia, which had very clear anti-Chinese implications, were also pushed vigorously from the middle of 1969.

As far as Washington was concerned, one may say that the whole period from the resolution of the Cuban missile crisis in 1962 was marked by tentative efforts to move to some easier and less risk-laden *modus vivendi* with either or both the Soviet Union and China. Just before Kennedy's death, a trial balloon was being floated, in the form of a speech by one of his chief advisers on Asian affairs, looking towards the eventual prospect of recognition of Peking.[14] In Johnson's time a new policy towards the Soviet Union, known as 'peaceful engagement', was being cautiously launched.[15] However, the preoccupations of Vietnam so absorbed the time and energy of the presidents and other policy-makers that not a great deal came of these tentative initiatives. It is impossible to put twenty years of very complex diplomacy into a few pages without leaving out a great deal that was important: but one might summarize the process in a metaphor by saying that the seeds of detente were sown about the midwinter of Cold War in 1953; the shoots began to show a little above ground in 1955, and there was a period of gradual though somewhat blighted growth through the 1960s until circumstances and Dr Kissinger constructed the fragile diplomatic hothouse in which it flourished and bore fruits after 1969. It is to that period that we must now turn our attention.

CHAPTER 2

Dr Kissinger: The Policy-Maker as Theorist

Dr Kissinger's role in the architecture of detente has been so central as to justify exploration of the intellectual background he brought to office as policy-maker.[1] And the first thing that may be said about the doctrines and concepts with which he had been identified as an analyst of world affairs before 1969 might be that they do not, at first sight, suggest the probability that a more co-operative relationship with the two great powers of the Communist world would be the major outcome of his time in power. At least this is certainly the case if one assumes (as many people have done) that the case for detente is somehow dependent on undue optimism about the nature and future of Soviet policy. For Dr Kissinger had always been rather conspicuously tough-minded, even pessimistic, in his estimate of Soviet policy-making. His writings were flattering about neither the Soviet system nor its leaders, and rejected the 'convergence' thesis, popular in the 1960s with many intellectuals, which held that America and the Soviet Union were becoming more alike through the process of social change. Indeed he had even implied that any resemblances were those between the vices of the Communist world and those of capitalism, rather than their respective virtues. The irony of communism was that most of the evils it ascribed to capitalism – many of which were real enough – had become magnified and more intractable under the communist system. Communism's managers, like feudal lords, combined economic and political power, and their authority was difficult to assail by those below them. He did not place much faith in the process of industrialization or education, or even the critical spirit, to foster liberalism in the Communist world, holding rather that it was only the affirmation of some absolute value that transformed societies. He saw the leadership of communist states as a sort of priesthood of power. Given the hazards, historically demonstrated, of life in the Soviet political leadership, 'Only an enormous desire for power can impel a man to enter such a career. Anyone succeeding in Communist leadership struggles must be single-minded, unemotional, unsentimental and dedicated. Nothing in the experience of Soviet leaders would lead them to prize peace as an end, or accept protestations of goodwill at face value.'[2] The Soviet leaders were restrained by consciousness of the dangers of nuclear war, the instability of their own leadership group, and the difficulty of dealing with other communist powers, a sphere of problems that they found ideologically uncomfortable. He was disdainful also of the notion of the mellowing of Soviet society, thinking that to wait for the Soviet Union to become bourgeois was an off-loading of the problem onto future generations. The communist powers were, however, in general rather cautious, and their challenge moral rather than physical. It was necessary to understand Leninist doctrine in order to appreciate their view of diplomacy as just one tool among others in the international class struggle. The doctrine of 'peaceful coexistence' he saw as justified in Soviet thinking 'primarily as a tactical device to overthrow the West at minimum risk'.[3]

His view on detente itself as an element in Soviet diplomacy might be called particularly mordant or disillusioned:

> Peace offensives, of course, are not new in Soviet history. Peaceful coexistence has been avowed since the advent of Communism in Russia. It was stressed particularly between 1924–1939; between 1941–46; at the time of the Geneva Summit Conference of 1955; again on the occasion of Khrushchev's visit to the United States in 1959, and following the Cuban missile crisis in 1962. On each occasion the reason for the detente was some internal or external strain on the Soviet system. In 1924, it was the struggle between Stalin and Trotsky which was followed by the forced collectivisation of agriculture and the purges; in 1941–46 it was the German invasion; in 1956 it was the succession struggle after the death of Stalin; in 1959 it was part of a Soviet attempt to push the Allies out of Berlin; since 1962

it has been caused by the shock of defeat in Cuba and the internal strains on the Soviet system.

On each occasion the period of relaxation ended when an opportunity for expanding Communism presented itself. The period of tranquility after 1924 was ended by the annexation of Bessarabia, the Baltic States and one third of Poland as well as an attack on Finland. World War II led to the creation of the satellite orbit in Eastern Europe. The spirit of Geneva gave way to an attempted penetration of the Middle East and a crisis over Berlin. And the spirit of Camp David was succeeded by another Berlin crisis which did not end until the installation of Soviet missiles in Cuba.[4]

Scepticism about the prospects for the Soviet Union's evolving into a liberal society had of course considerable relevance to policy choices on detente, but pointed in quite the opposite direction to what might be supposed. From the earliest days of the Cold War, two Western theories about how it might be ended have existed in competition with each other. They may be called the 'domestic change' and the 'diplomatic accomodation' theses. The 'domestic change' view has said in effect: 'We will not be able to make agreements of any viable sort with the Soviet Union until it evolves or is pressured into becoming a society more like us – a society with liberal values.' Thus, paradoxically, the emphasis on domestic liberalism as an assumed precondition of international good behaviour tends to entail logically the prospective near-permanence of cold war. The other theory has said: 'The Soviet Union is *not* going to become like us, and anyway the question of whether the Russians share our values is not necessarily relevant to the question of whether we can live at peace with them. International history is crammed with wars between societies having near-identical values, but it also has plenty of instances of societies with incompatible values (religious, political, social or economic) learning to make a *modus vivendi* with each other. Like Moslem and Christian or Catholic and Protestant. The way to end the Cold War is diplomatic accommodation, *not requiring mutual trust but only mutual interest.*'

In terms of the old definition of liberals as the party of hope and conservatives as the party of memory, Dr Kissinger must certainly be classed as conservative by philosophy and temperament. His policies, more than those of any other secretary of state, seem related to the special data-bank of memory comprised in European diplomatic history. However, in the contemporary foreign-policy debate in America, the name conservative has been pre-empted by the right-wing segment of opinion, whose attitudes include a sharp rejection of detente, and whose general doctrines might more accurately be described as a somewhat abrasive and simplistic nationalism, expressed as much on issues like the Panama Canal as on relations with the Soviet Union. Since there is no quarrelling with established usage (though one may wince at a usage implying that Mr Ronald Reagan is the political heir-apparent of Burke and Disraeli) I shall use the term 'traditionalist' for the intellectual position taken by Dr Kissinger and various other analysts, such as Walter Lippmann,[5] on this question. Traditionalists and some liberals have espoused the 'diplomatic accommodation' thesis about the mode of ending the Cold War with the Soviet Union. True radicals, like conservatives, have tended to adhere to the 'domestic change' thesis, only the society in which they have demanded change (or said it was necessary before real progress could be made) has of course been the United States. The group known as 'cold war liberals', which includes Senator Jackson, has adhered to most of the propositions of the conservative 'domestic change' thesis. A good many other liberals have been ambivalent, their dislike of Soviet domestic repression almost outweighing their dislike of cold warriors. Perhaps the central point of difference between the traditionalist position and that of American mainstream liberalism is the traditionalists' philosophical scepticism or pessimism: the consciousness that most of human history has been a story of failures. Mainstream American thought tends to an optimistic assumption that representative democracy, social mobility and the market economy will together solve most human problems. The radical rejects this because he believes that the market economy will always produce the exploitation of the weak by the strong. The traditionalist rejects it, as far as foreign policy is concerned, because of his scepticism of the assumption that the other side's adoption of Western value-systems is either a sufficient or even a necessary condition of a reasonable *modus vivendi* on the diplomatic plane, still less a guarantee of general international harmony.

The political rhetoric that assumes that democracies are by definition peace-loving and autocracies (whether of left or right) are aggressive, has not much historical backing, though it can of course always point to the experience of the inter-war years, when one of the dictatorships at least was genuinely bent on war. Since the Second World War, right-wing autocracies have mostly been installed in relatively weak powers, who have often been allied to the West, so their theoretical war-bearing potential has not been much dwelt upon. If the familiar liberal equation between dictatorship and aggression is to be applied to the present central balance powers, it has to impute aggression to the communist party dictatorships of the Soviet Union and China, though many left–liberals, even in America, find this discomforting. At any rate, it is the ghost of this theory (which can claim very respectable antecedents in Kantian philosophy) that may be seen in the view that only when the Soviet Union has somehow been transmuted into a liberal democracy will what is usually called 'a true detente' be possible.

If the origins of Dr Kissinger's theory of detente are not to be found in any optimism about the 'liberalization' of the Soviet Union, or of communist societies generally, or in belief about their economic and sociological 'convergence' with Western societies, where is it to be found? At the risk of over-simplifying a complex intellectual analysis, one would say it arises from a concept of the relation between what he calls 'a legitimate order' and 'a revolutionary order', and the way in which diplomacy may be used to turn the tension between them towards a creative direction. Most of the arguments that bear upon these issues are to be found in *A World Restored*,[6] which seems in many ways the most personal of his books, even though it is formally about the diplomacy of the early nineteenth century.

The Harvard graduate student who sat down to write a thesis about how Metternich and his fellows restored a viable world after ruinous wars, brought on by the revolutionary nationalism of Napoleon, clearly had strong personal reasons for seeking a pattern that might help illumine the contemporary world and its possible futures. The darker pathological nationalism of Hitler had shaped the pattern of his own life to that point. A Jewish boy born in Bavaria in the year of Hitler's first *putsch*; expelled from his grammar school as the Nazis consolidated their power; fleeing with his family for their lives as the 'final solution' got on its terrifying way; living as a disconsolate adolescent refugee in New York (making a living as factory-hand and messenger-boy in a shaving-brush factory and getting an education at night-school); returning to Germany seven years after he had fled, as part of a conquering American army, and acquiring early administrative responsibilities as a sergeant in army intelligence during the occupation: his experience cannot be called a comfortable prelude to the scholarly life, but undoubtedly one likely to involve a historical imagination strongly with the problems of international order in a revolutionary epoch and with the meaning of history.

A World Restored is often described as being about the balance of power, but in fact it is about the working of *a concert of powers*. The distinction between the two is important for an understanding of its relevance to detente. Obviously a balance of power underlay the nineteenth-century concert of powers, or it would not have proved viable, just as a balance of power is now necessary as the foundation of the detente, which is not yet a concert of powers. As Castlereagh once said, in a concert system the Powers feel a common duty as well as a common interest. A balance of power may be regarded a sort of force of history that tends to assert itself almost automatically in any system of independent sovereignties. A concert of powers, on the contrary, must always be a construction of conscious statecraft. So has been the detente: not something arising spontaneously or demanded by popular clamour, but something consciously manoeuvred into being by a few high policy-makers in pursuit of their respective calculations, which were not necessarily in line with the expectations of their respective societies. (This last point seems to have been particularly the case for China: the astonishment and resistance even among high party cadres, as reflected in the downfall of Lin Piao, has had no precise equivalent in Moscow or Washington.)

I am not of course implying that the notion of a concert of powers played any part in calculations in Moscow or Peking; it is the *strategy* that the three sets of decision-makers have in common, not the objective. Their objectives have been entirely disparate. Nor do I want to imply that the notion of a concert of powers has been widespread even among Western policy-makers or Western fellow-travellers. Obviously it is familiar to the Europeans, since it derives from their diplomatic history, but any workable concert system for the late twentieth century, as against the early nineteenth, would of course have to include non-European members. One can perhaps see emerging in contemporary international relations what might be called the candidate-members of some prospective world concert of powers, in countries like Brazil or Nigeria or Iran, and the regionalist tendencies of contemporary economic organization rather help this trend, but it is as yet quite embryonic.

One of the most interesting ambiguities of detente as a concept is that it may, as it were, be 'adjusted' to various levels of expectation. When the 'intelligence community' puts up estimates for Washington policy-makers of future Soviet building of a missile-system or such, the convention is to put up high, medium and low projections. One might do something similar with projections for detente as a strategy. In a very hopeful and ambitious mood, it may be seen as a mode of attempting to transmute 'a revolutionary order' (which the twentieth century clearly has been, and remains) into 'a legitimate order', by spinning a sort of web of common interests and arrangements between the revolutionary and the status quo powers. In a less optimistic, run-of-the-mill mood one would see it more modestly, as I defined it earlier, as just a strategy for managing adversary power. In a still less optimistic mood one might see it as at most a device for reducing the probability of nuclear war. On any of these projections, detente could of course be justified as the best available option. The prevalent level of American policy has been the medium one, but it is possible to catch echoes of all three levels of expectation in various statements of Dr Kissinger's. In his case also I think one might say that detente has been a strategy that suffused most of his policies. Vis-à-vis other powers than the Soviet Union or China the process had admittedly not got very far, but some of his 1975 economic diplomacy vis-à-vis the Third World, for instance, began to produce a detente in the North–South confrontation that might in due course develop into something more ambitious.

To argue for the notion of a concert of powers as one possible outcome of an extended period of detente is not, of course, to assume either that the late twentieth century will reproduce the nineteenth, or that Dr Kissinger thinks it will. He has specified the differences: 'Many of the elements of stability which characterized the international system in the 19th century cannot be recreated in the modern age. The stable technology, the multiplicity of major powers, the limited domestic claims and the frontiers which permitted adjustment are gone forever.'[7] Given the circumstances of the late twentieth century, when any viable concert of powers would, as I said, have to be on a world basis not a European one, and would involve at least two communist powers and possibly more, the notion might seem to imply a romantic optimism, rather than the Spenglerian pessimism usually attributed to Dr Kissinger. The characteristic assumption of most theorists and practitioners of *realpolitik* is that the perpetual quadrille of the balance of power (as one of its historians calls it) is itself the objective of the exercise. A really optimistic American view of cold war would presumably hold that the Soviet Union could somehow be made to shrink as a power, allowing Eastern Europe to regain its autonomy and ending any serious military threat and any possibility of the expansion of Soviet influence overseas. But that is a very unrealistic expectation, and is not at all what the more sophisticated enemies of detente maintain. Their view is in many respects more pessimistic than Kissinger's, arguing in effect that the Cold War is the best that can be expected, and the West must remain under psychological pressure to run as hard as it can merely to stay in the same place, in terms of power. There is an ambivalence on this point, as on a good many others, in Dr Kissinger's intellectual position. His general level of short-term expectation is undoubtedly sober, even sombre. The nuclear age permits only a choice between evils: even understanding the potential for disaster does not necessarily avert it. The warning of the oracle does not suffice to avert the doom, because salvation resides not in knowledge but in acceptance. Nothing is more difficult for Americans to believe than the possibility of tragedy. Yet this expectation of the worst did not operate to produce acquiescence in damage to the Western interests, but determined and wily efforts to avert it. One might also say that he used his well-known pessimism as a tactical device in short-term crisis situations, a technique quite apparent during the revolutionary phase in Portugal, and at the time of the Italian elections, or even during the Middle Eastern and Southern African negotiations. It is often difficult to distinguish in his statements between temperamental enjoyment of a luxurious historical melancholy or *weltschmertz*, and immediately useful signalling related to the crisis of the moment.

The tendency to assume that not much can be expected from the other side, that a certain amount of double-dealing is par for the course, was in a curious way a factor in preservation of the detente, especially for instance in the early part of the Middle East crisis, through the shrugging off of what might reasonably be interpreted as Soviet bad faith.[8] Despite the effort to 'spell out' mutual rules or conventions for the detente, his basic assumptions did not require surprise when the other side bent or ignored these rules, as might have been the case with a more sanguine or less machiavellian policy-maker. The 'passing-grade' for the adversary powers was not high, because his expectation of what their system would allow or require them to do was not high. Some critics argued that Kissinger, as negotiator with the Russians, might have got more if he had expected more, but on the evidence this seems over-optimistic. Those who expected (or at least tried to get) more from the

Russians, like Senator Jackson,[9] mostly found themselves with a broken deal, or no deal at all, as also in the cases of the Japanese with their efforts over the Northern Islands, or the Chinese with theirs over the disputed frontiers. The Russians have not been generous bargainers.

The other candid preoccupation of Kissinger's writings is with power and its management, including the threat or use of military force as one element of power in international relations. The most characteristic of his maxims is 'The test of a statesman is his ability to recognise the real relationship of forces and to make this knowledge serve his ends'.[10] But he was considerably less inclined than some earlier secretaries of state to assume that military power can be translated directly into diplomatic influence, weight for weight, so to speak. His pessimism extends to a discounting of excess claims on behalf of military or strategic ascendancy, and this again was important in preserving the detente, particularly in the SALT negotiations of 1969–72.

The dichotomy between optimism and pessimism in Kissinger's case is resolved at least for practical purposes, if not philosophical ones, by an assertion that ambiguity is the necessary condition of political action. The policy-maker 'must be allowed the modicum of ambiguity that is sometimes inseparable from a situation in which you cannot, at the beginning of a process, know completely what all the consequences are'. This view was not the result of office: it appears in the 1969 edition of *American Foreign Policy*.

> The dilemma of any statesman is that he can never be certain about the probable course of events. In reaching a decision he must inevitably act on the basis of an intuition that is inherently unprovable. If he insists on certainty, he runs the danger of becoming a prisoner of events. His resolution must reside not in facts as commonly concerned but in his vision of the future.[11]

In more generalized terms, it appears as early as *A World Restored*:

> Nations learn only from experience: they 'know' only when it is too late to act. But statesmen must act as if their intuition were already experience, as if their aspirations were truth ... [the statesman] must bridge the gap

between a society's experience and his vision, between its tradition and its future.[12]

The process by which the large diplomatic objective is advanced by means of the small tactical agreement is called 'linkage':

> Our approach proceeds from the conviction that in moving forward across a wide spectrum of negotiations, progress in one area adds momentum to progress in other areas. If we succeed, then no agreement stands alone as an isolated accomplishment vulnerable to the next crisis ... We have looked for progress in a series of agreements settling specific political issues, and we have sought to relate these to a new standard of international conduct appropriate to the dangers of the nuclear age. By acquiring a stake in this network of relationships with the West, the Soviet Union may become more conscious of what it would lose by a return to confrontation. Indeed it is our hope that it will develop a self-interest in fostering the entire process of relaxation of tensions.[13]

The most striking perception of *A World Restored* (especially considering it as the work of a graduate student) and the idea most relevant to Dr Kissinger's later diplomacy, is the reflection that insecurity is as endemic to international life as mortality to human life: the very essence of its being. It is a bleak enough insight, at odds with the liberal–optimist colouration of most American thought on international politics. The essential elements in his landscape of the society of states are insecurity, ambiguity and risk. Since insecurity is the condition of international society, the demand for total security on the part of any one state means the imposition of total *insecurity* on others. Most of his negotiating technique, later, was based on persuading various parties (the Pentagon, the Russians, the Israelis, even the Rhodesians or South Africans) that holding out for complete security is self-defeating: the acceptance of a measure of insecurity must be the first condition of accommodation and of progress towards stability and perhaps ultimately peace.

Peace must be sought, not directly, but as a sort of bonus pay-off from the achievement of stability in the system. If it is sought too directly, all states will be at the mercy of the most ruthless power in the system, since the demands of that power must be accepted to maintain the peace.[14] (This was written in the context of reflection on the nineteenth century but seems clearly inspired by reflection on the 1930s and the failure of appeasement as a policy.) If peace is to be a pay-off from stability, stability in turn is dependent on self-restraint, especially on the part of the great powers, on an acceptance (more or less) of the 'rules of the game', and on agreement about the nature of 'workable arrangements', which permit diplomacy to operate for the adjustment of differences through negotiation.

This preoccupation with power relations in the world undoubtedly concentrated his interest at the top of the power hierarchy, the central balance that determines most other relationships. The main structural change in the central balance, beginning in the late 1950s but confirmed and made public only after 1963, was clearly the schism between the Soviet Union and China, and the resulting situation was the basis on which he began and continued his pursuit of detente with both parties. He implied as much in 1970:

> The deepest international conflict in the world today is not between us and the Soviet Union but between the Soviet Union and Communist China ... Therefore, one of the positive prospects in the current situation is that whatever the basic intentions of the Soviet leaders, confronted with the prospect of a China growing in strength and not lessening in hostility, they may want a period of detente in the West, not because they necessarily have changed ideologically, but because they do not want to be in a position in which they have to confront major crises on both sides of their huge country over an indefinite period of time.[15]

It is ironic that almost all the attacks on detente have come from conservative opinion, since as a strategy it is itself conservative in a triple and literal sense, oriented to conserving the peace, conserving the sphere of American power, and conservative also in the sense of aiming at economy of means. In my view it is the only strategy that could have served these ends simultaneously. As to whether peace or the American power sphere would have been given priority in the event of an irresolvable clash between them, one can only speculate, but of course it was Dr Kissinger's central task to prevent such a clash from occurring, and his crisis-management operated successfully to that end. This equal orientation towards the preservation of peace and the conservation of power was however the origin of much of his political and even moral vulnerability. Right-wing opinion tended to object to those policies that were directed to reinforcing the peace, like arms control and economic rapprochement. Left and liberal opinion tended to object to those policies that were directed towards maintaining and reinforcing the American power sphere, like the cultivation of military autocracies as allies if they happened to be strategically useful (Greece in the junta period or Spain under Franco). Thus, whereas most secretaries of state confront criticism from one quarter only (usually the left, though in Acheson's case the more damaging attacks were from the right), Kissinger came under fire from both quarters, the criticism often being cast into the form of moral reproach. The accusation of 'having no values' normally means 'not adhering to my values', whether those values are of the left or right.

In fact the most interesting and controversial aspect of detente is not its level of success as a strategy, but the way it crystallizes within itself the central moral tension, not only of international politics but of politics in general: the tension between order and justice. 'A legitimate order', in Kissinger's definition, is merely an order accepted by all its major members: it does not imply adherence to a common constitutionality or ideology and, he adds firmly, 'it should not be confused with justice'.[16] On the other hand, if any of the major powers within such an order is suffering from so acute a sense of injustice as to provide that state with a motive to break the whole framework of the system, the legitimate order will have been transmuted into a revolutionary order. Thus the provision of a reasonable measure of justice is a requirement for a stable legitimate order. This view was re-echoed in a speech just before he became Secretary of State:

> The history of the post-war era has been a never ending effort to maintain peace through crisis-management. The structure of peace we envisage would instead, be sustained by a growing realization on the part of all nations that they have a stake in stability, and that *this stability is ensured by acting from a sense of justice and with moderation*. The world is beginning to see that its purpose need not be the captive of its fears, that they can be shaped by its hopes and dreams.[17] (Italics added.)

But obviously this attempt at a resolution of the two sets of claims did not satisfy all the critics of detente, and when pushed he would usually imply that peace had the higher priority:

> Where the age-old antagonism between freedom and tyranny is concerned, we are not neutral. But other imperatives impose limits on our ability to produce internal changes in foreign countries. Consciousness of our limits is recognition of the necessity of peace – not moral callousness. The preservation of human life and human society are moral values too.[18]

There is an eerie premonitory echo of the argument between Kissinger and Solzhenitsyn in what Kissinger had been preoccupied with as a graduate student, twenty years earlier. The nineteenth-century policy-makers about whom he was writing, Metternich and Castlereagh and their colleagues, provide archetypes from their own time for this perennial dilemma and how it was resolved or lived with for a span of years that makes twentieth-century efforts look rather feeble. It is unwarranted to describe Kissinger as an uncritical adherent of Metternich; he is clearly beguiled by that personage's cleverness, but regards him with some disapproval as a moral lightweight: 'His face was delicate but without depth, his conversation brilliant but without ultimate seriousness.' He was a great tactician, but a mediocre strategist, a man who never came to terms with his age, devious and guilty, his life spent in shoring up decaying buildings, which is not a pursuit worthy of a serious man. If his goals were fixed, they were also sterile: there was an aura of futility about him. Most demanding rebuke of all: he lacked 'the strength to contemplate chaos, there to find the material for fresh creation'. Castlereagh is presented as a more congenial, or at any rate a luckier conservative, in that his conservatism was based on tradition rather than rationalism.

What grips Kissinger's imagination (so that he returns to it in later books) is the conflict between the conservative, whom he sees as statesman, and the revolutionary, whom he sees as prophet. Though he clearly identifies with the conservative, his empathy with the revolutionary is noticeably strong:

> ... the prophet is less concerned with manipulating than with creating reality. What is possible interests him less than what is 'right'. He offers

his vision as a test, and his good faith as a guarantee. He believes in total solutions: ... He objects to gradualism as an unnecessary concession to circumstance. He will risk everything because his vision is the primary significant reality to him. Paradoxically, his more optimistic view of human nature makes him more intolerant than the statesman. If the truth is both knowable and attainable, only immorality or stupidity can keep man from realizing it ... To the statesman, negotiation is the mechanism of stability, because it presupposes that the maintenance of the existing order is more important than any dispute within it. To the prophet negotiations can have only symbolic value – as a means of converting or demoralizing an opponent; truth by definition, cannot be compromised.[19]

It was a nice twist of irony that the prophet/moralist appointed by history to be the thorn in Kissinger's own flesh in the matter of detente was the special kind of revolutionary most likely to evolve in a society that itself maintains a system of oppression rationalized in the name of revolutionary justice: that is, a counter-revolutionary. For certainly Solzhenitsyn's prescriptions, if applied in the Soviet Union, would amount to a revolutionary reversal of most of Russian history since 1917, or at any rate since the downfall of Kerensky, since Solzhenitsyn clearly sees the root of Soviet evil in Lenin, not merely in Stalin.

As a premonitory justification of Kissinger's own stand against the absolutist political moralities, which obviously have great force and appeal, one might use his account of the rationale of the statesman/conservative:

The statesman lives in time: his test is the permanence of his structure under stress. The prophet lives in eternity ... his test is inherent in his vision. The encounter between the two is always tragic, because the statesman must strive to reduce the prophet's vision to precise measure, while the prophet will judge the temporal structure by transcendental standards. To the statesman, the prophet represents a threat, because an assertion of absolute justice is a denial of nuance. To the prophet, the statesman represents a revolt against reality, because the attempt to reduce justice to the attainable is a triumph of the contingent over the universal. To the statesman, negotiation is the essence of stability because it symbolizes the adjustment of conflicting claims and the recognition of legitimacy: to the prophet it is the symbol of imperfection, of impure motives frustrating universal bliss.[20]

Many analysts have argued that the moral 'cool' of a balance of power policy is so unfamiliar and so uncongenial to the American electorate that it must fail through lack of public understanding and support. Pointing to the fervour generated by the old anti-communist containment consensus, Stanley Hoffman has written: 'The subtleties of the balance of power, the apparent coldness of a policy that gives up both the most extreme claims of force and those of evangelism, that tries to curb both disembodied idealism and the imperial strivings of a self-interest licenced by idealism is not likely to strike a similarly responsive chord.'[21] This may well be true, but might not necessarily have proved a drawback for policy-making in contemporary and foreseeable circumstances. The assumption that the American electorate needs to be fired with moral indignation against adversaries, or with moral enthusiasm for allies or for collective security, is essentially a hangover from the Cold War years, when a possible retreat into 1930s' isolation appeared a danger that had constantly to be averted. There was little sign that this remained the case in 1977. Balance of power concepts seemed to have percolated down to the political grass-roots in some odd and even comic[22] ways without exciting any particular revulsion. Dr Kissinger's 'approval rating' in the polls, at the end of eight years as policy-maker,[23] was higher than that accorded much of the time to an insistent moralizer like Mr Dulles. His critics were on the whole not recruited from 'grass-roots opinion', but from rival foreign-policy intellectuals, and political spokesmen with party axes to grind. The self-doubt and disillusionment generated by Vietnam and Watergate had apparently (at least temporarily) produced a pervasive scepticism about earlier assumptions of special virtue in the American way of life, a scepticism logically appropriate to existing and prospective foreign-policy necessities. 'The claim to moral superiority leads to an erosion of all moral restraint.'[24] That was written by Kissinger of Czar Alexander, but it could have characterized some earlier American policy-makers: Mr Dulles in the massive retaliation policy, for instance. A disenchantment with claims of this sort – after Vietnam, Watergate, Lockheed, and the innumerable investigations of the C.I.A. – appeared for a time in 1975–6 to be well established. The policy-makers of the late 1970s and 1980s, entitled neither to the heroic assumption of the early Kennedy period that American strength alone was sufficient to carry all conceivable international burdens (and that the American people were willing to pay any price demanded), nor to the complacent assumption of a remoter day that the American national interest was barely distinguishable from the laws of God, might therefore (it seemed) find reason to build an international consensus compatible with that national interest, through the traditional modes of the balance of power.

However, the early weeks of the Carter administration appeared to demonstrate a sharp reversal of that trend.[25] An audible renewal of emphasis on morality (or perhaps moralizing) as a strand in American foreign policy seemed to be the most notable break with the spirit of the Kissinger period. It was not yet clear, at the time of writing, how persistent this style would prove as the new President encountered the actual dilemmas of policy or how far it would affect substance as well as style, but the change of mood in Washington in early 1977 was striking, and indeed disconcerting to some of America's allies.

CHAPTER 3

Dr Kissinger: The Theorist as Policy-Maker

It would be entirely possible to argue that theory is not often a help and may well be an active burden to a policy-maker: a sort of Old Man of the Sea that cannot be dislodged from his intellectual back, and will only discomfort him with digs from its sharp knees and elbows as he makes his way through whatever minefield history has laid for him. Not enough U.S. secretaries of state have been in any sense theorists to bring historical evidence to bear on this proposition. Mr Dulles committed himself to a book or two, but they are really polemical works, of not much abiding interest. Dean Acheson, the other strong innovative secretary of the post-war period, was a practical lawyerly man, rather impatient of theories. On the face of it, one would say that in any case the probabilities are against any translation of theory into practice. The decision structure of American foreign-policy-making is so complex, and incorporates so many veto-groups, that any stream of thought would seem unlikely to make its way through to consistent embodiment in policy decisions. Yet despite all this, the skeleton of theory does appear quite visibly through the substance of policy in Dr Kissinger's time, even though with an occasional limb that seems to belong to some other corpus sprouting awkwardly from it.

This is the more surprising when one contemplates the situation as it existed in early 1969. By that date, the textbook description of American foreign policy as a constitutionally provided battleground for the struggle between president and

Congress seemed to have been superseded by a condition resembling a scrimmage between raiding parties from a dozen different seigneuries. In part this was because of the long decline of the Department of State as the primary policy-maker, a decline that began with the McCarthyite attack of the early 1950s and Mr Dulles's failure to resist it. There is perhaps usually some tension between a strong-minded secretary of state and the Department, whose top echelons are full of other able and strong-minded men, quite attached to their own views on policy matters, and quite inclined to think of the secretary as a temporary phenomenon to be put up with – as he sometimes has been. In Mr Dulles's time, it was said that he kept American foreign policy in his hat-band. No doubt the same remark would have been applied to Dr Kissinger if he had been more given to hats. Between Mr Dulles's death in early 1959 and Dr Kissinger's promotion in September 1973, there was really no strong figure as secretary, and this succession of weak monarchies allowed a great strengthening of the competitors for the policy-making role. The presidents themselves and their 'courtiers', especially in Mr Nixon's time; the enormous bureaucracy of the Pentagon, especially when Mr McNamara was Secretary of Defense; the vastly ramified 'intelligence community', especially the C.I.A.; the Chiefs of Staff jointly and severally; the congressional leadership, and through it assorted lobbies and pressure groups: all these represented competitors, and rather often successful ones, in the formulation of policy. Most of them had views on detente, and *prima facie* not many of them seemed likely to be favourably oriented to it. Yet the policy survived.

Let us look first, in search of explanations, at the top of the decision-making process, the two presidents, Mr Nixon and Mr Ford, and Dr Kissinger's relation to each of them. Both president's were and are identified with the centre–right of the Republican party, hard-line anti-communists, hawks of long standing on Vietnam, with strong personal connections to big business (including the multinationals in Mr Nixon's case) and a firmly capitalist attitude to the problems of the world economy.

How did it happen that Dr Kissinger as the agent of both administrations was able to secure presidential endorsement for a policy whose central concepts have included detente not only with the two major communist powers, but even with the minor but more resented communist power in Cuba?

In some ways the answers are more obvious in Mr Ford's time than in Mr Nixon's, though he was perhaps the further right of the two. He, of course, 'inherited' Dr Kissinger at a moment when the Secretary of State's prestige was enormously high, not only for the foreign-policy successes vis-à-vis China and Russia and the Middle East, but for the interpretation (in inner Washington political circles) of his role in the dangerous final phase of Mr Nixon's exit. The Secretary of State represented an element of continuity with the one successful strand of the Nixon administration, at a time when every strand of continuity, legitimacy and success in the American governmental process was cherished. And Mr Ford himself was not a man given to the analysis of foreign policy. Mr Nixon had undoubtedly represented a competitor of sorts for Dr Kissinger in the policy-making field, especially in the first two or three years, and one whose views inevitably prevailed when it came to the crunch. The latter point was formally true of Mr Ford also, but the level of probability of a competitive strategy was always much less. Various *ballons d'essai* were floated after Mr Ford's succession about a new 'Ford foreign policy', as distinct from a Kissinger policy, but these appear to have come from White House staff, usually at moments when foreign-policy issues looked as if they might prejudice Mr Ford's chances in 1976, rather than from the President himself. And the content of any such new policy was left very vague, the implication being rather that the style of policy would be different – more open, less secretive, more 'principled'. There was not really much indication, in the various crises of the period from August 1974 until after the 1976 election, that Mr Ford contributed anything more to America's foreign relations than an amiable, direct personality (certainly in that a contrast to his predecessor) and a willingness to take the advice of his Secretary of State. On the one important occasion on which he had to appear alone, without anyone to prompt him, the foreign-policy TV debate with Jimmy Carter, he proved so maladroit verbally on Eastern Europe as to damage his own intellectual reputation and electoral chances. If he had had any serious differences with Dr Kissinger over detente, they would presumably have shown at the time when he had to choose between the latter and Dr Schlesinger, and on that occasion he opted for Kissinger. Admittedly the President did drop the word itself, which had never exactly seemed a natural part of his vocabulary, as the election approached, and acquiesced in a foreign-policy plank at the Republican nominating convention that seemed rather to repudiate the concept also. But these were gestures under political pressure rather than true changes of policy or, as far as one can discern, of his personal attitude to the Secretary of State.

There were a good many more riddles and ambiguities in the relationship between Mr Nixon and Dr Kissinger, and perhaps will continue to be even after both men have written their memoirs. How did it happen that Mr Nixon, who as vice-president seemed to out-Dulles Dulles in his readiness for war in the 1954 Vietnam crisis, and who had held the angry 'Kitchen Debate' with Khrushchev in 1959, chose a National Security Adviser of Kissinger's well-known views ten years later? The choice had an element of unexpectedness on the personal as well as the doctrinal level, since Kissinger, a long-time adherent of Nelson Rockefeller, was widely reported, at the time Mr Nixon got the nomination, as saying that the candidate was not fit to be president. A prescient enough view as far as domestic political honour was concerned, and one that must have reached Mr Nixon's ears, so the offer of the post regardless seems to indicate a certain generosity on the then president-elect's part, not often seen in his actions. The relationship obviously remained armed, double-edged, and wary on both sides, despite their joint successes. Kissinger was on the point of resignation several times, including the period of the final delay over Vietnam, late 1972, and the penultimate phase of Watergate, spring 1974. And he did not precisely work at concealing his opinion of the President, or his courtiers, though he did praise Mr Nixon's 'demonic courage' and his capacity for decision.[1]

Mr Nixon once said (before Dr Kissinger took service with him) that the secretary of state was of no great importance in foreign policy: the president was everything. One can perhaps see this view reflected in his initial appointments: Mr Rogers to occupy a blatantly figurehead position as Secretary, the President himself to play the *beau rôle* as manipulator of the world, and Dr Kissinger as the talented but initially-intended-to-be-rather-anonymous 'brains-truster' in the back-room. The process by which Dr Kissinger escaped from that assigned role will no doubt make an interesting study in itself some day. His qualifications as the intellectual source of new initiatives were to be seen in the lines of potential policy he had been drafting for the speeches of Nelson Rockefeller, and also in his efforts on behalf of President Johnson towards a negotiated end of the war in Vietnam. He had been engaged in secret diplomacy on that matter since 1967,[2] and the experience may have been his decisive claim in Mr Nixon's eyes to eligibility for the post of adviser. The president-elect had just seen Vietnam destroy the political life of President Johnson, a man with a much wider base of personal popularity and more political charisma than he himself had ever had. He did not want that fate: he wanted to be a historic peace-maker (outdoing Eisenhower) and certainly he wanted (as he so disastrously sought) to ensure a second term as president.

During the final eleven months of painful stumble downhill for the Nixon administration, its foreign-policy successes were often cited as the main argument against the President's impeachment. But though Mr Nixon was initially vital to the success of the new policies, by 1974 that was no longer the case. In more than one sense, he had worked himself into a situation in which he was dispensable. The realization that the foreign-policy successes were the President's last shield against impeachment inevitably drew some of his adversaries' fire towards Kissinger: he was given some rather pointed hints to walk away or find himself getting hurt. But within the inner circle, the state of the President and the uncertainty as to what he might conceivably do were the strongest possible arguments against the departure of those sustaining policy in the final days.

It was undoubtedly fortunate for American foreign policy that the ultimate fatal revelation that the President had known about the break-in only a few days after it had occurred, and was already then instigating the cover-up, was made so devastatingly clear by the tapes. Even a man with Mr Nixon's talent for the more painful and embarrassing forms of self-destruction could hardly cling to office after that damning piece of evidence came to light. The choice (voluntary or not) of resignation rather than impeachment was a final valuable service, on his part, to America's ability to act in the world. For during an impeachment process, which could potentially have lasted several months, the possibility that the adversary powers would assume paralysis on the part of American decision-makers might have presented great dangers to the world. Even though this possibility did not come about, the conduct of American diplomacy was hampered during Mr Nixon's final six months to a degree that was necessarily concealed by Dr Kissinger at the time, but that has become apparent since. In fact, Kissinger admitted at the end of 1974 that the major satisfaction of the year was that the transition to Mr Ford's presidency had been achieved without disaster.[3]

The detente with Russia was the policy potentially most vulnerable to the fall-out from Watergate, in that during this final period, the first half of 1974, it was reaching a critical stage of bargaining for a new round in SALT and other negotiations, and still more in that it had been personally identified with Mr Nixon (as against the grain of his party), and that the Russians themselves for a long time, almost to the very end, tended explicitly to interpret the whole Watergate saga as a conscious and deliberate plot against the detente. One cannot, of course, say how far this published interpretation was believed by the chief Soviet decision-makers, but it is reasonable to suppose that it seemed plausible even to them, for what was actually happening was totally impossible to reconcile with the official Soviet orthodoxy of the nature of American political reality. That the American head of state should be publicly shown to have been guilty of a piece of alleged political wrong-doing (the keeping of concealed watch on political rivals would be conventional practice for the Soviet leadership) and forced to resign by the pressure of public feeling as orchestrated through the media and Congress, was far too 'democratic' an episode to be accommodated in Soviet (or for that matter Chinese) interpretations of how the American system works. Therefore the assumption that it was a conspiracy organized against the detente, a conspiracy whose victory must be seen as a success for the more war-minded members of American 'ruling circles', was inescapable. Since this has been shown not to be the case, the Soviet explanation, if one is still found necessary, must ascribe it to personal rivalries.

Though one may say that the chief danger to the detente in the Watergate episode lay in Soviet misinterpretation of its nature, it had other repercussions, especially in the discussions in Moscow in June 1974, only a few weeks before the President's fall. According to the conservative columnist, William Safire, who was one of Mr Nixon's speechwriters and reasonably close to him even at this late stage of decline, the differences in interpretation of detente as between Dr Kissinger and Mr Nixon almost reached the surface on that occasion. 'President Nixon, a graduate of the John Foster Dulles school of international affairs, carried a hardliners' suspicions of long-range Soviet intentions into his planning for a structure of peace. His goal as he came into office was for a limited peace, with power-centres co-operating to keep out of war, but with the ideological struggle continuing until, in some far distant future, forms of democracy would persevere over forms of communism.'[4] According to Safire, in the earlier years of his administration Mr Nixon would reshape and modify Dr Kissinger's drafts on foreign policy; in his final phase of weakness he had to accept them, as in his defence of detente in a speech of June 1974, which has some clearly Kissinger rather than Nixon phrases: 'We cannot gear our foreign policy to the transformation of other societies ...

Peace between nations with totally different systems is also a high moral objective.'

If this interpretation of the Nixon (as against the Kissinger) concept of detente is true, one might say that for the President it may have been rather more a tactic than a strategy: that the cold warrior of Mr Dulles's time was still lying in wait behind the artful web of Dr Kissinger's detente diplomacy. That interpretation would in a way give more coherence and consistency to Mr Nixon's general foreign-policy stance and thus it has a certain plausibility, except that coherence and consistency do not seem attributes of the Nixon style in political life.

The troubles of the Watergate period throw light upon one of the more interesting ambivalences of Kissinger's own career as both theorist and policy-maker: his uneasy relationship with the most important of all the pressure groups that influence American foreign policy, a pressure group so pervasive as to be invisible and hardly mentioned in the text-books, which are indeed mostly written by its members. In Britain it is called the Establishment; American political scientists (especially of the left or the far right) sometimes tend to call it more ponderously the 'Eastern liberal–intellectual foreign-policy elite'. Its members are well-informed, prosperous, influential persons who take a strong interest in foreign policy: professors, journalists, lawyers, bankers, industrialists with large international interests, directors of transnational corporations, senior officers of the armed services. Undoubtedly this was the group of people who made American foreign policy from F.D.R.'s time up to and including Vietnam. It might appear that Kissinger, a Harvard man whose first study of contemporary international politics had been written under the auspices of the Council on Foreign Relations (the main club of the foreign-policy establishment), would naturally be one of its favourite sons, but this was not really the case. His status was more reminiscent of those many characters in Russian plays and novels who are 'with' some great and powerful family rather than 'of' it: the talented but somewhat difficult tutor or protégé of the true 'in-group'. The establishment is predominantly Anglo-American, from long-settled families with a good deal of 'old money' to bless themselves with, and connections through the more expensive private schools as well as Yale, Princeton or Harvard. Dean Acheson would be its archetype: son of a bishop, Yale man, corporation lawyer, liberal Democrat. And, until March 1968, the most determined of hawks on Vietnam.

This last point is significant, for Vietnam was the great failed cause of the American liberal establishment, originating in the Truman period, proclaimed with 'gung-ho' enthusiasm in the Kennedy period, and abandoned with guilt and anguish in the Johnson period. Kissinger was not an adherent of the strand of opinion that originally sponsored the war, and was rather conspicuously not among the large Harvard contingent embarked for Camelot by Kennedy in 1960, though he did have some consultant status with the President for a while on European affairs. He first visited Vietnam in 1965, returned clearly sceptical of military success for America (I heard him lecture at Chatham House on his way home from this visit, in January 1966, and was much struck at the time by the degree of his consternation) and was engaged from 1967 in the secret efforts of President Johnson's time to end the war.[5] Yet the mood of guilty disillusionment dominant among American intellectuals (especially former Democratic policy-makers) after 1968 severely damaged his own standing, especially with the liberals. The process of extrication of American forces from Vietnam as he conducted it for President Nixon from 1969 to 1973 seemed agonizingly slow to anti-Vietnam activists, including some of his colleagues and ex-colleagues in the National Security Council and at Harvard, who had themselves been still convinced Vietnam hawks when Kissinger was beginning the efforts to a negotiated end in 1967. It is difficult to know how far policy decisions on the conduct of the war during this negotiation phase were his responsibility, as against that of the President or the military. It does not seem probable, for instance, that at the time of the Cambodia secret bombing of early 1969 or invasion of 1970 (when he was still very much 'on approval' in the White House) he had any great ascendancy over the making of what was obviously military policy, intended to disrupt the supply of material to the Vietnam fighting fronts. General Abrams' tactical requirements for a breathing-space on the southern battlefields appear to have been the origin of these ultimately disastrous decisions. General Westmoreland, in his memoirs, has said that he wanted them in 1968.[6]

Covert operations like the Cambodian bombing were already familiar policy expedients in Washington, and had been at least since Eisenhower's time, taking then the form for instance of the secret armies for the Guatemala and Cuba invasions. A tendency for their details to be leaked to the press was equally familiar. The technique of fighting decisions you do not like, especially if they are agreed by the chief of your own department, through 'selective leak' to a sympathetic journalist, might be called the dominant Washington art-form. So it was inevitable, when the Cambodia bombing story leaked in April 1969, that the source should be sought among Kissinger's subordinates at the National Security Council and the journalists who frequented its corridors. Nixon's reaction to the leaks was less philosophical than Kennedy's had been when something similar happened during the preparatory stages of the Bay of Pigs invasion, but then Kennedy's past experience had been as the blue-eyed boy of the media: he could afford to be relaxed with them. Nixon, on the other hand, had long been their *bête noir*. There was a Washington joke of the time which went: just because you're paranoic, it doesn't mean they are not out to get you. It perhaps expressed the essence of the President's relations to the press.

The slowness of the Vietnam disengagement, and some of the measures taken to improve the prospective military viability of 'Vietnamization', were undoubtedly the major original reasons for the alienation between Kissinger and the left–liberal wing of the foreign-policy elite, especially in the universities. The telephone-tapping charges raised against him during the Watergate episode were both an outcrop and a symbol of the vendettas created during that particular battle over policy.[7] And this alienation in turn cut him off from those who might have been his natural allies as far as detente was concerned, the sceptical and revisionist intellectuals who rejected the conventional accounts of the origins of the Cold War.

There is an ironic twist to the respective relations of Dr Kissinger and President Nixon to the establishment. If Dr Kissinger was, as I have said, not *quite* a member, he was certainly an admired and indulged (if patronized) protégé, a prospective adopted son, and ultimately a potential *éminence grise*, succeeding Lippmann. Mr Nixon was not *possibly* a member, any more than Joe McCarthy had been, and for much the same reasons. The criterion for exclusion is not right-wing views, but ungentlemanly conduct of a political life. To revert to my Russian metaphor: if Dr Kissinger was the isolated and temperamental tutor with the powerful family, Mr Nixon was the boorish and faintly sinister *nouveau riche* who had once occupied a humble position on the estate but had now become powerful enough to threaten a take-over of the cherry orchard. The President certainly felt this 'outsider' status acutely, as the ramblings on the Watergate tapes show, even attributing his final disaster to it, in a conversation with John Dean: 'The basic thing is the Establishment ... they have got to show that despite the successes we have had in foreign policy and in the election, they have got to show it is wrong...'[8]

In the jungle of Mr Nixon's Washington, a streak of paranoia was perhaps a necessity for survival, though the President himself took it to damaging excess. In Dr Kissinger's case, it seemed to emerge in a predilection for casting himself as a 'loner', expressed in rather Walter Mittyish fashion in one famously indiscreet interview, rashly using the folk-myth of *Shane*: 'The Americans love the cowboy who comes into town all alone on his horse and nothing else ... He acts and that is enough, being in the right place at the right time, in sum a Western. This romantic and surprising character suits me because being a loner has always been part of my style.'[9] His rather abrasive relationships with the foreign-policy bureaucracy in the State Department and the intelligence community probably owed something to this self-image.

To sum up the Nixon–Kissinger relationship, one must concede that at this stage most of the questions about it still remain unanswered, though it is clear that it changed a great deal in the years of their joint rearrangement of the world. Kissinger could from the first supply the ideas, the techniques and most of the hard work. But until the last few months it had to be the President who supplied the political authority and endorsement, and originally also a good deal of the courage. He took ultimate responsibility for breaks with the past (on China policy and Russia policy and on Vietnam) that better presidents and better men had not been able to face. His credentials as a tough anti-communist, even the fact that he had discreditably made his career in the McCarthyite period as a *professional* anti-communist, were positive assets during this crucial decision-making. They operated as a sort of protective colouration or camouflage for policies that would probably have raised great alarm and resistance on the Republican right and in 'Middle America' if they had been sponsored by a liberal Republican, like Rockefeller, and still more if they had been sought by a Democrat. Even the eventual necessity of accepting the departure of American troops from Vietnam without a victory might have been almost an impeachment matter for a different kind of president.

As the President's constituency was gradually washed away by Watergate, Congress reasserted an authority in foreign-policy matters that it had not enjoyed since before F.D.R.'s time in the 1930s. One might in fact say that the major problems of negotiation for Dr Kissinger from late 1974 were neither with allies nor with adversaries, but with Congress. This was inevitable in the political and constitutional circumstances. Neither the new President nor the new Vice-President had any mandate from the people. The sole source of political legitimacy was Congress. Moreover, the appointment of Mr Ford as Vice-President, after the disgrace of Mr Agnew, had been imposed on Mr Nixon by a powerful group of right-wing Republicans headed by Mr Melvin Laird, the former Secretary of Defense, who is reported to have cherished thoughts of being Secretary of State, and whose views included an undisguised distrust of the notion of detente.

So one might say that immediately after Mr Nixon's fall the situation constitutionally was that Congress was not only the sole fount of political legitimacy, but was thoroughly alienated from the presidency by the long struggle over Watergate. The media, always inclined in America to consider themselves a political 'Fourth Estate', had been unprecedentedly strengthened vis-à-vis constituted authority in general by their role in Mr Nixon's fall. The orthodox right wing of the Republican party had 'evolved' a new president, in a way fascinatingly similar to the manner in which the Conservative party in Britain used to evolve its new prime ministers. Political authority generally was at a sharp discount in the country. And naturally enough in these circumstances, the congressional elections at the end of the year returned an exceptionally large number of new recruits, mostly liberal Democrats full of the glow of reforming virtue and the determination to reassert 'Congress's rightful role', in a very ambitious definition, in foreign policy.

Thus it was probably inevitable that the two years following Mr Nixon's fall should provide the roughest patch of the road for Dr Kissinger as policy-maker and for detente as a policy. The world outside America was, for a variety of reasons, also rather unamenable to management during this particular period of history. The most damaging issue, as far as his general capacity to secure co-operation from Congress was concerned, was Cyprus. The crisis in the island came to a head just as Watergate went into its final spasm, and for that reason undoubtedly received less effective attention than it might have done. The immediate domestic result was the creation of a large, angry and powerful lobby of the 'friends of Greece' in Congress, not balanced by any countervailing 'friends of Turkey' lobby, since most congressmen have many Greek constituents, but few have Turkish ones. Moreover, this particular lobby could to some extent make common cause with a still more powerful and much longer-established one, the 'friends of Israel'. That group, which could regularly expect support from some seventy senators, was anxious at this period about the possibility that Dr Kissinger might put an undue amount of pressure on Israel to secure a further step in his Middle East peace-making. Furthermore the situation in Vietnam was at this time moving rapidly towards the final end, though this did not become publicly apparent until about January 1975. And in general the Democratic presidential hopefuls in Congress, enlivened by what already appeared the near-certainty of a Democratic victory in 1976, were becoming intent on showing off their respective paces, with an eye to the nomination, and were thus wishful to demonstrate that they could put together better foreign policies than the Secretary of State. (Since foreign policy was the one area of success of the Republican administration, it was especially desirable to show that a Democrat could more than compete there.)

So altogether Dr Kissinger's policies had to take rather a heavy battering, and some received considerable damage. The most real and possibly long-term ill was done to American relations with Turkey, through the insistence of the House of Representatives on maintaining an embargo on arms deliveries, after the misuse of American arms in the Turkish invasion of Cyprus. That created resentments in what had previously been a very cordial relationship, possibly reorienting the whole direction of Turkish policy away from identification with the West towards re-identification with the Islamic world and even an inclination towards non-alignment. The Angola crisis and the final stages in Vietnam and Cambodia were also marked by some abrasive arguments between the Secretary of State and Congress, but those were perhaps episodes destined to be lost causes even without that complication.

As to the detente with the Soviet Union, the objective in the last few months of the Ford administration had necessarily to be securing its survival, rather than its advancement. There was really no progress to speak of on arms control between the Vladivostok meeting of November 1974 and the 1976 election, and the general political relationship went downhill in those two years, mostly because of Angola. There was not, however, much pressure against detente from the Democrats, other than during Senator Jackson's brief showing as a possible nominee. The serious pressure was that from the Republican right, from late 1975 to August 1976. The main formal success for this sector of opinion came at the end of the period, in the foreign-policy plank adopted at the instance of Mr Reagan's supporters during the Republican convention. If election planks had to be taken as the actual basis of post-election policy for the party concerned, it might well have been assumed that detente would not survive in a new Republican administration, for the party appeared to endorse the views of the most eloquent of the policy's opponents, and conveyed a deliberated snub to Dr Kissinger:

> The goal of Republican foreign policy is the achievement of liberty under law.... We recognize and commend that great beacon of human courage and morality, Alexander Solzhenitsyn, for his compelling message that we must face the world with no illusions about the nature of tyranny. Ours will be a foreign policy that keeps this ever in mind. Ours will be a foreign policy which recognizes that in international negotiations we must make no undue concessions – that in pursuing detente we must not grant unilateral favours with only the hope of getting future favours in return.

However, this was not, of course, likely to be construed even by foreign observers as a serious forecast of actual change in policy in the event of a Republican victory. The Republican party faithful, serving as delegates to the convention, represented the activist minority of what was itself a dwindling minority (about 22 per cent) of potential voters. As the party shrank in numbers, those who remained naturally tended to be the hard core 'true believers' of Republicanism, rather than average possible supporters of Ford as presidential candidate. There is a sense in which one can say, nevertheless, that the sort of instinctive nationalistic conservatism they represented was more in line with the traditional Republicanism of Mr Dulles's day, for instance, than the innovative policies devised by Kissinger under the authority of Nixon and Ford.

The policy lines suggested before the election by Mr Carter seemed on the whole (though this was naturally not dwelt upon by the spokesmen of either party) at least as much in accord with existing or potential detente patterns. One of the few specific proposals he put forward as candidate was that of a multinational agreement to reduce the sale of arms round the world. Whatever one thought of the feasibility of such a proposal, it was quite clear that it would have little chance of Soviet agreement, save in an atmosphere of detente considerably warmer than even the best achieved during the Republican administration. Arms sales are one of the major means by which the Powers bind their friends and allies to themselves and secure formidable holds over their decision-making capacity in crisis situations. To suppose the Powers agreeing with each other to give up this useful asset is to suppose their reaching a more marked degree of mutual trust and sense of common interest than had thus far appeared. On the other hand, Mr Carter also implied that he would institute a tougher and more forceful mode of detente bargaining than Mr Ford, demanding better Soviet compliance with the human rights provisions of the Helsinki declaration and an easing of the restrictions on Jewish emigration. Moreover, he hinted that in the case of another Soviet venture like that in Angola he would use economic weapons against the Soviet Union, including a 'total withholding of trade'. (However, Congress in 1975 had refused use in Angola of even the minor expenditure of a few million dollars of arms-aid, whereas 'total withholding of trade' would affect, merely on the grain deals, interests running at about a thousand million dollars a year, so it might well in actual practice encounter domestic and congressional obstacles of a serious kind, even in the hands of a president likely to have greater leverage with a Democratic Congress than Mr Ford.)

Most of the Democratic criticism of Dr Kissinger's diplomacy in the final debates concentrated on matters of style rather than of substance.[10] The President-elect was clearly in agreement on a highly activist U.S. foreign policy, based on maintenance of the alliances with Western Europe and Japan, the cultivation of as good relations as could reasonably be secured with China and the Soviet Union, and the pursuit of initiatives like those in southern Africa and the Middle East. There were marginal differences with existing policy on matters like the prospect of withdrawing troops from Korea, but no hint of neo-isolationism or of real possibility that the armed forces would be cut to a degree that would undermine the balance of power, either of which might be fatal to detente.

Yet the assumption that the 'Kissinger style' in diplomacy (with its emphasis on privacy in dealings between the Powers, and a concession of the reality of 'unlikeness' between societies) was a superficial matter that could easily be discarded with benefit to the substance of the relationships was in fact misleading, as the earliest initiatives of the Carter administration had begun to show by March 1977. One might say that Dr Kissinger's style was a sort of shorthand indication of a theory or set of concepts about the nature of the relation specifically between independent sovereignties, and the purposes and limits of diplomacy and influence in that particular context. Mr Carter's style, by contrast, insofar as it was visible in the first weeks of his administration, seemed to indicate a transposition of the values and techniques that had made for his great success in American domestic politics directly into his dealings with other governments. As an enterprise it had initially considerable public appeal, but its incompatibility with the theories held in other sovereignties was readily apparent.

CHAPTER 4

Strategic Doctrine and Arms Control: The Nature of Stability

I suggested earlier that detente should be seen as a diplomatic strategy for the control of adversary power. The heart of the problem of the adversary's military power, for both the United States and the Soviet Union, is the other's capacity for nuclear strike. The effort to control the size, nature and mode of deployment of that capacity is what we are essentially concerned with in looking at the arms-control measures of the detente, though conventional forces have also entered the arguments and are coming to be more important in them. There is, however, a slight ambivalence, even a paradox, in the relationship of arms-control measures to detente in general. The strategy as a whole rests on, and demands, a reasonably stable balance of power, and ceases to be viable if that essential infrastructure is weakened. Most people tend to equate the balance of power with something that is rather different, less complex and more quantifiable: the existing balance of armed forces. The balance of armed forces can be, and is, published every year,[1] and contrasts between numbers of divisions or tanks often look rather more dramatic than they actually are. Thus the political confidence on which the viability of detente rests, as far as the Western powers are concerned, requires that the strategic balance, posture and doctrine that underlie it should not only *be* sound, but should *look* sound when published to the electorate. The 'apparent balance' or 'perceived balance', as against the real balance, must not provide too available a psychological handle for politically ambitious persons, out to advance their electoral fortunes by arguing that existing office-holders are neglecting the country's security interests. And this has been one defining and limiting condition of arms-control measures, over the detente period, for both sides.

To put the matter in this way may seem to underplay the significance of arms control. Some comments on the Strategic Arms Limitation Talks (SALT), for instance, give the impression that arms control and detente[2] are wholly dependent on each other, unable to sustain life separately. One may sympathize with the use of this argument, since it is tactically valuable to the friends of arms control, which does not have much of a constituency except among left–liberal intellectual opinion and is a project that needs any tactical advantage it can contrive. Detente *with* arms-control measures should undoubtedly be both more creative (since fewer useful resources will be wasted) and more viable (since what Mr McNamara used to call the action–reaction syndrome in arms-building feeds back into the political relationships) than detente *without* arms control. Nevertheless, detente has proved a useful thing in a number of political ways even when it is not productive of arms control, as obviously in the case of the America–China detente or the Germany–Poland detente. Even if it should become impossible to maintain the measures of arms control achieved or indicated as likely so far between the U.S.A. and U.S.S.R., there would be a case for salvaging the remaining elements of the America–Soviet detente for their own value and for their general diplomatic influence. Indeed, though disarmament or arms control is one of the more dramatic ways in which the world may be made less dangerous, and in which the waste of useful resources may be reduced, it is not the only pathway to these desirable objectives, and historically speaking it has often proved rather a blind-alley. Disarmament, if unilateral, has even occasionally strengthened the forces making for war. In assessing the costs and benefits of the moves towards arms control in the contemporary detente, one must avoid a simplistic 'armaments bad – disarmament good' assumption. The Western powers reduced or neglected arms budgets during the 1930s: it did not enable them to avoid war. In fact, one might argue that higher arms spending by Britain, France and the United States, from 1931 on, would conceivably have shortened the depression, lessened the political disasters it produced, and discouraged Hitler's fantasies of democratic decadence and the Thousand-Year Reich. Even if the Western powers had still been obliged to embark on war in 1939, they would have done so on better terms, and possibly found victory sooner – even perhaps before the atomic bomb became feasible.

I write this paragraph not in order to cast doubt on the achievements of SALT, which I think very valuable (rather more on a political than a strategic basis), but to underline the fact that arms-control proposals must be related to the underlying forces-balance and political reality of their time if one is to discern whether they will make for peace or war. And if one is thinking of arms-control measures extending through, hopefully, a long period of detente, they must be related to strategic doctrine, as well as to the immediate or foreseeable military balance. The primary objective must, I will argue, be stability at the lowest level of arms that is politically acceptable for both sides. But if there is a forced choice between a higher level of arms *with* stability, or a lower level *without* stability, the higher level must be the prudent option. One might compare the world's situation to that of a tight-rope walker. No doubt he would be best off on the ground of general and complete disarmament, but for a variety of reasons he is unlikely to make that rational choice. He may be able to choose only between fixing his tight-rope ten storeys up to somewhat crumbling brickwork, or twenty storeys up to a firmer stanchion in domestic political reality. Either ten or twenty storeys leaves him equally with the prospect of 'overkill' if he should prove less than surefooted on his unreasonable pathway. But the higher level may, in defiance of apparent common sense, be the lesser danger or irrationality if it can be an *agreed* level that will not suddenly be jacked up at either end. For who would choose to walk an uphill tight-rope?

Strategic Doctrine and Arms Control: The Nature of Stability 57

This is somewhat the way one might look at prospective levels of both nuclear and conventional arms over the foreseeable future. Even given the optimistic assumption of a long period of detente, one should not expect them to be dramatically lowered. The basic factor in fixing the levels remains the Soviet government's ambitions, or its sense of its own vulnerability, and even the troubles of the capitalist world in 1974–6 did not necessarily reduce this sense of vulnerability. There are many reasons why the Russians will want to maintain a high level of armaments, no matter how cosy their relationship with the Americans and the West Europeans may become. First, it has been the Russian tradition, as much in Czarist as in Soviet times. Second, there is the sense of danger from China, which may even be increased by some of the side-effects of the crumbling of the Western ex-colonies (since Maoist doctrine has some built-in advantages over Russian in societies of this sort) and which seems to be rooted in a kind of Russian folk-memory of the 'golden horde' of the Mongols, and a rather guilty half-suppressed consciousness of how much territory the Czarist Empire won from the Chinese Empire only a century ago. The recent territorial disputes keep these memories alive, and China's progress as a nuclear power is not likely to quieten them. (One can see the back-lash of this in the first SALT treaties of 1972. One of the reasons why 'zero ABM' – no anti-ballistic missile systems – which some Western arms-controllers argued for, was not feasible for the Russians is that it would have required them to dismantle the 'Galosh' ABM system round Moscow, which is no use at all against American capabilities but might catch a stray Chinese missile. Thus the American acceptance then of two ABM systems, though apparently irrational – since the U.S. negotiators believed them at best useless and at worst destabilizing – was in fact realistic and produced the later agreement to move to one system each.) Thirdly, there is the wish to control and garrison the East European buffer-zone, which the Russian leaders see as the one undeniable gain for Russian security through the agonies of the Second World War. The events of 1970 in Poland, 1968 in Czechoslovakia,

1956 in Hungary and elsewhere, and 1948 in Yugoslavia can hardly have left the Soviet leaders with any illusions as to what is likely to happen to this buffer-zone if they dismantle the armies that garrison it. Whether it is rationalized ideologically as making permanent the gains of the socialist revolution (as in the Brezhnev doctrine), or nationalistically as a necessity of Russia's defence, or materialistically on the basis of the usefulness of these economies to the Soviet consumer, there is very little doubt that the Russians will continue to want to maintain the garrisons, which are not small: about thirty-one divisions at the moment of writing. So that obviously the amount of actual reduction they have been likely to accept through the arms-control talks in Vienna (MBFR) is not very large. This is one of the points on which the political and the strategic or military aspects of detente interact in a very complex way: the encouragement of unrest or dissention in Eastern Europe obviously reduces any chance of Soviet arms cuts there. One might say also that there is a kind of built-in defensivemindedness enforced on Soviet decision-makers both by Russian historical experience over many centuries (the experience of invasion and disastrous battles on Russian soil) and by Soviet ideology, which theoretically at least is bound to have in mind one final desperate attack by the allegedly dying capitalist world.

With all these motives towards high force-levels, it may even seem surprising that the Soviet Union has used arms-control negotiations as anything other than broadcasting systems for propaganda. But there are reasons for supposing that though the Soviet Union wants to keep force-levels high, it also wants them controlled, especially vis-à-vis America. Firstly, if there were a true uncontrolled out-and-out arms race, the Russians would be quite likely to lose it. Neither in the essential contemporary skills like computers and lasers, nor in the general level of industrial strength, have they yet caught up with the United States. Secondly, they can afford a true arms race much less well than the Americans. When the U.S. economy falters, it tends to do so from deficiency of demand. A rapid rearmament programme, as from the outbreak of the Korean War, tends to produce economic boom, rather than hard times. America does not need to sacrifice butter for guns: on the contrary, the fact that the guns are being produced makes it *more* likely that practically everyone will be able to afford butter ('military Keynesianism', as Professor Galbraith calls it). The Soviet Union, on the contrary, is still an economy of comparative scarcity: if the steel has to go into making tanks, the waiting list for cars becomes even more hopelessly long.

Finally, one might say that the Russians want some measure of arms-control agreement (again with the Americans rather than the Europeans) because of the political and economic fringe benefits that flow from it. In fact one might argue that the political leadership (especially Brezhnev) has been enabled to impose some strategic restraint (not actual cuts, but a ceiling on demands) against the resistance of the military leadership in the name of the economic benefits of detente. The process by which the political leaders of a country enforce their own priorities on their respective military chiefs is quite a delicate one, even in countries so remote from the tradition of the military coup d'état as the United States and the Soviet Union. Military leaders have a professional commitment to anxiety about the capabilities of the other side, and one might say a professional scepticism about detente. 'Othello's occupation's gone' is an unadmitted worry, but may be a formidable one, especially where, as in the Soviet Union, there are few lobbies as politically powerful as that of the professional officer corps. One of the apparent reasons for the fate that overtook Mr Khrushchev in 1964 was that among the 'harebrained schemes' of which his colleagues accused him, the officer corps discerned the possibility of seeing themselves made redundant by his enthusiasm for missiles. At any rate, his projected scheme for a revolutionary change in the structure of the Soviet armed forces, which would have deprived half the young officers in the country of their chances of promotion and the careers for which they had been trained, was swiftly buried by his successors.

Dr Kissinger, in his press conference after the abortive effort at new SALT guidelines during Mr Nixon's final days, seemed to feel the same kind of military recalcitrance as a limit on what he could achieve: 'My impression from what I have observed is that both sides have to convince their military establishments of the benefits of restraint, and that is not a thought that comes naturally to military people on either side.' And later, in answer to another question, he seemed to be continuing an argument with some obdurate military man: 'And one of the questions we have to ask ourselves as a country is what in the name of God is strategic superiority? What is the significance of it politically, militarily, operationally at these levels of numbers? What do you *do* with it?'[3]

Of course the consciousness of the professional security preoccupations of the officer corps is not unique to the two present super-powers. Lord Salisbury felt it well before the space age, in 1892: 'If you believe the soldiers, nothing is safe ... If they were allowed full scope they would insist on the garrisoning of the moon to protect us from Mars.' It has been a familiar assumption of the American arms-control community that no project can get far unless it can manage to 'keep the Chiefs of Staff on board', and no doubt the same is true for the Soviet Union. In fact the process of unadmitted bargaining between political and military authority seems fairly symmetrical in the two cases, which is probably rather useful for the prospects of agreement. Even the business of looking to a possible alternative political leadership, which was inherent for instance in the situation of the contenders for the presidency in their criticisms of administration policy, and the support that could be indicated by Pentagon figures for particular candidates, is not very different from the way the Soviet 'top brass' looked beyond Mr Khrushchev to the alternative political leadership of Mr Brezhnev in the days before the change of chief decision-maker there.

Thus it is a major point in favour of the degree of arms control thus far achieved or foreshadowed that it is compatible with the strategic doctrines likely to remain dominant for the rest of this century. The chief element in these strategic doctrines is the 'hostage' situation of the cities of the two adversaries. That is, since the two hundred or so main areas of human habitation on each side are known to be targeted or targetable by the strategic nuclear missiles of the other side, and since there is no means of defence against these putative strikes, the inhabitants of those places are all necessarily and ineluctably 'hostages' to the other side. The first SALT treaties in effect stabilized this hostage relationship by agreement not to attempt anti-ballistic missile systems, save the two then in existence or prospect (reduced by the agreement in 1974 to one each side – the Russian one round Moscow and the American one round the ICBM sites in North Dakota). It also put some interim restrictions on numbers of offensive missiles. The second phase of attempts at control, in the Vladivostok guidelines of 1974 and since, has been concerned with seeking agreement to restrict the number of such missiles by establishing 'ceilings' for mirvs and launchers.

The central concept round which arms-control measures must be organized, whatever details may be debated of numbers, throw-weight, megatonnage or 'lethality', is that of 'essential equivalence'. It is a concept that involves scrutiny of conventional as well as nuclear forces, since in a world in which nuclear forces had reached a true equivalence, but in which the West was in a situation of marked conventional inferiority, threats of the use of nuclear weapons might fail to appear convincing, and the whole concept of deterrence would be undermined.

Some approach to essential equivalence between the forces on the Central Front, as between Nato and the Warsaw Pact, is not nearly so remote as might appear from the figures often cited. It is certainly not so remote that it must be dismissed as an impossible dream for the Western powers, whose peoples are in fact more numerous as well as a great deal richer than those of the Warsaw Pact countries. It is only a species of nationalist self-indulgence and failure of political will that has prevented them from deploying forces fully equal in strength to those of the Warsaw Pact.

That failure of political will has very often been attributed to detente, and used as a major part of the case against it. But in fact it was just as characteristic of the Cold War period. As early as 1952, just after the first spurt of Western conventional rearmament, and in the coldest and most apprehensive years of the Cold War, the Western powers were already in process of failing to live up to their announced ambitions with respect to conventional forces, and that pattern persisted for the following twenty years, though there was some accretion of strength when German forces began to be raised after 1955, and a spurt of general concern about conventional force-levels in the early Kennedy–McNamara period, 1961–2. The reasons for this consistent quasi-failure are deep-seated in the politics and psychology of the Western powers, and in the nature of the contemporary strategic dilemmas. If the problems had really been created by the detente, that would be a heavy and damaging charge against it, but any history of the military development of Nato will prove the point of their being just as troublesome during the Cold War.[4] The military strength of the Soviet Union has been growing steadily for more than thirty years, as Dr Kissinger has often pointed out, for reasons that have to do with population and resources and the political system and are not determined by the diplomatic climate of cold war or detente. That is a formidable fact, one that must partially govern the policies of the Western powers and China for as long as it persists, and one that the West has never quite come to terms with, though the margin of deficiency is much less than is usually alleged.

There is one way, however, in which the concession of 'essential equivalency' on the nuclear side, characteristic of the arms-control measures of the detente, might potentially help to remedy the weaknesses that have so long plagued the West on the *conventional* side. One of the reasons why a measure of this particular brand of inferiority has always been regarded with relative calm by Western decision-makers (except during the yearly effort to get defence budgets through Congress or Parliament) has been the policy-makers' unavowed assumption that the Western edge in nuclear strike-power was enough in fact to inhibit any serious Soviet military adventures in Europe.

Strategic Doctrine and Arms Control: The Nature of Stability 63

Until the last few years, Soviet naval weakness had the same inhibiting function for Soviet adventures outside Europe. One of the most interesting lessons of the Cuba missile crisis of 1962 was how Soviet power to act was blocked on the conventional plane by naval inferiority in the area concerned, and on the nuclear plane by overall strategic inferiority. The lesson was not lost on the Russians: their attention to both fields of armaments after that last and most dramatic crisis of the true Cold War has quite transformed both balances, so that by 1976 the Russians could be interpreted as having the naval capacity for 'global imperialism', at least in the mode of Angola. And in Europe they might be judged as likely to feel less inhibited by a sense of strategic nuclear inferiority from military adventures for a number of reasons, including an intensive civil defence effort to obviate the 'hostage' situation of their cities, on which the main structure of deterrence rests.

It is this last consideration that provides incentives for the Nato powers to improve their conventional forces towards a closer and more obvious approximation of 'essential equivalency' on that plane also. If the Nato forces were as wildly inferior as is often represented in political argument, that might be a lost endeavour. However, the Western disadvantage in numbers on the Central Front, according to various evidence, is both less substantial and less important than the figures usually cited would appear to indicate, and this assessment is sometimes confirmed by official spokesmen. Dr Schlesinger, for instance, once said that the difference was of negligible military importance.[5] It is not that the statistics that seem to show otherwise are false, but putting them together is rather like composing a bouquet: there is a considerable range of blooms between which one may choose to produce a desired effect. Alain Enthoven, who was Mr McNamara's chief lieutenant as Secretary of Defense, has demonstrated in some detail how this is done.[6] One may for instance, if needing to justify higher arms budgets, maintain that Nato is 'outnumbered on the Central Front by 68 divisions to 24'; alternatively, one can say that the two sides are in a state of effective rough military balance on the Central

Front, with about a million men each in ground and air forces. In tanks, the Warsaw Pact forces appear to have a large advantage in numbers, 15,500 against 6,000, but the true balance in this field is tanks versus anti-tank defences, the strategic missions of the two armies being quite different.[7] Analysts (except when they are talking for budgetary effect) tend to maintain that the Western weapons are the more advanced. Nato also has or had a large advantage in tactical air-power, aircraft capable of carrying 2.5 times the payload of the other side, and equipped with 'smart bombs'. One of the reasons why the statistics can be made (without actual fiddling) to give quite disparate pictures is the position of French forces. The French army amounts to 332,000 men, and though France must formally be rated in peace-time as no longer a participant in the military affairs of Nato, in fact the French high command has always remained represented at Nato headquarters, and French forces are tacitly written into the contingency planning and are deployed in Germany. It would clearly be absurd to assume that, in the event of actual hostilities, the unwilling East European governments and armies, which are at present captives in the Soviet sphere and have to be garrisoned by Russian troops, would be reliably enthusiastic for forwarding Russian military purposes, whereas the French government and army would fail to construe its own interest as dependent on the Western line holding, in a situation in which if the line does *not* hold, the Red Army is estimated as likely to reach the Rhine in forty-eight hours. But the official statistics cannot be changed to take account of this reality while France remains formally outside the Nato command.

French defence policy as reformulated in mid-1976 by President Giscard d'Estaing and his Chief of Staff, General Gui Méry, went some distance towards making this difficulty almost entirely formal and statistical.[8] In the June issue of the French *Revue de Defense National*, and in subsequent discussion at the defence academy, General Méry said that it was 'by no means excluded' that France should take part in the first battle (i.e. that on Nato's forward defence line) and that indeed it would be extremely dangerous for France willingly to stay out of that battle, since its own fate might be then decided, and that therefore there must be exercises with Nato forces to perfect 'interoperability'. The 1976 budget proposed to double defence expenditure by 1982, raising it from seventeen to twenty per cent of the national budget, and spending most of the money re-equipping the army. The *force de frappe*, the great Gaullist symbol of France's strategic independence of the United States, was considerably down-played. Plans for building a sixth nuclear submarine were scrapped, and the implication was allowed to appear that French nuclear forces should be construed as only dissuading *nuclear* attack on France: other forms of attack must be met by conventional means.[9] These changes in French policy and doctrine were described and resented by both the Gaullist right and the socialist and communist left as an abandonment of France's independent strategy, and so in all logic they were, though political tact precluded their being acknowledged as such by the President or his official spokesmen, or welcomed as such by France's allies. With the dropping of his Gaullist Prime Minister, M. Chirac, for M. Barre in August 1976, President Giscard d'Estaing may be said to have moved away from the Gaullist interpretation of French personality and destiny in more respects than those of defence.

Bearing this in mind one may argue that such inferiority as may be attributed to Western forces is not a matter of deficiency in either manpower or resources, but of various self-inflicted wounds, which are essentially curable, though troubling. In particular, the Western mode of organization has produced far fewer combat divisions from a given number of troops. Also the use of a large number of competitive weapons types, for reasons of national pride and economic interest, is supposed by some analysts to have cost Nato thirty per cent of its combat efficiency. The deployment of Western forces has not been adequately related to the essential strategic function of stopping a massive offensive by the Soviet tank armies, which are the most formidable aspect of Warsaw Pact strength.[10]

The outcome of the Helsinki 'summit' of 1975 and the strategic debate of early 1976 seemed to indicate some prospective effort at progress in the field of control of conventional and tactical–nuclear forces. It was perhaps exaggerating to refer to these talks as negotiations up to 1976, since the participants in them spent the first three years of their meetings in peacefully spinning a small substance of proposals into a large cloud of words. This temporizing procedure was probably inevitable, since neither the Nato side nor the Warsaw Pact side had any great enthusiasm for cutting the forces concerned. The talks were in effect required of the European parties by domestic pressures in America; they could be regarded as among the fringe costs of the Vietnam War. The anguish generated in Vietnam spilled over into congressional suspicion and dislike of all stationing of U.S. forces abroad, and thus put real steam behind the perennial impulse in Congress to cut the American forces in Nato. The West Europeans, confronted by the prospect of unilateral American cuts forced on the U.S. administration by the Mansfield amendment,[11] felt that the hazard might be averted or delayed or turned to some compensating advantage by well-drawn-out negotiations for reductions on both sides. And (more surprising at first sight) Mr Brezhnev appeared to feel the same way. How else can one explain his choosing to make a speech in May 1971, just a week before the Mansfield amendment was presented, declaring the Soviet Union in favour of negotiated reductions, and challenging Nato to stand by its previous declarations on this point? His timing could hardly have been more obliging, as far as the U.S. administration and the West Europeans were concerned, if Dr Kissinger had suggested it.

At the time concerned, late 1970 and early 1971, it was not unreasonable for the Russians to prefer negotiated rather than unilateral American withdrawals, or even (despite the long Russian campaign against the American bases on Europe) to feel that the existing situation had considerable advantages. The 'Europe of the Ten' that seemed to be arriving at this time (not long after Mr Heath's electoral victory) looked a good deal more formidable in prospect than contemporary Europe does in actual being. Economically, Europe did in 1970 seem to be acquiring a giant's strength, and to have even turned the tables on the Americans. The effect of the envisaged American unilateral cuts in forces assigned to Nato might be, it then seemed, to galvanize this apparent developing titan into a successful effort, finally, towards political and defence integration, and the building of European armed forces that might produce an approximation to strategic independence of the U.S.A. There was even talk at the time of a possible 'European nuclear force', produced by joint targeting of the British and French forces. Thus Mr Brezhnev had several reasons to prefer negotiations (especially if fruitless) to unilateral American cuts. They averted the prospect of any such galvanic shock to the European system, and constituted at the same time a painless contribution to the general mesh of detente relationship with the United States – and detente relationships with the United States looked particularly in need of reinforcement from the middle of that year, with the first Kissinger journey to Peking.

At the time the talks actually opened, in October 1973, these factors were probably still of some assumed importance. It was the changes of the year that followed (the Middle East War, the oil embargo, the demonstrated economic vulnerability and political weakness of Western Europe, the replacement of Heath, Pompidou and Brandt by Wilson, Giscard d'Estaing and Schmidt) that made 'third force Europe' vanish rapidly as a mirage. The Russians did not produce their own figures for their forces in the prospective control area until July 1976, and these figures were still at the time of writing theoretically confidential, but they were reported to claim 805,000 in ground forces and 160,000 in air forces. If that claim were in due course accepted as valid by the Western powers, it would mean that parity or even a slight Western advantage in fact already exists, for the Western figures for Nato-plus-France in the control area are 792,000 in ground forces and 210,000 in air forces: the West is thus 12,000 below the Warsaw Pact on ground forces but 50,000 up on air force personnel. However, the conventional Western figures normally cited are at variance with the Russian, ascribing to the Warsaw Pact 899,000 in ground forces and 204,000 in air forces.[12] Clearly the statistical discrepancy needs to be reconciled, and the Western proposal of a common ceiling adhered to. But assuming the problems of statistics and classification can be overcome, and given completion of the changes in organization and weapons procurement policy initiated in Dr Schlesinger's time, something like parity in manpower (or at most a differential of about ten per cent) may be attained, or conceded to exist, on the Central Front, and that may make a common ceiling agreement feasible. It is not likely to be initially as low as the original Western suggestion of 700,000. Perhaps 800,000 in ground forces and 200,000 in air forces, which would be more or less an approximation of present existing levels, would prove acceptable. The same technique of initially writing-in existing levels as ceilings and aiming to lower them was adopted in SALT, first for ABM systems and then for mirvs and launchers, and has shown more promise than most arms-control techniques.

The size of Soviet tank armies was more troubling to Nato than manpower discrepancies, and the concrete Western proposals of 1976 were mostly designed to secure the retirement of some of these forces from central Europe, against reduction in the numbers of Western tactical nuclear weapons (which at 7,000 were far in excess of any conceivable strategic requirement).[13] The lessons of the 1973 Middle East War seemed to be to the effect that the Warsaw Pact advantage in tank numbers might, however, prove a relatively doubtful one. The antitank weapons entering service in the Western armies, with immensely sophisticated guidance systems, were believed by some expert opinion to effect a remarkable transformation in the potential capacity of the Western forces to hold their ground. It is usually argued that the forces taking the offensive need something like a three-to-one ratio in their favour in the conditions of the contemporary battlefield: Russian tank forces had shown this ratio, and it had been assumed that their numbers reflected a strategic aim of pushing rapidly west along several axes in the first forty-eight hours of any hostilities in

Europe, and holding the ground won during any subsequent negotiations. The Russians offered rather a quaint rationalization for their insistence on maintaining this advantage: in effect that it is all because of the Chinese. If they incurred serious hostilities on their Far Eastern frontier, they argued, it might well seem to hawkish or dissident Europeans a good moment to start some trouble on the Central Front in Europe, to take advantage of the Russians' embarrassment. Therefore they must maintain enough local conventional superiority to deter any such project. The spectre of the two-front war appears to have more substance to Russian strategists than it would to Western observers, who tend to discount the possibility of major hostilities by China.

The Vienna talks have not yet produced any arms reduction, but they were undoubtedly helpful in the cause of containing the congressional pressure for unilateral cuts. As the Vietnam trauma died, the Mansfield Resolution was more easily deflated (it was not put to a vote in 1975, after failing of a majority in 1974, and not even presented in 1976) and the U.S. forces in Europe were actually strengthened in 1975, both in numbers and in the proportion of combat troops. Further, the 'professionalization' of the U.S. army proceeded on schedule,[14] as did the reduction of the earlier U.S. contingents in Asia. So, altogether, the strains on American conventional forces were much reduced by 1975, and the Nato forces in Europe benefited accordingly.

It would seem probable that if the next phase of talks proceeds as expected a bridge will be built between nuclear and conventional arms control, as for instance through the Nato proposal to reduce the number of Western nuclear warheads in Europe against the reduction of Soviet tanks. The real unresolved problems of Western strategic posture for a long period of detente are financial, or more broadly economic. The demands of the defence budget on America's G.N.P. have been falling from about fifteen per cent in the coldest war years (1952-3) towards six per cent, though with an upturn in the Vietnam years. The same pattern holds true for the other members of Nato, but in a more extreme form. As a proportion of the tax dollar, defence costs are down from about sixty cents to about twenty-six cents. Even given a rapid recovery of prosperity after the 1974–6 recession, one would expect continuing pressures, more still in Europe than America, behind the demand that these figures should not be allowed to rise beyond their present levels. Western strategists must accept this political fact of life as a 'given', and devise the optimum strategic posture that can be sustained on five per cent (or rather less) of G.N.P. for Nato countries as a whole. And this is a situation that should, one would think, reconcile even the most intransigent general to some measure of arms control. For only the political leadership in Russia can impose any kind of similar restraint on Soviet arms budgets, and only a continued sense of the usefulness of detente is likely to induce them to do so. Up to 1976, C.I.A. assessments of Soviet defence expenditure ran at about the level of six–eight per cent of G.N.P., but in 1976 the estimates were raised to eleven–thirteen per cent. This apparent doubling, however, represented a change in statistical method in Washington rather than any assumption of a sudden leap in expenditure. That is, Soviet military procurement was seen as more expensive, in terms of alternative Soviet goods and services, than had previously been calculated, and thus a greater burden on the Soviet economy. The comparison of Nato and Warsaw Pact defence budgets is a vexing business, full of statistical pitfalls.[15] On the one hand, one might say that since the absolute level of real national incomes is very much less in the Warsaw Pact countries than in the West, eleven per cent of Pact national incomes would represent about the same level of real resources as six per cent of Nato incomes. On the other hand, Pact forces are mostly low-paid conscripts, and Nato forces are increasingly turning over to fairly well-paid professional armies, so the 'defence rouble' buys a good deal more manpower than the 'defence dollar'. But the point remains: if Western defence budgets must be, as seems likely, kept at or below five per cent of G.N.P. by the electorates' demands for alternative goods and benefits, then Western military capabilities can only be kept at a reasonable match for Russian military capabilities by the success of arms-control negotiations.

There is luckily a factor, common to all three of the dominant powers, that already operates as an incentive in one field of arms-control measures, and may become more important. This is their common aversion to further nuclear proliferation. The number of nuclear powers at present might be regarded as five and two halves, the nuclear capacities of Israel and India being each rated as half-strength. There is probably now no way of preventing the last two from putting on further nuclear muscle, but there are various modes, other than the non-proliferation treaty, of preventing new entrants to the club. For instance, the powers that export various kinds of technology essential in the field can come to a tacit agreement to restrict supply, and had indeed done so in principle by January 1976, through an exercise in secret diplomacy. China was not a party to these negotiations, and it used to maintain that the spread of nuclear weapons, even to minor Third World powers, was a commendable revolutionary development. But this clearly had changed, even before the agreement. Mr Mohammed Heikal has given us an account of Chou En-lai's reactions when the Libyans tried to buy atomic weapons.[16] In general it seems clear that new members of the nuclear club rapidly become convinced of the inconvenience of letting in others, and restrict their export of technology accordingly. The Indian acquisition of the means of entry seems to have been from Canada, itself voluntarily a non-member, but careless about controls on its exports. The beginnings of the Israeli nuclear capacity came from France, during the period of tacit alliance between 1956 and 1967. The negotiating process for the control of nuclear proliferation, from the earliest days of the test ban treaty in 1962–3, has had a *political* importance very much greater than the somewhat meagre results in the way of actual arms-control agreements. The danger of nuclear war is sufficiently felt as a universal apprehension to, as it were, 'license' adversaries to talk to each other on this particular matter at times when it was not really politically feasible for them to talk about other issues.

The preservation of existing alliance structures in good repair and credibility would seem to be one political condition helpful in restraining proliferation. Countries seek nuclear weapons mostly because, like India and Israel, they feel vulnerable or disadvantaged. Mr Attlee similarly began Britain's nuclear effort in 1946 before Nato was set up and at a time in the post-war period when America looked likely to retreat from Europe. France began to work seriously at its nuclear effort in the late 1950s as it became discontented with its place in Nato. Practically all the countries on the nuclear threshold, technically, are within either the American or the Russian nuclear protectorate, and will probably step over that threshold only if their respective alliances break down. Japan is the clearest instance. It could become a nuclear power within two years of making a political decision to that effect. But so far the memory of 1945, and its status within the American nuclear protectorate, have operated to prevent a Japanese decision to this effect being made. The Chinese interest in maintaining that state of affairs provided the logic behind Mr Chou's urging of Dr Kissinger to keep America's alliance with Japan in good repair.

To revert to the central strategic relationship of the world, that between the United States and the Soviet Union, the first essential for the survival of the detente is that this strategic relationship be so structured that neither party sees advantage to itself in surprise attack (either nuclear or conventional) or has reason to fear pre-emptive attack by the other party. The condition most likely to achieve this measure of strategic stability is possession of nuclear second-strike forces as nearly invulnerable as possible on both sides, with consequently no real first-strike capacity, plus conventional forces of 'essential equivalency', even if it has to be at a high level, on the Central Front in Nato to discourage any short-term or impulsive local adventures.

There appeared no reason, in early 1977, why the journey to those objectives, admittedly still distant, should not shortly be resumed with reasonable prospects. The years 1975 and 1976 more or less had to be a period of marking time, not only because of a two-year run-up, after Watergate, to the U.S. presidential election campaign (Senator Jackson was off and running from the time of the Vladivostok guidelines) but also because of the advent of a new American weapons system, the cruise missile, which proved to be much more important in strategists' calculations than was originally expected, and because of the cooling political relationship between the United States and the Soviet Union, especially after Angola. Two of these problems, the election campaign and Angola, were of diminishing impact by 1977, but the cruise missiles had imposed extra complexities in the business of verifying the 'ceilings' proposed at Vladivostok.

Nevertheless they also seemed to suggest that the technique of 'putting the missiles out to sea', originated in SALT I, might prove of continued usefulness. Cruise missiles may of course be airborne or land-based as well as based on submarines or surface craft: the difficulties they present for arms control arise precisely from their being versatile, relatively cheap and easily concealed, and in general potentially a 'poor man's delivery system' for nuclear warheads.[17] They are not, however, an innovatory weapons system, being descendants of the V1 flying bombs used against London in the Second World War, and short-range cruise missiles are standard weapons in many armouries including that of the Soviet navy. What changed their apparent potential, both as battlefield and strategic weapons, in 1974–5, was the vast improvement in range and accuracy achieved by American technology, and the fact that they could be used with conventional or nuclear warheads, perhaps to redress the battlefield balance in areas where it was unfavourable to the West, such as the Northern Front of Nato. Considerable resistance was thus generated within the Pentagon to arms-control proposals that might affect their deployment: the arguments seemed to be important enough even to have played a part in the departure of Dr Schlesinger.

The cruise missile operated to increase the advantages of sea-based systems by making fixed-site land-based missiles still more vulnerable to counter-force strike. It was implied in some of the arguments that even cruise missiles with conventional warheads in German hands, for instance, might be targeted on Soviet missile silos in Eastern Europe. The United States has an edge in this field whose importance is usually, perhaps deliberately, played down. A much smaller percentage of American 'throw-weight' is in the vulnerable land-based form, as against Soviet 'throw-weight'. Possibly seventy-five per cent of Soviet strike capacity is 'targetable', at least in theory and possibly in actuality, by American or other Nato counter-force capacity: a wholly successful American first strike (though improbable in itself and never advanced as a desirable strategic option by responsible policy-makers) would therefore leave the Soviet Union with only about twenty-five per cent of its strike capacity in being. On the other hand, even a successful Soviet first strike against U.S. land-based missiles would still leave perhaps seventy-five per cent of American strike capacity in being.[18]

The strategic doctrine of the 'Triad' (a doctrine, perhaps originally devised to keep the peace between the Services, which holds that nuclear capacity must be shared between sea-based, land-based and airborne weapons) is probably strong enough to prevent a total reliance on sea-based nuclear forces, except for the minor nuclear powers (Britain and France, at the moment, but with some indication that China may also be moving in this direction). There are command-and-control advantages to land-based systems, and also some remaining advantage in accuracy, though sea-based systems are rapidly catching up in that respect. If one is contemplating a long period of detente, in which the function of strategic nuclear forces is reduced to that of inhibiting resort to an all-out war of conquest, and in which the total number of missiles has been controlled by overall ceilings, then the most desired 'platform' for missiles must be the least vulnerable. The least vulnerable, for the foreseeable future, are undoubtedly those based in the most advanced types of submarine: the American *Poseidon* or *Trident*, or the Russian *Delta*.

Thus a number of factors (including the consideration that Jimmy Carter is a former naval officer trained in nuclear submarines) incline to encourage the belief that submarine-based systems will continue, and even increase their dominance in American nuclear capacity, though considerations of expense, and aversion to having all the eggs in one basket in case of a breakthrough, will operate as some inhibition on this evolution. If the Americans do take that option, the Soviet Union must follow suit, or over the long run face a situation in which its silo-based systems are targeted by American sea-based systems of impressive accuracy that are not themselves vulnerable to Russian targeting, at least in the present or foreseeable state of the art. That clearly would be an unacceptable prospect to the Russian political and military leadership.

The growth of the Soviet navy, which has provided one of the most dramatic-seeming changes in the overall balance of forces since the late 1950s, is in itself an index of the strength of Soviet determination to match American capacity as nearly as they can. Even before the Soviet period, the Russians, with four widely separated and disadvantageous sea coasts to guard, tended towards a large naval strength on paper (not necessarily matched by effectiveness during hostilities as the record during the Russo-Japanese war and the First and Second World Wars indicates), but the Politburo decisions of the late 1950s and through the 1960s that created the present Soviet navy seem clearly to reflect Soviet observation of the usefulness of naval forces to American crisis-management (the Lebanon crisis of 1958 and the Cuban missile crisis of 1962, for instance), as well as consciousness of how large a proportion of the American capacity for nuclear strike at the Soviet Union is carried in sea-based systems, and, of course, memory of how vulnerable the Western powers were to German submarines during the Second World War, and a tendency to assume that there might, after all, be another battle of the Atlantic like the last, despite the strategic changes.

It is important to note that the Soviet naval build-up, though visible mostly since the detente, arises from strategic and political decisions taken during the Cold War. This must obviously be the case, bearing in mind that the 'lead-time' for a large ship (i.e. the time from the decision to build to the ship's actually entering service) is up to ten years. So decisions taken before 1969 will be affecting ship deliveries to the Soviet navy up to 1979. But actually the rate of delivery of ships was already dropping quite fast by the mid-1970s. The rate of delivery in the 1958–68 period (i.e. ships both commissioned and delivered during the Cold War) was 45.5 per annum. The rate of delivery during the detente (1969–76) had already fallen to 17.4 per annum, and these would also in part be ships commissioned during the late Cold War years. The Soviet rate of delivery is less than the present U.S. rate, which is 19 ships per year. Moreover, the Soviet ships tended to be much smaller than the American ones. The Russians use a lot of vessels under 3,000 tons, frigates and such, to guard their coasts, whereas the American navy has not until very recently favoured ships of this size. It has been developing very fast surface-effect craft (hovercraft), capable of up to 60 knots, instead of ships, for use as missile platforms. It also has built, of course, huge aircraft carriers, of which the Russians have only one first quasi-approximation, the *Kiev*. In total tonnage the U.S. navy has outbuilt the Soviet navy 3.3 million tons to 2.6 million tons since 1958. In the detente period (since 1969) the Americans outbuilt the Russians by twelve per cent in ship numbers, as well as by seventy-one per cent in tonnage.[19]

At mid-1970s' rates of building and obsolescence, the Soviet fleet would fall from its existing 750 vessels to 435 in the early 1980s, whereas the U.S. fleet (which has already passed through the phase of 'block obsolescence' that has yet to affect the Soviet fleet[20]) would remain stable at about 480 vessels. But there was quite a strong probability (especially given an ex-naval officer as president) that a proposed long-term U.S. ship-building programme would be put into operation that would raise the number to 600. The Russians could try to match this, of course, but there are factors impeding Russian naval effectiveness, no matter how determinedly they build. The four Russian coastlines are all subject to 'choke points' that would be a source of vulnerability in actual hostilities, especially in a slow-motion naval and maritime war of attrition, such as is sometimes envisaged. The

Strategic Doctrine and Arms Control: The Nature of Stability 77

Northern Fleet must make passage from the Barents to the Norwegian sea south of Svalbad, and then passage through the 'Iceland gap', well controlled by Nato. The Black Sea Fleet has to pass through the Bosphorus, under the eye of the elaborate system of Nato surveillance in Turkey and the Eastern Mediterranean. The Pacific Fleet has to pass from its bases at Vladivostok and Nakhodka through the Korea, Tsushima, Tsugaru or Soya straits, again subject to intensive American watch from Japan. The Baltic Fleet has to pass through Oresund, which like the Black Sea and Japanese exits would be subject to blockade by Western or American action if the situation were grave enough to warrant it.[21] Compared with the extensive open coasts of the Western powers, and their many overseas bases, the Soviet navy is very ill-served by geography, and its base-complexes on the Kola peninsula in the Far North and at Petropavlovsk–Kamchatka would be vulnerable to massive strike, conventional or nuclear. Practically all the other noteworthy navies of the world are Western or West-oriented and allied to America (Britain, France, Japan, Canada, Australia), a factor usually passed over in the straight U.S.–Soviet comparisons. Such bases as the Soviet Union has obtained in non-aligned countries have proved rather impermanent, as with Egypt. Syria, Libya, India, even Vietnam, have been cautious or recalcitrant. Berbera is about the only success story.

So altogether, though the rise of the Soviet navy is a genuinely dramatic variation of the traditional pattern of power distribution, it by no means indicates as catastrophic a reversal of Western ascendancy as can be made to seem apparent in the election addresses of politically ambitious U.S. admirals. Moreover, the Soviet naval build-up, on the statistics, was a product of the Cold War rather than the detente, and its rate has been declining, not increasing, during the detente period, though the fact of its creation does mean Soviet capacities of a sort never previously existing.

To return to the central question, of what kind of strategic doctrine and balance of forces is appropriate to a long period of detente (if it can be maintained) and how it can be made to lead to effective arms control, one has to reassert the concept of 'essential equivalence' in both the nuclear and conventional sphere, and perhaps propose also a doctrine of 'symmetry', bearing in mind that capacities should not only *be* equal but *look* equal. The strategic balance over the whole period since 1945 may be said to have moved from a situation of 'balance-with-asymmetry' towards 'balance-with-(relative)-symmetry'. That is, in the early part of the period American nuclear and naval superiority offset Soviet conventional superiority: a balance existed, but not a symmetrical balance. With the loss of decisive Western superiority in nuclear strike power and naval power, this mode of balance is no longer feasible, and the West must therefore match, and be seen as matching, Soviet capacity in conventional ground forces. But this situation does offer some prospects for arms control, since like can be balanced against like, instead of against unlike. And there is an incentive for the two dominant powers to work at this process vis-à-vis each other, since only when they reach some mutual agreement can they hope to exert control over arms proliferation (nuclear as well as conventional) in the rest of the world. And this is a situation dangerous to them both, though also profitable not only to them but to other suppliers of arms and nuclear plant like France, Britain and West Germany. The secret agreement reached among nuclear exporters in London in January 1976[22] will need to be enforced and reinforced if it is actually to control the growth of membership of the nuclear club, and there is some conflict between efforts to prevent further nuclear proliferation and efforts to restrain the proliferation of conventional arms. Vulnerable or ambitious powers like Israel and Iran are in a position successfully to insist that they will only accept restraint on the nuclear plane on condition of very lavish supplies on the conventional plane. The dominant powers have thus to weigh a choice of evils: conventional proliferation, or the possibility of nuclear proliferation. Problems of this sort will be difficult to control even on the assumption of detente, but totally recalcitrant if the detente breaks down. Jimmy Carter, as I noted earlier, said as candidate that he hoped, if elected, to negotiate an agreed restraint on sales of conventional weapons. An agreement of that sort would only be feasible and viable in a much more secure detente than has so far been created.

To sum up, one might say that the probable defence structure likely to evolve over a long period of detente would be invulnerable second-strike nuclear forces, predominantly submarine-based on both sides (and perhaps ultimately so for China), serving only to deter all-out bids for military conquest by either party, conventional forces constructed as a solid shield (not a tripwire) on the Central Front in Nato, to deter anything short of such an all-out bid, and presumably similar Chinese forces facing the Russian troops at the other end of the Eurasian continent. With a reasonably stable military balance of this sort between the dominant powers,[23] their prospects of controlling local arms races and preventing further nuclear proliferation would be at least substantially better than they will be in the event of breakdown of the detente and reversion to a true arms race. That obviously is not a picture of a disarmed world, and must seem incongruous to those who assumed disarmament to be a natural consequence of detente. But though disarmament is no doubt a good in itself, it is a less important good than the actual prevention of war. Detente pursued without adequate attention to the balance of forces, which is its necessary infrastructure, might have consequences reminiscent of appeasement, and would be an equally poor strategy for maintaining peace.

CHAPTER 5

The Middle East War: Some Rather Loud Signalling

No aspect of detente has evoked more anxieties in assorted foreign offices than the question of how it would affect relations between the dominant powers and their dependent allies (client states) in crisis situations. At first sight, the logical probability appears to be that it might provide both reason and opportunity to reduce the diplomatic leverage of the client states concerned by encouraging either or both dominant powers to offer up the interest of the small ally as a sacrifice on the altar of detente. The Middle East War of 1973 was, among other things, the occasion of a crisis in detente diplomacy, and the most dramatic potential exemplification as yet of that possibility. It had, of course, many larger and more humanly absorbing aspects that it is not possible to explore here (the psychological impact of the hostilities on Israel and the Arab states for instance), and to look at it chiefly as an episode in the diplomatic calculations and manoeuvres of the Powers may seem a kind of callousness. Yet, if one is to understand the influence of detente, some abstraction of these calculations and manoeuvres from the rest of the drama is necessary.

Much of the comment of the time, insofar as it related the war to the detente at all, was to the effect that it illustrated the bad faith or duplicity of the Russians, or the alleged fact that detente was an illusion or a confidence trick and bound to operate against the United States.[1] Three years after the war, with Soviet influence in the Middle East almost everywhere in retreat, the Soviet alliance unilaterally denounced by the Egyptians, the possibility of a successful Arab attack on Israel lower than it had been for many years, Americans (but no Russians) officially installed in Sinai as the guardians of the peace, the Soviet fleet expelled from Alexandria and American influence predominant almost everywhere from the Gulf to Morocco (with the exception of Libya), the Middle East War was still being cited by some of the candidates in the 1976 U.S. election as evidence that detente had been dangerous to American interests. I shall argue, to the contrary, that the maintenance of the detente was essential to the overwhelming success of American diplomacy in this complex episode, that Dr Kissinger was able to use the central phase of the crisis to 'spell out' the limits of detente, and that the Russians were persuaded to acquiesce in his efforts to move the Middle East towards a diplomatic settlement mostly because of the value they placed on the detente's continuance.

The logical point at which to begin consideration of this process seems to be the Nixon–Brezhnev communiqué of May 1972, after the Moscow summit meeting. The affairs of the Middle East were dismissed in this communiqué in a brief and non-committal paragraph: the Arab leadership were not given any consoling or promising words to induce belief that their great and powerful friends in the Kremlin were inclined to press the case of their Arab allies in any way that would jeopardize the detente with America. President Sadat has since made it clear how much this increased the burden of irritation he already felt against the Russians:[2] in effect it seems to have been the moment of resolve that he must press the situation to a new crisis in order to force the dominant powers into a crisis-intervention that would in the upshot serve Arab (or at least Egyptian) national interests. President Sadat was at a kind of strategic crossroads at this point. To undo the consequence of the 1967 war (the advance of the Israeli frontiers) he had theoretically two options: military action or diplomatic leverage. Military action depended on maintaining his connection with the Soviet Union, since it was only from that source that he could hope to get the advanced weapons he needed to dislodge the Israelis from Egyptian territory. On the other hand, the difficulty and uncertainty of translating Soviet-provided military resources into effective pressure on Israel had already been well demonstrated. Only the Americans, in actuality, could put effective pressure on the Israelis. Theoretically, the Russians might be induced to put pressure on the Americans to secure concessions from the Israelis, but it had appeared that in conditions of detente they were not going to do so.

Thus, the possibility of a more direct diplomatic rapprochement with the Americans, a repair in the almost total breach that had followed the 1967 war, in the hope of securing a more even-handed (from the Arab point of view) American policy in the Middle East had become a more attractive option. The Arabs had had some indirect encouragement from Dr Kissinger to hopes of this kind. With the rather unnerving candour he sometimes used, he had indicated the American interest eighteen months earlier:

> We are trying to get a [Middle East] settlement in such a way that the moderate regimes are strengthened, and not the radical regimes. We are trying to expel the Soviet military presence – not so much the advisors but the combat pilots and the combat personnel – before they become firmly established ... But we certainly have to keep in mind that the Russians will judge us by the general purposefulness of our performance everywhere. What they are doing in the Middle East poses the gravest threats in the long term for Western Europe and Japan and therefore for us.[3]

To summarize, one might say that the strategic problem confronting President Sadat at this point was so to manage events that he could first use the military capabilities given him by the Russians to upset the existing 'no war – no peace' situation, despite the fact that it suited the Russians themselves rather well, since it maximized Arab dependence upon them. Then he must use the resulting crisis to induce Russian pressure on the Americans to help secure from the Israelis a territorial settlement more acceptable to the Arabs; or at any rate to the Egyptians, because one of the differences between President Sadat and President Nasser as decision-makers, comparing 1967 with 1973, was not only Sadat's greater flexibility and subtlety in diplomatic manoeuvre, but his greater willingness to distinguish between Egyptian and Arab interests.

Sadat's policies might be regarded as an object-lesson in the complexities of negotiation from a situation of relative diplomatic weakness. That relative diplomatic weakness arose from the fact that he was a dependent and marginal ally for the Soviet Union, and the Russians had made this status undiplomatically clear. It is true that the connection with the Soviet Union had since 1955 secured for Egypt a large amount of economic and especially military aid, but the relation of dependence, the necessity of petitioning recalcitrant Russian policy-makers, had been allowed to become increasingly galling. No doubt there were differential appreciations of the usefulness of the alliance in Moscow, with the Soviet naval chiefs logically likely to be strongly in its favour for the sake of the facilities at Alexandria. Even the Soviet navy, however, had some reason for ambivalence about putting all the Russian bets on Egypt, since they were interested in the reopening of the Suez Canal, which would obviously require American and Israeli consent as well as Egyptian.

The level of irritation of both sides within the Soviet–Egyptian relationship showed clearly through the events that followed. The first of them was the Egyptian expulsion of Russian advisers from Cairo in July 1972. Some surprise was expressed at the time in Western comment that the Russians accepted this with calm, not to say apparent indifference. According to some reports, they had done a good deal to provoke it by treating the Egyptian army's pride very roughly, replying to Egyptian complaints about arms supplies with an implication that the arms the Soviet Union had already sent were quite all right – as had been shown for instance when they were in the hands of the Vietnamese – and that what was doubtful was Egyptian ability to use them correctly. This standard of diplomatic ham-fistedness on the part of the Soviet Union in its relations with Egypt was consistently maintained through the aftermath of the war, as for instance in the refusal of a visit by the Egyptian foreign minister in July 1974, and Mr Brezhnev's abrupt cancelling of a promised visit later.

The fifteen months between the expulsion of the Russian advisers in July 1972, and the actual Egyptian strike at Israel in October 1973, offer a neat illustration of the uses of what was perhaps accidentally ambiguous signalling, resulting in successful strategic surprise. President Sadat had proclaimed 1971 as the 'year of decision' in relations with Israel. It turned out not to be so, and his explanations of delay seemed lame. (In fact the Russian recalcitrance about supplying as many and as advanced arms as he wanted seems to have been at least part of the reason.) The impression of infirmity of political or military purpose was reinforced when the same proved to be the case in 1972. Therefore, when he *again* told the Egyptian armed forces in December 1972 to be ready for war in six months, neither the Israelis nor the Americans nor apparently even the Russians took the declaration as seriously as they might otherwise have done. In effect, the apparent stance of one 'willing to wound but afraid to strike' seems to have provided a successful camouflage for the reality of Sadat's intentions as they developed in 1973. The Egyptian contingency plans were known from April to the U.S. intelligence community, and presumably also to the Israelis, since there were close connections. The increased supply of advanced Soviet weapons as from about February 1973 was also well known: President Sadat himself proclaimed how well satisfied he was with it in an interview in April with an American journalist.[4]

Yet despite all this, the actual attack achieved a remarkable degree of strategic surprise. Dr Kissinger received no warning until the morning it opened. U.S. intelligence may have been unduly influenced by Israeli estimates, which did not conclude an attack was imminent until 5 October, and then got the final timing four hours wrong. The Russians were apparently told the date of the attack only on 2 October:[5] the fact that they did not put up their observation satellites or pull out their dependants until 3 October perhaps indicates that they maintained their scepticism until the last moment. One may conclude that the unfulfilled threats of the previous two years had left a pervasive impression of military irresolution, and that this operated as a conscious or unconscious *ruse de guerre* for the Egyptians, causing clear evidence of intent to be discounted until a few hours before the attack was launched.

If this had not been so – if, that is, there had been a longer period when war was clearly seen to be impending, and preparations for it known to and obviously aided by the Russians – the wear and tear on the detente might have been greater. For the Russians ought theoretically (under the June 1973 agreement with America) to have warned the U.S.A. of any such threat to the peace. But given the general surprise, Dr Kissinger could shrug off this dereliction, if he thought it one, philosophically: 'in an ideal world, one would expect closer consultation, but given the particular volatility of the Middle East, it would have been a heavy responsibility to make known certain advance information.'[6]

The impression of Russian ambivalence, to the last, as to whether the Egyptians really meant it this time, and whether, if so, they were going to do any better than on earlier occasions also seems the most likely explanation for what was, according to Sadat, a Russian attempt to deceive or pressure him into calling off the war in its first couple of days. He has said that the Russians went so far, in argument with him, as to allege that the Syrians had already asked for a cease-fire, when he knew this to be a lie.[7] There is still a disparity between the Russian and the Egyptian accounts of this incident, the Russians maintaining that they were indeed asked by the Syrians to suggest a cease-fire, the Egyptians maintaining there was no such request from the Syrians, and President Assad himself, who could resolve the question, still maintaining silence on it up to the moment of writing. But the Soviet urging of cease-fire so early, even if there was some Syrian word that could be used to justify it, seems to indicate apprehension of another Arab disaster like 1967, or apprehension as to what the war might do to the detente, or a combination of the two. Obviously, this Soviet mood changed during the first week of the war, when it suddenly became evident that the Egyptian military performance offered prospects of unexpected success. The restoration of peace only returned as an urgent objective of Soviet policy with the turn of the military tide back towards the Israelis in the second week of the war.

It was this that precipitated the urgent invitation to Dr Kissinger to visit Moscow for consultations on 20 October. Though one must ascribe Soviet policy chiefly to an alarmed desire to put a stopper on further Israeli success in the drive into Egypt, it also appears to indicate concern to maintain the detente, and especially to use it as a basis for joint crisis-management. And this element in Soviet expectation was even more prominent in the next phase of the crisis, which I would tentatively describe as a Russian bid for, and an American refusal of, the idea of condominium.

This is the most interesting phase of the crisis, seen as an exercise in detente diplomacy, since it constituted, one might argue, Dr Kissinger's spelling out of the message that detente could not be parlayed into condominium. The theory that it could, and indeed the alleged probability that it would, had provided some earlier nightmares for many European and Asian policy-makers and analysts. The notion of condominium – a sharing of effective power in the world *only* with the Americans in a kind of permanent and somewhat institutionalized version of the power balance as at the end of the Second World War – had deep roots in the Soviet view of the world and of the international power struggle in its present phase. One could call it characteristic of Soviet policy-makers from Stalin's time on, bearing in mind some of his approaches to Roosevelt, as against Churchill.

Ironically enough, it was this potentially collusive element in the Soviet view of the U.S.A., rather than the competitive or adversary side of the relationship, that precipitated the brief 'confrontation' phase of the crisis, 24–26 October. It began with the Israeli breach of the first cease-fire, and the drive of the forces commanded by General Sharon to surround the Egyptian Third Army. This military success on the part of the Israelis confronted the Russians with the apparent prospect of an unacceptable level of defeat for their Egyptian allies, and a danger

The Middle East War: Some Rather Loud Signalling 87

that they would be obliged, in effect, to choose between sacrificing the detente or accepting a serious loss of face as protectors. The Egyptians met the situation by asking (presumably after consulting the Russians) that a joint Soviet–American force be sent to the Middle East. Mr Brezhnev indicated in a letter that has not been published, but that was somewhat forceful (the opponents of detente tend to refer to it as 'brutal', but the extract seen by me does not bear out that description), that the Americans must either accept this proposal or risk seeing the Russians act alone to send their own troops to the Middle East. At the same time the Soviet high command began various rather ostentatious moves that conveyed the possibility that they might be intending an airlift of troops to Egypt.

It is these signals that I would interpret as the bid for condominium, though with reservations as to how seriously it was really intended. Dr Kissinger was emphatic in refusal:

> The United States does not favour and will not approve the sending of a joint Soviet–United States force into the Middle East. It is inconceivable that we should transplant the great-power rivalry into the Middle East or, alternatively that we should impose a military condominium by the United States and the Soviet Union.
>
> It would be a disaster if the Middle East, already so torn by local rivalries, would now become, as a result of a U.N. decision, a legitimized theatre for the competition of the military forces of the great powers. And therefore it seemed to us that the political purposes would be best served if any international force that were introduced were composed of countries that have themselves no possibility of being drawn into rivalry as a result of being there. The plan for a joint U.S.–Soviet military force in the Middle East was never broached to us either publicly or privately until yesterday. And we immediately made clear that we would not participate in such a force and that we would oppose any unilateral moves ... The measures we took and which the President ordered were precautionary in nature ... We are not talking of threats that have been made against each other. We are not talking of a missile-crisis-type situation ... We are attempting to preserve the peace in very difficult circumstances ... The alert that has been ordered is of a precautionary nature and is not in any sense irrevocable. It is what seemed to be indicated by the situation.[8]

The 'alert of a precautionary nature' that had been authorized by the President was that called 'Defcon Three', a standby alert for troops, including strategic nuclear forces, to await further orders. It was cancelled on the 26th, and Mr Brezhnev made rather a conciliatory speech on the same day, so the 'confrontation' period may be reasonably regarded as confined to those three days. Probably the true crisis was much less than this, perhaps only a day. This phase of the events of the war is sometimes cited by opponents of detente, such as Admiral Zumwalt, as constituting proof that the U.S. government was obliged to yield to a 'savage' Soviet 'ultimatum' to prevent the Israelis from 'annihilating' the Egyptian Third Army, which they had encircled. That interpretation is hardly consistent, however, with the fact that American policy, well before the Soviet note, was clearly bent on saving the Egyptians from another humiliating defeat, and this objective was already a visible aspect of Dr Kissinger's management of the situation. The more machiavellian interpretations of his control of resupply to Israel during the first ten days of the war, for instance, imply that he 'nailed the Pentagon's shoes to the floor' in the matter of the airlift of supplies at this stage, in order to restrain Israeli capacity to take the offensive.[9] Whatever the truth on that particular point (and if he did operate as alleged it was a very bold and far-sighted piece of crisis-management), it is probable that a new devastating defeat for the Egyptians, as against the 'honours even' situation that was actually produced or assumed to exist, would have renewed Arab fury at the U.S.A. and probably re-established Israeli intransigence, as after the 1967 war. Whereas the policy devised by Dr Kissinger, to the contrary, effected a positive *renversement des alliances* by the Arabs, with the United States replacing the Soviet Union as the paramount outside great power, the Egyptians (and even the Syrians) moving in the direction of a negotiated settlement, and the more militant Arab 'refusal front' checkmated, at least up to the time of writing, by the results of this course of action.

The most reasonable way to regard the American strategic alert and the Russian moves that evoked it, is as an exchange of rather loud signals – excessively loud, one might hold, and thus unnecessarily abrasive to the nerves of the world. But they probably needed to be loud, in order to carry over certain background noises, and to reach other ears than those of the American and Russian policy-makers concerned, who were, of course, perfectly well able to communicate in whispers, unless it was useful that others should hear. Who were the others whom it was desired should listen to the messages in this case? Primarily, in my view, the allies of the two dominant powers: the Egyptians, the Israelis, the Europeans.

Let us take first the Russian signals: the letter that Senator Jackson and Admiral Zumwalt have described as 'brutal', and the ostentatious military indicators. These apparently consisted of the alerting of airborne forces (50,000 men) and the phasing-down of the Russian resupply operation in such a way as to suggest that the transport planes used in it might be redirected to lift the airborne troops to Egypt or Syria. It is quite difficult to believe that these indicators corresponded to a serious military intention, unless it were to be one clearly given a green light by the Americans. But President Sadat's demand for action to make the Israelis return to the cease-fire lines of 22 October had obviously put the Russians in a situation in which they were obliged to make some démarche. If by any chance the Americans *had* agreed to a condominium arrangement in the Middle East (as some Western comment was eagerly and timidly suggesting), it would have provided an enormous 'pay-off' from the crisis from the Russian point of view. But such an arrangement could not be advantageous to the Americans in terms of the power balance, since they could, as it proved, do much better, and in any case it would not have been morally acceptable either to policy-makers or to the electorate in Israel or the U.S.A.

Dr Kissinger's press conference of the 25th spelt out emphatically, though in mild enough words, the refusal of condominium. The strategic alert, which seems to have lasted less than twenty-four hours, added the message 'nor unilateral initiatives either'. The main criticism one might make is that it was perhaps too loud a signal for the occasion, exaggerating the crisis. On the other hand, it had to carry through the domestic noise of Watergate, which might have misled the Russians into believing the

U.S. government incapable of action, and the noise of the intramural crisis in Nato, which will be looked at presently. It had to reach the Egyptians, to convey the reasons why the *Russians* would not act, and thus provide President Sadat's excuses for accepting the situation. It had to startle the Israelis, to convey the dangers of uninhibited military success, even to characters like General Sharon or General Dayan. And it had to reach the Europeans, where it was most necessary to convey the 'refusal of condominium' message, since that vision was one of their standard nightmares, and might seem to have been given more substance by these events. So altogether there was a very fair case for loudness.

Looking at the episode as an example of crisis-management techniques in general, one might define it as the use of an emphatic, entirely unambiguous American signal to reply to some ambiguous Russian signalling. Possibly one should not take what I have called the 'bid for condominium' from the Russian side very seriously, any more than the ostensible threat of unilateral action, but since the possibility was being raised by other policy-makers (such at this time as M. Jobert) as a weapon against America, it was useful to dramatize the refusal even of a bid that may not actually have been made. One cannot be sure it was not: the Russians had indicated this line of thought on other issues, such as in the SALT negotiations. A less wary American policy-maker than Dr Kissinger, in a tighter corner than this one actually was, might conceivably have seen such an arrangement as necessary, or even desirable.

One of the side-effects of the war was an intramural crisis within Nato. It was produced chiefly by the Arabs' belated discovery of how powerful a weapon oil could be, or rather their belated use of a weapon long theorized about. The crunch came in the second week of the war, over European recalcitrance concerning the American resupply operation to Israel. The Europeans undoubtedly put more obstacles in the way of this effort than either the Russians or the Arabs. The U.S.A. first asked the Spanish government for loading and refuelling rights at Spanish airfields. They were refused even passage through

Spanish air-space. Portugal permitted refuelling stops at Lajes air-base in the Azores, but forbade any mention of it in Portuguese newspapers. Herr Brandt's government in Germany not only demanded a halt in the resupply of Israel from U.S. dumps there, but announced in a Foreign Ministry press release that it had done so, which the Americans regarded as a particularly gratuitous slap in the face. Mr Heath's government in Britain put an immediate ban on arms shipments to the Middle East, which was damaging exclusively to Israel since it cut off the supply of spare parts and ammunition for the Centurion tanks whose survival was vital to the battle. There was also a sharp little row between Britain and America over the introduction of a possible cease-fire resolution at the Security Council, the British being told by Sadat that he would not accept it, and therefore failing to press the proposal. Dr Kissinger on the other hand had been told by the Russians that Sadat would accept, and is said to have conveyed his feelings about the British foot-dragging pretty crisply to the then ambassador, Lord Cromer, and to have reacted explosively to Mr Heath's demand that if the Cyprus base were used for reconnaissance flights, the planes should be provided with an unbreakable 'cover story'. The rest of Nato (with the honourable exception of the Netherlands) seemed to exhibit a panic anxiety to dissociate themselves from any connection with American aid to Israel, and the French seem to have been actively mischievous, encouraging the Syrians to remain intransigent to the American effort to secure a cease-fire and disengagement on that front.

It was not difficult to see the logic of these European attitudes: a consistent (if craven) determination to appease the Arabs in order to avert the threat to European oil supplies. In this objective they were more or less successful, but at a very heavy cost. For though an actual oil blockade was averted, the Arabs were taught how much they could exact both politically and economically from the industrialized world by the threat of cutting oil production, and they subsequently used that knowledge to set oil prices at a level that threatened some Europeans with balance-of-payments deficits for the foreseeable future, and that helped produce a world slump almost on the scale of the 1930s.

Nemesis seems to have worked overtime, gratifyingly, on the decision-makers responsible for this policy shambles. M. Jobert, Herr Brandt and Mr Heath all went out of office for various reasons, at least temporarily. In the British case, the then ambassadors in Washington and at the U.N. also vanished from those posts with the change of government. This surprisingly clean sweep, by electoral and other means, no doubt helped in a reasonably rapid recovery (within six months) of European–American equanimity. The complaints on the American side, that the Europeans had 'acted as if Nato did not exist', and on the European side, that Dr Kissinger had failed to consult them about the strategic alert, probably led to the more carefully maintained alliance relationship at the resolution phase of the crisis, and a general consciousness of the desirability of refurbishing Nato. One must regard the initial confusion and cross-purposes as an exemplification of the tendency for the links of alliance to be fragile in any such episode. One might also note in passing that it appeared to indicate that 'Europe' at the time was *less* than the sum of its parts: its members had not yet learned to act as an ensemble, but had lost their old capacity to act uninhibitedly as sovereign states. If one compares the reactions of Britain and France to the 1973 threat to their oil supplies with their reaction in the 1956 crisis to a much lesser threat to oil supplies, which were themselves then of less acute economic importance, one must regard the contrast as a case study in the progressive enfeeblement of political will. Deplorable and disastrous as the Suez adventure no doubt was, it showed some degree of European initiative and capacity to act, quite lacking seventeen years later, at which time not even a little ambiguous signalling on the possibility of retaliatory action against the Arabs could be undertaken by American policy-makers without audible panic among Europeans.

The measures of cease-fire and disengagement reached by the end of 1973 may be regarded as a resolution of the immediate crisis created by the October War. The three years of Dr Kissinger's diplomacy thereafter were directed to evolution of a Middle Eastern detente, and ultimately a settlement between Israel and the Arabs, on the basis of the new local balance demonstrated rather than created by the 1973 hostilities. The Israelis did not actually suffer a defeat: on the contrary, after the initial setback resulting from the Egyptian achievement of strategic surprise their resilience and military *panache* were as usual spectacularly demonstrated. But the almost costless ascendancy of 1967 was clearly gone, and conceivably for good. The casualty figures for the Israeli forces were not particularly high, given normal expectations of fighting between forces at equivalent levels of competence and armament, but they were traumatic for an electorate and a political elite that had lived by the legends of the effortless superiority of 1967. The Egyptian commanders' demonstration of a new military initiative, the Egyptian troops' demonstration of competence in the use of sophisticated Russian weapons, and the weapons themselves, especially the 'plane-killing' missiles that for the first week effectively neutralized the Israeli air force (the most telling source of strategic ascendancy in 1967): all these things effectively changed the military relationship that had underlain the diplomatic stalemate of 1967–73. Even the more hawk-like segment of the Israeli political elite had to recognize the fact that if Israel continued having to meet Arab armies of relatively equal competence to her own, over the middle and long term the cost of maintaining the security of the state by its strong military right arm and the 1967 territorial acquisitions would become exorbitant. Thus the case for an alternative mode of security, with borders more tolerable to the Arabs and some form of international guarantee, became more attractive – though still not really attractive to much Israeli opinion, especially on the right. A determined long-term military ascendancy and extended boundaries might well remain the desired option to a people with as hard a history as the Israelis, provided it were believed to be available. And inevitably there will always be a sector of the electorate and perhaps of the political leadership who will believe it available. But for the mainstream leadership, the demonstration of Israel's long-term military vulnerability was enough to induce reconsideration of possible alternative modes of security.

It was this change in the local military and psychological balance that provided the basis for Dr Kissinger's personal diplomacy vis-à-vis both the Israelis and the Arabs in the period that followed. It was not really surprising that the going often seemed to be easier with the Arabs (or at least the Egyptians) than the Israelis. The strain on Egyptian society of twenty-five years of bearing the brunt of the Arab effort to restore the rights of the Palestinians, without any substantial success, had been economically crippling. The Sinai disengagements[10] may not have impressed other Arabs as necessarily in accordance with the *Arab* interest (which for many is equated with the Palestinian interest), but they did seem to most Egyptians to be in accordance with the *Egyptian* interest. They began the process of the Israeli army leaving Egyptian soil, they restored the income of the Canal and the resources of the oil-fields, they provided a new, less abrasive and more generous diplomatic friend and quasi-ally to take the place of the Russians. President Sadat from 1974 to 1977 seemed almost incautiously eager to dispense with the Russian connection: no doubt an index of how irksome he and the Egyptian high command in general had found it. During his visit to Washington in October 1975 the reasons given included the Soviet refusal of his request to buy arms to replace those lost in 1973, and their refusal of a grace period for the repayment of debts. Some of the diplomatic snubs probably also rankled, especially by contrast with Dr Kissinger's emollient attentions. But though these irritations make Egyptian policy understandable enough, the quarrel with Russia left Sadat in no position for the foreseeable future to resume hostilities with Israel, even on the assumption that he might secure Western arms in place of Russian, since integrating such armaments into a defence structure that had been based for twenty years on Russian weapons would inevitably be time-consuming and imply a period of impaired military strength. The Israeli

The Middle East War: Some Rather Loud Signalling 95

armed forces were very amply resupplied by the United States after the war.

The Syrians, unlike the Egyptians, did maintain their arms-supply connection with the Soviet Union, and had a well-stocked armoury in the aftermath of the war. But the second Sinai disengagement, and the conflict it engendered between Egypt and Syria, effectively neutralized the Syrians as well, since they were far too vulnerable to contemplate launching an attack unless the campaign could be concerted with the Egyptians. At the moment of writing, any such prospect appeared still remote.[11] Thus the Sinai disengagement, though it had to be forced on the Israelis in the teeth of considerable apparent resistance and resentment, appeared to have served their security interests considerably better than the situation as at September 1973, which had, after all, allowed their two chief enemies to mount an almost successful surprise attack.

To revert to the argument about the detente inducing Soviet acquiescence in the American management of the crisis and its diplomatic aftermath: the Russian restraint on arms deliveries to Egypt during 1974 and 1975, which had left the Egyptians hardly in a position to go to war again even if they wanted to, was undoubtedly a contribution (perhaps an unconscious and accidental one) to the strength of the American hand vis-à-vis Israel. For Dr Kissinger and Mr Ford could hardly have put as much pressure on Israel for the second Sinai disengagement as they did in the spring of 1975 if the Israelis had been in immediate military danger from Egypt. The Russians did resupply Syria very lavishly, perhaps to illustrate to President Sadat what he was missing, but obviously in the knowledge also of the unlikelihood that Syria alone could consider war against Israel. These Russian-supplied weapons were in 1976 turned against the Russians' other allies in the Middle East, the Palestinians, during the Lebanese civil war.[12]

The Palestinians and Jerusalem remain the human and emotional heart of the Arab–Israeli conflict, but the Egyptian–Israeli confrontation has been its military heart, so that inducing a detente there was a logical prelude to creating the sense of security that might persuade the local parties that a longer term *modus vivendi* was possible without the sacrifice of their respective identities. The process was barely kept under way during 1976, a presidential election year not being a time when American policy-makers could put much pressure on Israel. Nevertheless, the outline of a potential settlement had become visible, though the Israeli political changes of 1977 perhaps made it more distant.

Whatever the timetable of change in local attitudes and adjustments, the context of great-power involvement within which they operated was clearly transformed by Dr Kissinger's initial crisis-management. In September 1973, no one would have dared to prophesy that within two years America would be restored to more influence in the Arab world than it had had since 1948; that an American president would have enjoyed a triumphal tour of the entire Middle East, and an Egyptian president been invited to address Congress; that American personnel would be stationed in Sinai at the request of both Israel and Egypt, and with the acquiescence of the Soviet Union; that Israeli cargoes would have been allowed through the Canal; and that Lebanon, the P.L.O., and Syria could each be nudged towards taking their places in the necessary change in diplomatic patterns. The prospect of settlement and the rise of American ascendancy were two sides of the same coin. Obviously Soviet policy-makers could not enjoy being edged into a back seat by this process, and the Soviet press grumbled insistently at Dr Kissinger's step-by-step technique, and demanded at regular intervals the reconvening of the Geneva Conference, at which their diplomats would have equal status with American. But the Russians did not really do anything much more than grumble and perhaps encourage the upsurge on the left in Lebanon, though that also redounded to their eventual disadvantage. It is difficult to think of Russian motives for this relative restraint, in a period during which they so visibly lost much of the diplomatic influence in the Middle East that they put twenty years into acquiring, save their wish to maintain the detente with America.

The Middle East War: Some Rather Loud Signalling 97

To sum up, looking at the three phases of the crisis – development, confrontation and resolution – one may say that in each of them care of the detente appears to have been one preoccupation of the Russians: perhaps pursued with some duplicity and with regard to preservation where possible of their local interests in the Middle East, but having precedence over care for the interests of their local allies, Egypt and Syria. One would not say the same of the United States. The detente was undoubtedly cherished with great zeal and subtlety by Dr Kissinger, but during the crucial confrontation phase the vital interests of the United States and Israel evoked a clear indication that Washington would if necessary break the detente: that was the meaning of the strategic alert. The differential priorities with regard to the detente reflected the fact that it was, in other respects, more necessary and valuable to the Russians than to the Americans. Some critics of detente speak as if this were one of its disadvantages, but on the contrary it is the reason why it provides diplomatic leverage for America. The more valuable the central relationship of detente is to the Russians, the less they will be inclined to put it at risk by 'pushing their luck' in crises in peripheral areas. (The case of Angola, which may seem to contradict that observation, will be considered later.) Even the Middle East may be a peripheral area of interest compared to relations with America. Dr Kissinger's was predominantly a diplomacy of carrots rather than sticks. He sought, and often contrived, acquiescence in his rearrangements of the world by showing the parties concerned that there was something in it for them: a better territorial settlement, or economic aid, or more security, or a reopened Canal, or the safeguarding of the flow of oil. In the Middle East crisis he used local inducements of this sort for local powers, but for the Soviet Union these would hardly have been enough (considering the level of their loss of diplomatic assets) without the more subtle network of inducements constituted by the detente.

CHAPTER 6

Europe: Security and Identity

One of the paradoxes of detente is that the European powers, which had to press the concept on recalcitrant American policy-makers in Mr Dulles's day, grew decidedly suspicious of its consequences as they came to full flower under Dr Kissinger's care. Though this may seem just an instance of the normal European tendency to feel that America's place is in the wrong, it has a certain logic to it. The current identities (even the borders) of Western Europe and Eastern Europe were created during, and partly by, the Cold War. Their respective security systems, Nato and the Warsaw Pact, were devised for Cold War conditions, and sometimes the system has looked as vulnerable to detente as an igloo to a heat wave. When the identity or the security arrangements that once appeared confining or oppressive suddenly begin to look perishable, it is natural that they should be rapidly revalued and that the losses entailed in their possible dissolution should loom rather formidably. Political institutions do not accept the necessity for change very readily. They acquire bureaucracies, conventions, vested interests, which all tend to resist it.

That is probably true of the Warsaw Pact as well as of Nato, but most of what follows will look at Western Europe because its reactions are so much more open to inspection than those of Eastern Europe. The infighting within Nato and the E.E.C. is in full view, and has had a liveliness and variety about it that sometimes causes its importance to be over-rated. There has been a good deal *less* in many Nato crises than has met the eye.

But there has been from the earliest post-war period an intrinsic tension between the needs of American security and the possible definitions of the European identity. This tension affected the transatlantic relationship even during the Cold War years, but, for reasons that will be explored, was at its most acute in the early years of the detente.

The survival of a military alliance for almost thirty years undoubtedly indicates that it is felt by the governments concerned to confer benefits. Let us look at the nature of these benefits on both the European and the American sides, and see how they were affected by detente. Nato was initially (and in essence substantially still is) an American protectorate extended over Western and Southern Europe, up to a clearly defined boundary. But if we compare it with other U.S. protectorates, such as that extended to Japan by the U.S.–Japan Security Treaty, or to Australia and New Zealand by the Anzus Treaty, we may say that at least it has been a protectorate in which the protected powers supply far more to the common defence than in those other arrangements. It would be disgraceful if this were not the case, given the real military capacities and traditions of the European powers concerned. They have (and have had since about 1955) the material potential to mount defences independent of American troops that could perhaps be adequate for their own security. But they have not had the political will to do so, because on the whole the Nato relationship has been a comfortable enough one for the policy-makers concerned (except de Gaulle) and the alternative always looked and was both more expensive and less stable. Nevertheless, that alternative has always been there, at least as a hankering in the European mind, and the vision it uses as an allurement is much older than the actual existing systems of the E.E.C. and Nato. A firm-minded traditionalist like de Gaulle was thus equipped to become its most eloquent spokesman, and an equally firm-minded traditionalist like Dr Kissinger to understand its attraction better than most American policy-makers. Much comment has been devoted from time to time in the American press to the expression of astonishment that Dr Kissinger, undoubtedly the most European of American secretaries of state, should have had various sharp passages of arms with his European allies. But of course it has been precisely *because* of his understanding of this strand in European diplomatic potentialities that frictions arose. The American policy-makers who saw no conceivable danger to the American national interest in the European movement were those who did not know much European history.

The alternative version of Europe's possible identity that I have in mind has usually been called Gaullist, which is unfortunate since the name imposes too large a load of that remarkable personage's preoccupations upon it. One might suggest rather the term Carolingian, which contains a small bow in the direction of *le grand Charles*, but indicates the true orientation of the concept, to Europe's ancient and long imperial glory, to the Rhine and to the reconciliation of Germany and France. Whatever it is called, it is a strong rival to the other concept of the European identity, which has always rightly been called Atlanticist and looks to the sea and the West and the friend-in-need (economic or military) across the ocean. The Atlanticist concept grew only out of the experience of Europe's weakness and fragility, its self-destruction in two world wars and its desperation after the second of them. It tends therefore to seem tame, unenterprising, even small-minded, in Europe's palmier periods. There is not much spiritual satisfaction in it for the true European romantic.

Worse, it was founded upon, and seems still to imply, a de facto partition of Europe into spheres of influence for the Americans and the Russians. The original military and political situations of 1945, with the Russian Army sitting solidly along the centre of Europe, with communist parties in France, Italy, Greece and elsewhere commanding the support of a large part of their electorates, and with the remnants of Grand Alliance sentiment making it rather embarrassing for America and Britain to put together an anti-Soviet alliance, let it originally seem an even chance that within five years Western Europe might be barely distinguishable in political complexion and diplomatic orientation from Eastern Europe. It was only by American economic strength and the diplomatic skills of Dean Acheson and others that the liberal 'welfare–capitalist' market economies of Western Europe were preserved, began to prosper again from about 1948, and managed to construct in 1949 the security system that has withstood both internal and external pressures ever since. The shoring-up of the defences of Western Europe necessarily meant relinquishment of what lay beyond the feasible perimeter, and thus an enduring sense of sacrifice and guilt and loss of identity.

That is, the necessities of security assured the victory of the Atlanticist concept during the Cold War years. With the detente, those necessities began to seem so much less pressing that the larger, older, more ambitious vision of Europe began again to glimmer alluringly on the horizon. I shall argue presently that after 1973 these glimmerings once more retreated to the status of a mirage, but let us examine first the reasons why they appeared to have real substance in the ten years or so before that time. The decade 1963–73 provided a number of reasons, independent of de Gaulle, for the American connection to seem less desirable as well as less necessary for Europe. First, there was the Vietnam involvement through practically the whole period, and no single episode of policy-making has ever provided as many opportunities for denunciation of America from every conceivable shade of European political thought (especially the left) as that excursion into quagmire. Second, there was the deeply disconcerting series of American episodes of domestic tragedy and disaster from the assassination of John Kennedy (the last American president that Europe really took to its heart) to the disgrace of Richard Nixon. It was indeed a staggeringly bad decade for the presidency, and the European notion of America tends to be excessively governed by the image of president and presidency. So that as between these assorted forms of international and domestic damage, 'American' practically came to be a pejorative term, and anti-Americanism quite a settled mode of life in Europe. As someone put it, anti-Americanism became the racialism of the intellectuals. And not only on the left. The most startling denunciation I have encountered of Americans as positively polluters of Western civilization was from a deeply conservative Catholic intellectual who is the foreign minister of a small European power – a man clearly moved by a conviction that American 'pop culture' in the forms of music and television series and comics and pot-smoking adolescents represented a greater danger to the values of his staid little society than marxism could ever be.

By the time Dr Kissinger came into office in 1969, these forms of damage to the American image were considerably advanced, and the years 1970–3 added a conjunction of personalities to translate it almost into a political movement. The election of June 1970 in Britain, which brought Mr Heath to power as Prime Minister, provided for the first time a British decision-maker who might conceivably have chosen against America in the competition of alternative possible identities for Europe. Unlike Churchill, Eden and Macmillan as earlier Conservative policy-makers, he had no special family feeling for the American connection. His enthusiasm for Europe, from the early 1950s, had been much greater than that of most members of his party. He was much more like the moderate pragmatic-conservative 'meritocratic' politicians and bureaucrats who 'made Europe' than the traditional, hereditary, aristocratic, distinctly Anglo-American political elite who had established the pattern of thinking of his own party up to this time. On quite another issue he had managed (accidentally or not) to isolate from the party the one charismatic right-wing nationalist orator capable of swaying Conservative grass-roots opinion against Europe, Mr Enoch Powell. And, of course, he was much more free than Mr Wilson or any other Labour prime minister ever could be from the pressure of back-bench opinion and vested interests suspicious of Europe on protectionist trade union grounds.

Mr Heath's rather brief stay in power was, however, much less important than the reality and then the legacy of de Gaulle. Until the *événements* of May 1968 weakened his authority, the sixties in Europe were really his decade. Something has already been said of de Gaulle's concept of the uses of detente: now we must look at his concept of the uses of Europe, and its relation to America. The most extreme definition of that relationship, as implied in the Gaullist *'tous azimuts'* ('all horizons') defence policy would imply that the U.S.A. was seen equally with the Soviet Union as a potential enemy and a potential target for the *force de frappe*. 'It goes without saying that this force would be based on atomic weapons either developed by us or purchased, but which belong to us, and since one will eventually be able to destroy France from any point in the world, our force must have the capability of being able to act against any part of the world.'[1] A sort of deliberate conscious extravagance in ideas and demands, a capacity and willingness to shock, was part of de Gaulle's diplomatic technique, and one may see it here. As he once said, one may demand the moon in the certainty that it will be refused and that the refusal will be a bargaining card in one's own hand. The 1958 demand that Nato be turned into a triumvirate of America, Britain and France possibly falls into this category of ploys that are useful chiefly on the assumption that they can be relied on to evoke refusal. Nevertheless, what seems to have defeated the Gaullist effort to redefine Europe's identity as against the American connection was just this stratagem of total intransigence. De Gaulle's immediate successors in French policy-making, Pompidou and Jobert, inherited the tradition of intransigence without inheriting the independent political strength or the historical personality that could make it acceptable to France's allies, especially the Germans. A great man is a hard act to follow.

Given this prelude, it was no doubt always on the cards that Dr Kissinger should encounter frictions with his European allies in the early 1970s. But the really difficult phase in the relationship, the six months from October 1973 to March 1974, was of course a side-effect of the 1973 Middle East War. As had already been demonstrated in 1956, the Middle East is the part of the world where American and West European interests were most seriously at odds, and are still decidedly competitive. Their respective objectives are closely aligned in Europe, and their conflicts can be shrugged off as of minor importance in most of the rest of the world now that the Europeans have effectively retired from much effort to exert influence there. But the Middle East imposes a different scale of priorities on the two sides of the Atlantic and demonstrates a different level of vital interests. For Washington the survival and security of Israel has been and remains at the top of the list of priorities, even though the strength of the 'friends of Israel' lobby in Congress and the media may have been a little diminished as the consequences of undue Israeli intransigence have been reckoned up. America can live without Arab oil and Arab friends if it must, though any secretary of state must work hard to ensure that this choice is not forced upon the country. For Europe, on the other hand, living without Arab oil implied in 1973 total economic disaster. The survival of Israel may be a moral obligation for European policy-makers, but the Israeli definition of Israel's vital security interests was much less likely to be accepted in even the friendliest European capitals than it was in Washington. Therefore, if the adversary powers were seeking an issue on which to divide West European policy from American, they could hardly locate a more promising one than the Middle East.

The hammer-blow of the changed relationship with the oil-producers fell the more heavily on the European economies because the long European boom of the 1960s had in fact been fuelled by cheap Middle Eastern oil. The Marjolin report of 1962 had come down heavily for 'cheap energy', interpreted without question in those days as Middle Eastern oil. No one doubted the assumption that it would always be as urgent for the Arabs to sell the oil as it would be for Europe to buy it, and that prices would continue to be set by market forces largely favourable to consumers. These assumptions seem in part a legacy of the Suez crisis of 1956, in which the opponents of the military venture argued that military influence over either the oil-bearing real estate or the route by which it was transported to Europe was quite irrelevant to the quantity made available or the price at which it could be sold. There was little realization that Arab states might find it advantageous to leave some of their oil in the ground, in order to raise the price at which the rest could be sold, and also for the sake of their grandchildren. The coal production on which the earlier economic development of Europe had been based was phased down; the nuclear power stations which might have replaced it were not built. Cheap oil thus became a source of diplomatic as well as economic vulnerability over the medium and short term for Europe (and over the long term as well, unless alternative energy technologies are pursued more vigorously).

On oil, as on other matters, the French had more resentments against 'the Anglo-Saxons' than other members of the E.E.C. As early as the First World War, policy-makers in Paris had been irked to note that British and American companies were successfully moving in on French sources of oil in the Middle East. The loss of influence, especially to the Americans, continued in the 1930s and 1940s, and the French had good reason to be specially sensitive about this matter: their dependence on oil is greater than that of Britain or Germany, for instance, because they have less coal.[2] In the early stages of the 1973 crisis the Quai d'Orsay, or the Foreign Minister M. Jobert, seem to have seen the episode largely as an opportunity to retrieve French influence in the Arab world. The result was rapid deals with Libya, Algeria and other Arab states, and some intensive manoeuvring with the Syrians. Dr Kissinger was not unnaturally irritated by these démarches, since they tended to undermine his efforts to produce an Arab–Israeli settlement, as well as a joint front by oil-consumers towards producers. The issue therefore became a sort of extension of the battle in progress over the 'Year of Europe'.

This was an American project, rather incautiously unveiled in April 1973,[3] for a sort of moral and intellectual redefinition of the Western alliance to see Nato into its second quarter-century (which began in 1974), and to take account of the enhanced strength and status of Japan, as well as Western Europe; perhaps even to parlay the Atlantic Alliance into a sort of Oceanic Alliance for the advanced industrialized non-communist world. Most of the Western powers had no particular objections to cosmetic or inspirational attentions to Nato, even if they did not propose to take them seriously. But early 1973 was an inopportune moment for the burnishing of Atlanticist concepts. The prestige of Mr Nixon's government was beginning to ebb, and M. Jobert, the French Foreign Minister, was able to seize with impish glee on the project as an opportune battlefield for France's rival redefinition of the European identity. However, in fact 1974 turned out to be the year of digesting the unpalatable economic consequences of the Middle East War, and the riveting American political melodrama of Watergate. History is not necessarily co-operative with anniversary intentions, or proposals for theoretical redefinitions.

Yet because rather than in spite of this, by 1975 one could say that Europe's identity crisis appeared to have been resolved, at least for the time being, in favour of the Atlanticist definition. Third force or Carolingian Europe looked as infeasible as it had done in 1947, and for much the same reason: the sense of economic vulnerability that had vanished in the quarter-century of boom was back in full force under the impact of the new oil prices and a major recession, along with the possibility of a new war and a new embargo. The connection between security and prosperity, and the dominant role of America in both as far as Western Europe was concerned, was recreated by the suddenly returned sense of vulnerability, not only as regards the Russians but also the newly intransigent raw-material powers of the Third World, led by the Arabs. Thus the apparently destructive battles of late 1973 to early 1974, which at the time seemed likely to devastate the alliance, in fact resulted in a system that by 1976 was working in a way not at all unlike that projected in the 'Year of Europe' speech, and even enjoyed the co-operation of France, to an appreciable degree. One factor in this transformation scene was the remarkably rapid 'turnover' of European political personalities in 1974: the death of President Pompidou, the relegation of M. Jobert to the back benches, the replacement of Mr Heath by Mr Wilson, the fall of Willi Brandt, and the emergence of President Giscard d'Estaing and Chancellor Schmidt as the dominant

European personalities of the mid-1970s. In a sense the alternative definition of Europe – Carolingian Europe that might have turned into third force Europe, theoretically as likely to exert its strength against the United States as against the Soviet Union – seemed to be left without any articulate True Believers in positions of power. The Atlanticist concept held the field, hardly challenged.

During this complex transition, detente with the Soviet Union was vital to American capacity for manoeuvre. The conceivable alternative joint leadership of Europe – the Germans and the French – were each in their separate ways using detente as a concept within their own diplomatic strategies. Something has been said earlier of the French hopes for it. The far more substantial German version of detente, the *Ostpolitik*, has a literature of its own and its achievements (the improved status of Berlin, the German–Soviet treaty, the German–Polish treaty) are well enough known to need no analysis here.[4] The point to note in considering American choices is that any tendency to a dragging of heels on detente at this point by Washington, any tendency to reassert cold war concepts, could only have divorced American from German objectives, to the advantage of French ones. It would have helped Paris in effect to outbid Washington as a friend to the German national interests and hopes already firmly committed to the vehicle of the *Ostpolitik*.

This is a major point to be borne in mind in interpreting American policy in the prelude to the 1975 Helsinki conference. To describe that meeting as a peace conference after the Cold War was rather an exaggeration, since its 'Final Act' was specifically not a treaty, but it did fulfil one of the normal functions of peace treaties: it defined the status quo produced by the hostilities.

The most striking aspect of the European status quo as defined at Helsinki was not, however, the level of Russian influence but the level of *American* influence. West European dependence on the United States seemed actually greater, more accepted and prospectively permanent in 1975 than in 1965, as great as it was in 1955, not all that much less necessary, militarily, than it had been in 1945. That is, the thirty years' march of the post-war period, including the six years of detente, seemed to have done very little, at this milestone, to have divorced the two sides of the Atlantic. The West European identity remained Atlanticist.

The very widespread misgivings expressed in America about Helsinki[5] ('another Munich') before and immediately after the conference may be seen, at this distance, to have had little basis. The declaration conferred no legal force on the Soviet hegemony in Eastern Europe. The article on the inviolability of frontiers did not rule out the prospect of peaceful changes, since the Germans could not have signed if it had done so. In fact it specifically ruled such change *in*, and included a provision that may be useful for an East European power that wants and someday has a chance to leave the Warsaw Pact:

> They consider that their frontiers can be changed, in accordance with international law, by peaceful means and by agreement. They also have the right to belong or not to belong to international organisations, to be or not to be a party to bilateral or unilateral treaties, including the right to be or not to be a party to treaties of alliance: they also have the right to neutrality.[6]

At most it again conceded what had been tacitly conceded on many occasions since 1945: that the West was not prepared to upset Soviet hegemony by armed force, or take the risks of war to assist those already captive in the Soviet sphere. Western inaction in the crises of 1953 (over East Germany when the Soviet regime was at its post-Stalin weakest point), 1956 (over Hungary) and 1968 (over Czechoslovakia) had already made that point abundantly clear. The Russians in effect wanted it in writing as well, but their insistence on seeking this was based on a miscalculation of Western political opinion, and has proved counterproductive to their hopes. Far from creating a Western sense of the *legitimacy* of the Soviet power sphere, the Helsinki arguments seemed to reawaken the half-forgotten guilt-feelings of the West about abandoning the East Europeans.

Critical comment in America on the conference tended to imply that President Ford's attendance was in some sense a gratuitous concession to the Russians, without any *quid pro quo* for the West. But in fact it was part of a complex bargaining sequence from which the Russians, two years on, seemed to have emerged with very little except the couple of days of champagne and speeches of the meeting itself, whereas the East Europeans had been able to enhance their diplomatic leverage in ways important to them, and the Americans had been able to avoid any damage to their alliance relationships, and to gain at least some useful points for themselves. As Helmut Sonnenfeldt (Dr Kissinger's chief aide in this field) remarked at the time, they had sold American co-operation on Helsinki for the German–Soviet agreement, sold it again for the Berlin agreement, and then yet again for the MBFR talks.[7] (Despite the lack of actual progress in arms cuts through the MBFR talks, they have been politically very useful to the Western powers, as was pointed out earlier.)

Helsinki and the long prelude to it must be seen as an elaborate, rather traditionally European exercise in diplomatic finessing for all its thirty-five participants, and of the four main sets of national interests being more or less deviously advanced by means of this balance of power quadrille (the Russians, the Americans, the West Europeans and the East Europeans) the Russians might at the time of writing be judged to have come off to least advantage. Mr Brezhnev admittedly did well as far as his personal political situation was concerned, since the assumed successes of his diplomacy seem to have helped him fend off any challenges to his ascendancy posed by rivals within the Politburo. But that was no damage to the West. If the rivals for the eventual succession in Moscow are allowed to see that a detente policy may 'pay off' in personal terms, it must surely encourage them in its pursuit, and even the opponents in the West of detente do not on the whole want the *Russians* to return to a cold war strategy, complete with Berlin crises and such. They prefer to argue as if this were an option that could be reserved to the West.

The Russian drive for a European security conference dates back to Mr Malenkov's time, in 1954, and if we compare what was hoped from it then by Russian policy-makers with what actually happened at Helsinki, it will become clear that the Russians had been obliged to abandon more of their original ambitions for Europe in the intervening twenty years than the Americans had done. When the proposal was first put forward by Mr Molotov, its objective was to prevent the rearmament of West Germany, induce the retreat of American power and American bases from Europe, and dissolve Nato. It was to be a conference of *Europeans*, with no intrusive North Americans, and at the time that idea did excite quite a lot of interest in Europe. By 1975, even the Russians had given up trying to exclude the Americans, though it was still called a European conference. The Europeans themselves – both East and West Europeans – were insistent on the American presence: the U.S. President was the centrepiece of most manoeuvring and bilateral deals. *This acknowledgement of the American commitment and future in Europe was a far newer and more transforming element in European history than the acknowledgement of Russian power in Eastern Europe.* The princes of Muscovy have been a power in that part of the world for a good many centuries. The level of their presence waxes and wanes: since 1945 it has been at high-water mark, and Helsinki did not offer much sign that the tide could be induced to ebb. But it did seem to show the contours of the East European countries maintaining themselves ruggedly enough in their submerged fashion.

In particular the policy-makers of Poland, Romania, Yugoslavia and Finland managed to assert their individuality and security interests by means of the years of diplomacy that led up to the conference, through the accompanying visits by President Ford, and even in the language of the declaration itself. The principle of inviolability of frontiers (which in the Russian text is conveyed by a word that means something more like 'immutability' or 'untouchability') strengthens Polish leverage against Russia, in the sense that it reduces Polish apprehensions of German revisionism, and thus undermines the Polish sense of having to depend forever on Russian military power for their own national integrity. The Poles also managed to make a profitable side-deal with the Germans to release about 125,000 people of German ethnic origin to go to the West, a deal that can be included with the fringe benefits of detente in offsetting the human costs of the division of Europe.

The Yugoslavs, the Romanians and the Finns also made gains in their respective campaigns to enhance their own security, or capacity for self-assertion against Soviet pressures. The Yugoslavs got a visit from President Ford to signal U.S. interest and the beginnings of an arms deal for the supply of American TOW anti-tank missiles, a rather pointed contribution to their envisaged territorial defence against the Soviet tank columns that might conceivably be used in some post-Tito Russian attempt to force or manoeuvre Yugoslavia into the Warsaw Pact fold. They were also able to use the conference process to ease relations and border problems with Italy, Bulgaria and Austria. Even the old project of the early 1950s for a Balkan Alliance (with Bulgaria and Romania added to the original membership) was helped towards some revival, and this also must be seen as Yugoslavia taking out insurance against diplomatic isolation in case of future Soviet attack.

Militarily, the defence of Yugoslavia against Soviet pressure or attack must depend very much on the attitude of Romania, since Romanian co-operation or acquiescence would be vital to the security of Soviet lines of communication, even if Hungarian or Bulgarian territory were used by Soviet forces. Thus a co-operative – even collusive – relationship with Romania was of the first importance to Yugoslavia, and it appeared to be developing well at the time of Helsinki and during the following year. The Romanians have a territorial quarrel with the Russians over Bessarabia (disputed between the two since the early nineteenth century) and in a subdued way they were not allowing it to be forgotten. They do not permit Russian troops to be stationed on their soil, nor passage through the country, except by negotiation. They were developing a fighter-aircraft in conjunction with the Yugoslavs: they invited British, French, Italian and Greek defence ministers to visit, rather than Warsaw Pact ones; they continued to cultivate diplomatic relations with Israel and close and cordial links with China. A year after Helsinki, in the summer of 1976, they were not only maintaining their assertive foreign-policy independence of the Soviet Union, but visibly edging towards the status of non-alignment already enjoyed by the Yugoslavs: seeking and obtaining observer participation in the non-aligned conference in Sri Lanka, for instance. In short, from a Russian point of view, not behaving at all like a biddable and reliable satellite, and even hinting to Western visitors that they believed the Russians would not risk another 'Czechoslovakia 1968' operation, and that the West should resist Soviet imperialism more in places like Angola.

The case of Finland, as compared with that of Romania, brings up a distinction that might be useful in considering the future of Eastern Europe as a whole: the distinction between a Soviet sphere of influence and a Soviet sphere of hegemony. Finland incontestably lies within the Soviet sphere of influence, but not under Soviet hegemony. The term 'Finlandization', though much disliked by the Finns themselves, is unfortunately the only one available to denote a situation differing from that of an actual satellite because the country concerned is able to choose its own domestic political values, though at the cost of practising a sort of self-censorship in foreign and defence policy, deferring to the known views of a large inescapable neighbour. Undoubtedly such a status would represent a *decline* of freedom for Western Europe, but a marked *improvement* in freedom for Eastern Europe: it would have permitted the Czechs, for instance, to continue with their 'socialism with a human face' while remaining within the Warsaw Pact. It seems the only mode by which a restored political pluralism in Eastern Europe could be made compatible with the Russian's insistence on maintaining the area as a buffer-zone for their own security. Such an outcome may be difficult to be optimistic about, even given a long period of detente, but is less impossible to envisage than if one assumes a return to cold war. The West has considerable advantages in this subdued long-term contest, provided communication and economic relations remain easy – i.e. provided detente is maintained. The economic strength and elan of Western Europe, the attractions of its lively and consumer-oriented societies (as they become visible through travel) are far more alluring to East Europeans than the austere, puritanical, bureaucratic, nose-to-the-ideological-grindstone life of the Warsaw Pact countries is to Westerners. Even the young revolutionary left in the West is not attracted to Soviet-style societies, though it may still romanticize China or Vietnam, which are safely remote from inspection. Within the Warsaw Pact, the Soviet case for imposing communist orthodoxy on Eastern Europe is diminished by detente. German revanchism used to be a real fear in the countries occupied in the Second World War, but it has now almost lost its capacity to raise alarms, though the German army has in fact become quite formidable in the last few years, for the first time in the post-war period. And the other standard communist bogy, American imperialism, also looks a good deal less convincing in a period in which Poland as well as Russia itself are dependent on American grain.

The 'open' quality of Western societies, which is often presented as a serious handicap in the power competition with communist societies, may to some degree thus be turned into a positive asset, almost a weapon, against the Soviet Union. The Helsinki declaration is written in the language and to the prescriptions, by and large, of Western liberalism. The conventions it sets up as standards to be observed are normal Western practices, even in such minor-seeming matters as the availability of newspapers in the 'freedom of information' section. It is no cause of anxiety in Washington or London that *Pravda* and *Izvestiya* should be available for purchase on the local newspaper stalls and for reading in various libraries. They were there before the declaration. But if and when *The Times* and the *New York Times* are as readily available in the Gorki Prospekt it will be quite a revolutionary change. And until they are, there will be a demonstrable gap between actual Soviet policy and the 'declaratory policy' to which Mr Brezhnev subscribed his signature at Helsinki. The requirement for the disclosure of foreign trade statistics also represents a sharp deviation from Soviet traditions of secrecy, and so (much more) does the requirement for notification of military manoeuvres involving 25,000 or more men. This arrangement offers no problems to Nato, but the Warsaw Pact command clearly had to steel itself as for an ordeal, and at first seemed to be restricting its manoeuvres to below the agreed level in order to avoid complying, though it did issue invitations to two sets of manoeuvres in the first year after Helsinki. The West did not have any difficulty in preserving what may be considered a couple of its own cold war instrumentalities, the 'Cocom' embargo list, which was not even discussed, and the two broadcasting stations, 'Radio Free Europe' and 'Radio Liberty', which continued to be sustained, the American government voting $65 million for them a week or so after Helsinki. (The Russians continued to jam them, or attempt to do so.)

Though there was no legal sanction against the defaults that must be expected on many provisions of the Helsinki declaration, there was a diplomatic sanction in the form of the projected second conference two years after the first, at Belgrade in 1977. The Soviet government must want to avoid the loss of face that would arise from widespread accusations of breach of the Helsinki undertakings, and this was a sanction of sorts. The text of the declaration was laboured on so long by so many European foreign offices, the compromises were so laboriously achieved, that every European government had a sort of vested interest in its survival, and this was a matter in which American objectives were in line with East European as well as West European ones, whereas the Soviet Union was on the defensive.

Despite these advantages, the conference was still widely charged with having psychologically 'legitimatized' (if not actually legalized) Soviet hegemony in Eastern Europe. That would imply that some determinate group could be shown to regard Soviet hegemony as somehow more legitimate after August 1975 than before. But who precisely can be said to have taken that view? Certainly not the East Europeans: those prepared to be candid to Westerners on such matters saw the declaration as a weapon to resist Soviet hegemony. Equally, not the West Europeans: the arguments about Helsinki and Soviet default on its spirit did more than anything else to reawaken the resentments and misgivings, which had been rather quiescent since 1968, about the modes whereby Russians enforce their view of their security interests on the unfortunate East Europeans. Least of all in the minds of the American policy-makers themselves, whose actual viewpoint was spelled out in some detail early in 1976 through the medium of a row over the alleged 'Sonnenfeldt doctrine'. This was a storm in an electoral teacup, created by a charge in a television address by Mr Ronald Reagan that one of Dr Kissinger's chief advisers, Helmut Sonnenfeldt, had proposed 'in effect that the captive nations should give up any claim on national sovereignty, and simply become part of the Soviet Union. In effect slaves should accept their fate'. This curious interpretation of U.S. policy (explicable only as a desperate blow in the battle for the Republican nomination) had the side-effect of inducing publication of the actual text concerned, a candid report on the state of the contest over Eastern Europe, which it would normally have been undiplomatic to publish:

> The last thirty years have intensified the urges of East European countries for autonomy, for identity ... to break out of the Soviet straitjacket. There are almost no genuine friends of the Soviets left in Eastern Europe, except possibly Bulgaria ... The reason we can today talk and think in terms of dealing with Soviet imperialism outside of and in addition to simple confrontation is precisely because Soviet power is emerging in such a flawed way ... What we can do is affect the way in which that power is developed and used. Not only can we balance it in the traditional sense, we can affect its usage – and that is what detente is all about...
>
> We have to get away from seeing detente as a process which appeases or propitiates Soviet power. We have to see our task as managing or domesticating this power. That is our central problem in the years ahead, not finding agreements to sign or atmospheres to improve, though those have some effect. Our challenge is how to live in the world with another super-power and anticipate the arrival of a third super-power, China, in twenty years or so ...
>
> It is in our long-term interests to use these [economic] strengths to break down the autarchic nature of the USSR ... With regard to Eastern Europe, it must be in our long term interest to influence events in this area – because of the present unnatural relationship with the Soviet Union – so that they will not sooner or later explode causing World War III. *This inorganic unnatural relationship is a far greater danger to world peace than the conflict between East and West* ... [Italics added]

So our policy must be a policy of responding to the clearly visible aspirations in Eastern Europe for a more autonomous existence within the context of a strong Soviet geopolitical influence. This has worked in Poland ... A similar process is now going on in Hungary. Janos Kardar's performance has been remarkable ... He has skilfully used their presence [Soviet troops] as a security blanket for the Soviets in a way that has been advantageous to the development of his own country ... The Romanians have shown autonomy but they have been less daring and innovative in their domestic systems.

Finally, on Yugoslavia we and the Western Europeans, indeed the Eastern Europeans as well, have an interest which borders on the vital for us in continuing the independence of Yugoslavia from Soviet domination ... any shift back by Yugoslavia into the Soviet orbit would represent a major strategic setback for the West.[8]

The original leak of the story seems to have been motivated by a Yugoslav-oriented sensitivity to the use of the word 'organic', lest it should carry any suggestion that Soviet hegemony in Eastern Europe could ever be seen as a natural thing, whereas the speaker's actual purport was to consider how it could be made less oppressive – that is, how its crude power-enforced dominance could be modified. In fact, the East European alarm and visible bristling over a misrepresentation of a secret briefing for U.S. ambassadors, never intended as a matter of public comment, was in itself an indication of how important were the hopes attached by some at least of the East European regimes to American power and presence in Europe. The actual shape of American purposes is clear enough: discreetly sympathetic support to East Europeans hoping to erode away the Brezhnev doctrine (whose very existence the Russians themselves deny), allied with a consciousness that the process must be slow, patient, prudent and devious, since it is indubitably one that carries a risk of major war. Considering where the battlefields would be if hostilities did result, that measure of prudence is hardly one to which either East Europeans or West Europeans could reasonably object.

Even in the field of human rights within the Soviet Union, Helsinki clearly backfired as far as the Soviet authorities were concerned. The eminent dissident historian, Andrei Amalrik, who was sent into exile about a year after the conference, conceded that the regime had felt obliged to become somewhat more careful in its treatment of dissidents. He even claimed that the foundation in Moscow of the 'Group to Promote the Observance of the Helsinki Agreement' might perhaps gradually force the Soviet government to fulfil the obligations it had undertaken. European opinion was not induced to shrug off concern on these issues. The award of the Nobel Peace Prize to another Soviet dissident, Andrei Sakharov, the physicist who had been the father of the Soviet nuclear armoury (though ironic enough in that respect), was specifically a recognition of his brave campaign of resistance to the Soviet state in the field of human rights, and was one of the most pointed rebukes administered to the Soviet government in recent years by the European intellectual community, especially considering that it came through a sector of Scandinavian opinion that has frequently been rather neutralist in the East–West struggle. Perhaps the most favourable (to the West) of all the estimates of the outcome of Helsinki, and of detente in general, was that of the notable Yugoslav dissident, Milovan Djilas, whose book *The New Class* entitles him to be regarded as among the most perceptive firsthand observers of what actually happens to a communist elite after some years in power. He maintained that, in a continued period of detente, the Warsaw Pact powers would become more and more absorbed in their domestic problems. The Soviet bloc would eventually fall apart: within fifty years the present satellites would become 'Yugoslavias'. Communism was a spent force, the communist countries backward both economically and culturally, and the youth of those countries devoid of any enthusiasm for it. 'The U.S. has already won the Cold War, although it has not won it on its own terms. The important thing is that monolithic Communism is no longer a threat and that the future belongs to pluralism, even if it is a pluralism of Communist parties ... The ordinary man will be able to live better, to read more books, to travel, to lead a more normal life. In the long run, the detente will make East Europe free.'[9]

That seemed certainly an over-optimistic assumption, and one that would not be made in the West by even the most hopeful friends of the concept. Nevertheless, within a year after Helsinki some measure of 'Finlandization' seemed discernibly more likely in Eastern Europe than in Western. This was not only a matter of the restiveness of several Warsaw Pact governments against Russian strategic, political and economic control, but the restlessness of European communist parties against Russian intellectual and ideological guidelines. Tito and Berlinguer, both in their respective ways representing successful assertions of autonomy against Soviet purported authority, were the heroes of the European Communist meeting of June 1976, not Brezhnev. The phenomenon of 'Eurocommunism'[10] is one whose future import for the two alliance systems was at the time of writing still difficult to read, but since it represented an erosion or discard of Soviet predominance on the part of the whole establishment of the communist movement in both Western and Eastern Europe, it could hardly do other than reduce the usefulness of those parties to Soviet government purposes.

Thus most of the American apprehensions concerning Helsinki expressed before the event could make little claim to justification afterwards. The East Europeans had not been 'confirmed in slavery', or caused to desist in their efforts to create some breathing space for themselves against the oppressive Russian embrace. The West Europeans were not induced to dismantle their alliance, or concede the area of Soviet hegemony to be sacrosanct: on the contrary, some at least of them were spurred to mount a mild ideological counter-offensive, as for instance in the reiterated warnings of the British leader of the Opposition, Margaret Thatcher, against the growth of Soviet military power and imperialist purposes. The American connection with Europe was not reduced: it was strengthened, confirmed and visibly accepted even by the Russians. Willi Brandt, in a speech in London a few weeks after Helsinki, even went so far as to use the word 'integration' for the future of the relationship.[11] That may have seemed visionary to most of his listeners, but the system of consultation between the advanced industrial economies that appeared to be under way at the Rambouillet, Puerto Rico and London meetings did seem to correspond to the concerting of policies for that world, which the 'Year of Europe' speech had proposed. Even the French, in operational though not in declaratory policy, seemed by late 1976 to have rather conceded the battle and to be moving closer to Atlanticist positions. The redefinition of French strategy was so much in accord with the views of Nato as to rouse the remaining Gaullist faithful to vehement protest. On the economic side, while there were still Franco-American disputes over, for instance, the sale of nuclear reactors, the level of the French challenge appeared a shadow of its earlier self.

To sum up, one may reasonably interpret detente as a useful strategy for American policy in its relations with both Western and Eastern Europe in this period of transition. In Western Europe, the primary American interest was that the European identity should not be defined in a fashion incompatible with Atlantic security, and at the end of the period that objective looked better safeguarded than it had been for years past. In Eastern Europe, the American objective was that the hope and chance of more autonomy, more breathing space, should be kept alive without being encouraged into forms that would threaten the general peace. Mr Ford may have been verbally maladroit about it in the television debate with Mr Carter, but the policy itself was by no means maladroit.

CHAPTER 7

South East Asia: A Means of Disengagement

There is a special poignancy in the relation of the detente to America's disinvolvement from South East Asia, for it was the original involvement there, or rather its interminable costs, that produced the mutation in the American national mood that in turn permitted and required detente. The Cold War was a high-ambition, high-cost policy. If one takes its ideological rhetoric seriously, it was an unlimited-cost policy: 'pay any price, bear any burden', as the Kennedy inaugural said. There is always a gap between rhetoric and reality, so the unlimited-costs notion need not be taken literally, but it seems reasonable to say that no determinate limit was fixed by American policy-makers for the preservation of what were thought of as American or Western vital interests, like Berlin. The Cold War in Europe did not, however, actually *exact* heavy costs, save in money and nervous tension. Containment was accomplished on the basis of psychological deterrence rather than by actual military enforcement.

It was far otherwise in Asia. Containment was applied twice by military means, in Korea and in Vietnam. The first episode was costly in terms of American, Korean and Chinese lives, but relatively brief, relatively successful (at least it produced military stalemate and reasonable political stability for some twenty-five years) and relatively well-approved internationally. The second, Vietnam, was unendurably long, immensely costly in lives, destruction and televisual anguish, and almost unsupported internationally. Above all it ended in the gall and wormwood of defeat.

I shall argue that detente, primarily with China but also with Russia, was an essential element in the process by which America eased itself out of a lost cause in Vietnam. Though the extrication was deeply painful and somewhat damaging even with detente, it would have been more painful and probably more dangerous without it. The transition from an American 'high profile' to a 'low profile' in South East Asia inevitably imposed new strategic and diplomatic assessments on other powers in the area, and these will be looked at in due course.

In essence the process we are considering is the dismantlement of an American protectorate in South East Asia. The protectorate was part of an intended system of military containment of Chinese power: it was originally erected on the assumption of a probable expansion southwards of the Chinese *machtgebiet*, unless defences were erected against it. In the mood of 1954, when Dulles first confronted the issue, as he saw it, of replacing France as the 'containing' power in Vietnam after the French defeat at Dien Bien Phu, the obvious answer seemed to be American backing and guarantees for the more tough-minded and intransigent anti-communist nationalist leaders of the area. In effect the American creation and sustenance of the government of Ngo Dinh Diem in Saigon, in the teeth of French recalcitrance, was the heart of that policy. Its international framework was provided by Seato, which was established to form a multilateral facade for the American guarantee and visibly to spread its benefits to Thailand.

Though the first shadows of the American involvement in Vietnam belong to Truman's time, these political decisions of the Dulles period were the real turning-point towards what became the full combat commitment of the Johnson period. That development was probably inescapable, or nearly so, as long as the assumptions of the Cold War were maintained. If the original Dulles decision to preserve a Western-oriented government in Saigon was to be sustained, and if it proved (as it did) that South Vietnamese military capabilities were not adequate to the task, even with American equipment and training, then there was no alternative but the investment of American troops. But the cost, in lives and the domestic political consensus, of that investment of American troops was what broke the back of the whole policy. The moment of its breaking was March 1968, when Johnson decided that he could not put in any more troops, and would not try again for the presidency.

That moment really marks the beginning of the end for the American policy of military containment of Chinese power in Asia. It necessitated and permitted a new policy stance vis-à-vis China, a mutation in the almost unalloyed hostility that had existed between Washington and Peking since 1949. During the Kennedy and Johnson period some sporadic attention had been given to the desirability of a new initiative towards China: a speech by Roger Hilsman, for instance, not long before Kennedy's death, was designed as a 'trial balloon' to that end.[1] The notion was logically always subversive of the Vietnam policy then in operation: if you are seriously seeking a better *modus vivendi* with the communist great power in Peking, what exactly is the rationale of resisting militarily the establishment of a small communist power in Saigon? There were of course answers, but they were answers in terms of honouring a commitment that came to seem burdensome, pointless, mistaken, disastrous *ab initio* (as indeed it had been), rather than in terms of direct strategic power calculation. One might say that the Saigon regime was the bastard child of American policy-makers of the middle Cold War years, and by 1969 the original connection and its offspring had come to be bitterly regretted, but honour precluded a mere cutting of the throat of that offspring, however inconvenient and burdensome. So Dr Kissinger had to labour for four years to produce a settlement that might provide South Vietnam with 'a reasonable chance of survival', as he said at the time. Peace with honour really meant disengagement without immediately abandoning the vulnerable burdensome legacy of an earlier error.

'A reasonable chance of survival' in January 1973 could plausibly be interpreted as at least four years for political adjustment by Saigon, and perhaps more. For in January 1973 President Nixon had just won a landslide victory: no doubt appeared of his ability to keep up the supply of armaments on the one-for-one replacement basis allowed in the agreement. And most analysts assumed, as was spelled out in the confidential 'understandings', that if the agreement were broken by a massive North Vietnamese invasion of the South, that breach would be requited by the sanction of American air-power, at least in the form of air-interdiction strikes directed at the invasion routes. The agreement by that time would of course no longer be in force, having been broken by the other side.

It is quite possible to argue that the logical way out of the American involvement in Vietnam was simply to end it: to pull out American troops unilaterally in 1969, whatever the level of resistance by the South Vietnamese government. But aside from the horrifying local military problems that this would have involved, the enormous damage to America's credibility as an ally of so sudden and obvious an abandonment of a regime earlier American policy-makers had created, and the way it would have polarized domestic opinion, such a course was ruled out by the fact that President Nixon was no more willing than his predecessors to preside over an *undisguised* American defeat. It would be putting it rather cynically to say that the detente helped provide the necessary disguise: it was more a matter of its providing pit-props to shore up the shaky local balance while the American forces were extricated. Or one might say that both China and the Soviet Union were successfully seduced away, though only for a time, from any feelings of ideological duty to their Vietnamese allies by the prospective sweets of the detente with America. It is difficult to place any other interpretation on, for instance, the Soviet non-reaction to the American mining of Haiphong, which did not even produce a postponing of the Soviet–American summit of May 1972, or any visible friction there. This military option had been considered on a number of earlier occasions, as the Pentagon papers make clear, because it was the most obvious way of reducing the flow of sea-borne supplies (which were as much as two-thirds of the total) to the North Vietnamese. But before the construction of the detente it had to be rejected in case Soviet reaction should increase the general level of danger. Only with the detente did it become relatively safe.

One might also cite the Chinese rolling-out of the red carpet for Mr Nixon earlier in the same year, and its shrugging-off the final bombing of North Vietnam in December 1972. There was a cryptic Chinese message to Hanoi at that time, seeming to signal that the Vietnamese leaders had better sign the agreement or face a future of hostilities on the scale of the December bombings.

Thus, as I said, Dr Kissinger was able to use the detentes with China and Russia as international buttresses (in default of a reliable local military balance between North and South Vietnam) so that American power could be disengaged from this disastrous commitment without inducing immediate collapse in the South. Ought one to go on to say that the time thus bought was only two years: that China and/or Russia returned to full support of the North Vietnamese military conquest of South Vietnam in time for the final offensive of 1975?

This is a natural interpretation for the enemies of detente to use, but it does not correspond with what in fact occurred. The reasons why 'a reasonable chance of survival' was not translated into the *actual* survival of the Saigon government depended a great deal more on what happened in Washington and what failed to happen in South Vietnam than on decisions taken in Russia or China.

First, as to what failed to happen in South Vietnam. The 'Vietnamization' programme, which was billed to make the forces of the South equal in fighting capability to those of the North, obviously failed, despite the pouring-in of American supplies and techniques. Perhaps those techniques were always wrong for that war, sustained as it would ultimately have to be by the local economy. The account given by the victorious commander of the North Vietnamese forces, General Van Tien Dung, makes it clear that at the time of the final battles he had an overwhelming superiority in tanks and big guns because of the Congress-imposed decline in U.S. aid to the South. 'Nguyen

Van Thieu was then forced to fight a poor man's war. Enemy fire-power had decreased by nearly 60 per cent because of bomb and ammunition shortages. Its mobility was also reduced by half, due to lack of aircraft, vehicles and fuel.'[2] General Van also makes it clear that planning in the North for the final offensive in the South began within six months of the Paris agreements, and that the North originally expected, as did Western observers, that the final push would be timed for 1976. It was the Watergate-induced collapse of the Nixon administration, and the conflicts with Congress, that led the Northern planners to assume, correctly, that the decisive encounter might be brought forward to 1975. The fall of Phuoc Binh without U.S. intervention confirmed this conclusion. The brevity of the final campaign – only seven weeks – was due in part to strategic error or inadequacy by President Thieu or his commanders in the field: the withdrawal to defensive positions closer to Saigon was so badly executed that it disintegrated his armies and administration to the point at which only one small final battle, at Xuan Loc, was required to complete the rout.

Strategic error alone could perhaps hardly have produced so sudden and startling a political collapse, but it became apparent in the year or so after the communist consolidation of power that in fact the former regime was honeycombed with adherents of the other side, strategically and properly concealing their real allegiance, including many ensconced in positions of such eminence that the Americans had made plans to evacuate them on the assumption that this would be necessary to save their lives. That secret vanguard or fifth column meant in effect that the former regime was like a beam hollowed out by deathwatch beetle: just a little extra weight served to break it.

The other half of the process that vitiated the Paris agreements took place in Washington. There are few neater pieces of historical irony than that by which the shadow of Watergate finally darkened the most popular achievement of Mr Nixon's first term, the extrication of American forces from Vietnam. When President Thieu was coerced and bribed into signing the Paris agreements (which he had fiercely resisted and had no intention of observing), President Nixon was at the peak-point of success and apparent security of power: just returned to office with an overwhelming majority and an absolute mandate for his foreign policy. No one could conceivably have foreseen that within two years he would be politically broken and disgraced. Yet the worm was already in the apple of his political life. Watergate had already happened. And almost from the beginning of the period of operation of the Paris agreements, from March to April 1973, the consciousness of his personal vulnerability seems to have inhibited his power of decision as far as breaches of the cease-fire in Vietnam were concerned. Even before Congress placed an embargo on his power to act, in August 1973, the ingrowing consciousness of possible personal disaster seems to have operated to much the same effect.

Thus the 'private assurances'[3] of vigorous reaction never became operative. They could not, of course, ever have amounted to a 'secret treaty' since constitutionally the American Congress is always entitled virtuously and legally to repudiate any agreement not ratified by the Senate, and has not infrequently done so. Presidential assurances can never be any better than the political life and influence of the president who makes them.

The American intervention in Indo-China, from 1954, in effect imposed twenty years of delay on the victory of the forces that looked originally to Ho Chi Minh. But for the decisions of Mr Dulles and President Eisenhower in 1954 the victory would probably have been completed by 1956, by military or political means. The twenty years' delay cost America 55,000 dead, 150,000 million dollars, and a great deal in lost domestic political authority and consensus. It cost the Indo-China states an intolerable degree of destruction and anguish. Altogether the Indo-China intervention was probably the most painful and damaging single error in the whole 200-year history of American foreign policy, and no conceivable advantages bought by the delay can possibly justify the costs.

Relating this disastrous episode to the diplomatic relationships of the period, there are some points to note. The first is that though the final passing of Vietnam, Cambodia and Laos into communist control took place in the period of detente, the injury to American interests from the involvement as a whole undoubtedly had its origins in the Cold War period, and indeed in the central strategic–political doctrine of the Cold War, the doctrine of containment. If the detente with China had been instituted earlier, the apprehensions that brought American forces into combat might have been avoided, and therefore also the disenchantment with the burden of foreign wars, which seemed in 1975 to put a question-mark for a month or two over the whole future of America as an actor in international politics. Without the American intervention, Indo-China would undoubtedly have come under communist rule much earlier, since the seeds of the ultimate victory had already germinated by 1946, but the trauma to America would have been avoided. Victory for Ho Chi Minh's forces would not, in 1954–5, have meant defeat for America but only for France. Responsibility for the damage to America from Vietnam thus belongs at least as much to the Dulles decisions of 1954–6 as to the original Truman decisions that began the commitments, and to the Kennedy and Johnson decisions that raised them to the ultimate breaking-point. The American defeat of a French-sponsored attempted coup in 1955 probably marks the 'point of no return', after which the victory of the forces that looked to Ho could not seem other than an American defeat, though the degree and the visibility of that defeat enlarged steadily until 1968, as successive presidents made ever more desperate attempts to avoid it.

Though the changes in South East Asia in the period 1954–74 do not in any way justify or even substantially offset the costs imposed by Vietnam, there is a case to be made in mitigation of the final phase, the slowness of disengagement, 1969–72. The basic motive of policy was still the wish to avoid confronting the American electorate (and the policy-makers themselves) with the plain, rebarbative countenance of a defeat for American arms. When it finally arrived in 1975, the end was quite readily accepted by the American public at large, rather gloatingly welcomed by a few on the left, and was probably a source of secret relief even to some policy-makers, since if the final offensive had actually been delayed until early 1976, as was expected by both sides in late 1974, it would have dangerously and embarrassingly coincided with the U.S. presidential nominating process. But by that date the war had already been 'distanced' in American minds by the two years that had elapsed since their official disengagement, and the six years that had elapsed since they began to disown the war through the process of 'Vietnamization'. The final defeat therefore seemed a defeat for the Vietnamese, not for America. To the American man in the street the regime in Saigon by then was a remote, unsatisfactory bunch of people whom the U.S.A. had tried once to help, but who had not proved capable of 'making it', and who deserved nothing more of America, not even a final allocation of funds.

One may argue that the domestic damage of the defeat to the American political consensus was greatly reduced by this 'distancing' effect, compounded from the lapse of time and the abdication of responsibility. Less than a year after the debacle in Saigon, the scars from that final episode (as against the scars from the actual years of involvement) were hardly visible. Even the refugees seemed to have simply vanished into the great confluence of American ethnic minorities. And this mitigation of the blow to American national pride was perhaps beneficial, not only to America but to the society of states as a whole. Defeat is seldom good for the national psyche: it can poison it for a whole post-war generation, as with Germany after the First World War. Probably results as dramatic as those were never to be feared in America, but in the desperately polarized mood of 1969–70 a retreat into isolation in the manner of the 1920s, a turning of America's back on an ungrateful, unmanageable, intransigent world, would have been welcomed by a lot of Americans. And that really would have destroyed the patiently built Western coalition, which was the main achievement of the Cold War years.

In the event, with visible, undisguisable defeat postponed to 1975, very few ill-effects seem to have followed, not even a domestic witch hunt as after the most similar other such episode, the 'loss' of China in 1949. American troops had not actually been engaged in China: no lives were lost to the communists, no prisoners agonized over (save a vice-consul or two). Yet the 'loss' of China had long-term and damaging consequences in American political life: the rise of McCarthyism, the painful hysteria in political and intellectual life that it brought; the cry of 'twenty years of treason' and the consequent deformation of American foreign policy by twenty years of pointless hostility to China. By contrast, the 'loss' of Vietnam was hardly mentioned even during the presidential campaign of 1976, and former hawks competed with doves in promising more rapid development of the detente with China.

The assumption of a serious conflict of American interests with China by then seemed so ill-founded that it was almost difficult to believe it had been a basis of policy-making for twenty years. Yet it was. Perhaps the overprotective, sentimentalizing, moralizing quality of the original American relation to China, from the late nineteenth century until about 1948, was bound to produce a disproportionate reaction when the long-term protégé turned away towards a more genuinely potent adversary, the Soviet Union, in 1949–50. However, the irrational apprehension with which China was regarded during the 1950s and 1960s had been almost completely dissipated by 1975, and so the collapse of the Saigon regime hardly scratched the China detente.

The detente with the Soviet Union, in contrast, took a bruise or two, on the argument that most of the weapons for the final North Vietnamese advance were supplied by Moscow. That was no doubt true enough, though the disparity in weapon supplies to the North and South arose rather from Congress's refusal to vote funds for American supplies to the South than from the stepping-up of the level of Russian supplies to the North. Consciously or unconsciously, Congress acted as if aware that the only way of ensuring an early end to the war was to choke off supplies to America's own client state, and it hardened its heart (with popular support) to do so. Perhaps that kind of decision may more easily be taken by a collectivity like Congress, where guilt-feelings can be so spread as to be inconsequential, than by an individual policy-maker like the president or the secretary of state. Certainly the final few weeks in Vietnam showed an unusual reversal of roles, with Congress almost callously determined to make an end and Dr Kissinger pleading the case for the residual moral commitment to a regime for which he certainly had no love.

The decision to phase out Seato provides an appropriate gravestone for the damaging chapter of American policy that began with its foundation, though perhaps gravestone is too solid a metaphor, since Seato always looked more like a stage backcloth of unconvincing fortifications, quivering flimsily in every passing diplomatic breeze. The organization was never much more than a multilateral 'front', whose only solid reality was the substance of American containment policy in South East Asia. The general lines of America's successor policy have now been provisionally defined. The detente with China is its centrepiece, and is founded on the common strategic interest of the West and the Chinese in maintaining a countervailing balance to Soviet power. Economic relationships might prove useful in reinforcing this common interest: a grain-for-oil agreement might be as feasible with China in some years of low harvest as with the Soviet Union. But there are reasons, which will be looked at presently, for supposing that the relationship will remain limited to strategic and economic modes, and will be difficult to move to any greater political or cultural congeniality.

With Japan the alliance relationship returned fairly rapidly to even keel after the shocks of the transition period. The closeness of the economic ties appeared likely to ensure its continuance. Some of the transitional frictions, the 'Nixon shokku', perhaps arose from the ex-president's dislike of the Japanese,[4] as much as from the actual necessities of secrecy, but the forced Japanese realization that a free ride on the coat-tails of American power might not be part of the permanent order of the world was not necessarily counterproductive to the health of the alliance. With India the frictions of the 1960s and early 1970s appeared to have diminished into a relationship that was reasonably correct, even if not particularly close or cordial, and that may be as much as can be expected. As long as there is an understood sense in which China and the United States are permanently concerned with providing a counter to Soviet power, whereas India retains her suspicions of China and her quasi-alliance with the Soviet Union, India and the U.S.A. must be on opposite sides of the balance. With India there is neither the parallel strategic interest that America has with China, nor the closeness of economic and defensive ties that it has with Japan. And for much of the period the 'largest Asian democracy' argument used earlier was rather in abeyance. There could be no case for sacrificing the American relation with China to the improvement of that with India: such a move would be destabilizing to the whole system.

One might thus in general argue that American policy in Asia, after Vietnam, appeared to be on a relatively logical course as far as all three of the Asian great powers were concerned. For the medium and minor powers, by contrast, the context of detente was one that in some respects multiplied the uncertainties of their futures. After so long a time in which Asian spokesmen put down their difficulties to the tensions either between America and China or between America and Russia, there is some historical irony in this byproduct of the process by which both those tensions have been reduced. Lee Kuan Yew, a more candid spokesman than many, has offered an analysis of the situation as probably several of them saw it:

> An era has come to an end. America was the dominant power in South-East Asia for thirty years, since the end of World War II. Once America acknowledged that she could no longer intervene in Southeast Asia, it is fair to assume that the contest for influence over the peoples of the region will be mainly between the People's Republic of China and the Soviet Union ... The fate of Southeast Asian countries is to be caught in a competitive clash between these two.
>
> China has the advantage of historic associations with the region. Memories of past tribute paid, and an awareness of geographical proximity make all Southeast Asia anxious not to take sides with the Soviet Union against the Chinese, even though the Soviet Union is ahead on military technology.

Most hope to maintain equal relations with both China and the Soviet Union. But this may not be possible unless these two Communist centres cease to compete for ideological and nationalist supremacy – a prospect which appears remote.[5]

This disparity of advantages, which to some degree favours China over Russia for the long-term contest as far as most Asian societies are concerned, is rather the reverse of that obtaining in the central balance relationship. One of the major problems for American policy has become that of keeping the detentes with China and Russia reasonably 'symmetrical' with each other. Or rather, perhaps one should say, keeping the rapprochement with China in reasonable parallel to that with the Soviet Union. Of the two communist powers, China is obviously the more unlike the West in structure and assumptions. The Soviet Union is a state–capitalist society run by an oppressive authoritarian bureaucracy, but its intellectual life has been influenced by Western values, and its people aspire wistfully towards Western standards of consumption. It may not be a consumer-oriented society, but the pressures of those who would like it to be are reasonably formidable and have to be taken into account by decision-makers. China is something else: a revolutionary, puritan, self-denying society, still gripped by Maoist orthodoxy and the concept of 'self-reliance'. 'Self-reliance' is so large and central an element in the Maoist creed, and is so much in accord with China's rather bitter historical experience of the society of states since the nineteenth century, that it provided a kind of barrier against the web of interests that (in the Russian case) Dr Kissinger used to reinforce the detente. The natural adjectives for 'alliance' in the Maoist vocabulary are 'temporary' and 'tactical'. This meant, for instance in the economic field, that joint development of the Chinese off-shore oil resources with Japan or America or even Western Europe, in the way the Russians have envisaged for Siberian gas and oil, would probably remain unlikely. Possibly Western Europe, as the most remote of the three other powers, and the one that in Chinese eyes had parallel strategic interests to China against both super-powers, would have the best prospects of cultivating economic rapprochements. China's interest in Europe as, from its point of view, the 'second front', which must be made a 'first front' if possible, was almost obsessively voiced by Mr Chou and Mr Teng in their respective final periods of power. The mutation of the triangular balance into a four-power balance, with the emergence of an independent Western Europe, would be strategically desirable to China, but not its mutation into a five-power balance, since that would logically require an independent and probably nuclear Japan, and the Chinese policy-makers showed a clear preference for Japan's remaining under America's wing. Mr Chou apparently at one stage reproached Dr Kissinger with neglecting his Japanese allies. Chairman Hua, in early 1977, appeared to be adhering to Chou's general analysis of China's foreign-policy options.[6]

The present society of states remains on course, in Maoist thought, for either war or revolution: detente is strictly temporary, though war should be postponed as long as possible to allow China to recruit its strength. China after Mao showed little impatience over Taiwan and none over Hong Kong, and still seemed so preoccupied with the relationship with the Soviet Union that every other issue, including Taiwan, remained in comparative abeyance. One formula conceivably applicable to the transition period was that denoted by the cryptic phrase 'one China and two Hong Kongs': i.e. a silent, de facto Chinese extension to Taiwan of the 'settlement deferred' status already accorded to Hong Kong. In unspoken terms, this would mean the Chinese allowing it to be understood that they would not settle the issue by military means, and the Americans abrogating their defence treaty with Taiwan, removing their few remaining troops (in 1976 about 3,000) and transferring their embassy to Peking. The change would not mean that Taiwan became indefensible: the island would remain a formidable proposition even with local troops only, especially in view of the very substantial provision of U.S. arms in late 1976, presumably in agreed anticipation of the break. The Chinese guard their sovereignty fiercely, and could not endorse in words any implication that their relationship to Taiwan could be other than a domestic matter. Yet de facto there were both strategic and political reasons for postponing any encounter, as far as Peking was concerned. So the 'settlement deferred' situation was possible in practice, even without diplomatic agreement.

As for South East Asia, the still more cryptic maxim to 'beware lest in expelling the wolf through the front door you allow in the tiger by the back door' appeared still to be the Chinese policy prescription for the local powers. That is, Peking's main anxiety appeared to be lest any partial vacuum created by the American disengagement from South East Asia might be filled by Russian power. This was also a matter on which Chinese interests were complementary to those of the United States, since it would be galling for both to see, for instance, the great base that the Americans built at Camranh Bay become a Russian naval facility. The signs at the time of writing were that Vietnam would play a complex game, recruiting even the U.S.A. back into the balance by the cultivation of some links with the Carter administration,[7] so as to maintain with tenacity its long-preserved relative independence of the Soviet Union as well as China, in a situation in which the relation with China seemed by 1976 already quite abrasive.

The Asian power balance had thus become considerably more subtle, as the processes of detente were worked out, than it had been during the Cold War. At the time of Dr Schlesinger's visit to China, just after Mao's death, the new Chinese policy-makers appeared anxious to interest American policy-makers in the defence of China's frontier areas, and Dr Kissinger responded with a statement that China's security was essential to the world equilibrium, and thus a vital interest of America.[8] The old 'China lobby' and other forces inimical to full normalization of diplomatic relationships appeared unlikely to reassert any new blocking capacity in the foreseeable future. The post-Mao Chinese leadership remained apparently indifferent, at the time of writing, to the Soviet wooing directed towards them after Mao's death.[9] It was clear, however, that some redressment of the central triangle might in future become possible, with a degree of detente between China and the Soviet Union.

That would have considerable implications for South and South East Asia, but it would not necessarily be in any sense a disaster for Western policy. In fact, if detente is to be used ultimately to construct a concert of powers, some measure of it will be required in the Soviet–China relationship in due course, since both would be necessary members of such a concert.

One might argue that by late 1976 something like the old geopolitical concept of the 'heartlands' and 'rimlands' balance appeared to be developing: a dichotomy between the three great landholders of the Asian mainland – China, the Soviet Union and India – on the one hand, and the island fringe, dominated by sea-power, on the other. The 'rimland' powers – Japan, Indonesia, the Philippines, Australia – seemed likely to retain strong ties with the maritime great power, the United States. The minor powers on the mainland had to make their accommodations with the heartland powers as best they could, with Bangladesh in the post-Mujib period perhaps the most uncomfortably pressured, between Pakistan and China on the one hand or India and Russia on the other.

In such a system, the peninsulars (Korea especially in this case) may be regarded as debatable ground, and so it appeared in 1977. The main American 'asking-point' vis-à-vis China was for Chinese influence to restrain the North Korean regime from any military adventurism against the South. In terms strictly of the local balance of forces, South Korea ought readily to be able to fend off any such attack, since it is far richer and more populous than the North. Yet with local decision-makers as erratic as those in power seemed to be, crisis or collapse could not be ruled out, and the effect on Japan's concern about its own security would be severe. Thus the American need for Chinese restraint of North Korea, and also over Taiwan, was substantial and seemed in early 1977 to be evoking some response. The inducements that America could offer in exchange would potentially include advanced defensive weaponry – radar warning systems, anti-tank guided weapons and the like – which would be of help in China's stance against the Soviet Union. Some foreshadowing of such a potential supply may be seen in

American approval of the British sending Rolls-Royce Spey engines for military aircraft to China. A licence for these engines had previously been refused through Cocom.[10] It was the part of political tact that such military goods for China should, at that time, come from European sources rather than from American, and in this instance they served the useful purpose of providing contracts for the hard-pressed British aerospace industry as well as improving China's defensive capacity without the direct American military aid that would undoubtedly have been upsetting to Soviet policy-makers.

About a year after the end of the almost-thirty-years' war in Indo-China (in which the American involvement had been an episode generated in the Cold War and ended in the detente) the American national interest thus appeared to be well guarded. A more or less even-handed rapprochement towards the Soviet Union and China had endowed Washington with some of the classic freedom of manoeuvre of the 'balancer' in that triangular balance. A general situation of 'equidistance' did not preclude a hinted 'tilt' towards one party or the other as occasion might require. Relationships with the 'rimland' powers appeared on even keel and viable over the long term. The options of the small mainland powers were somewhat reduced, but not necessarily to the detriment of their respective peoples, since the necessity of providing for their own security by domestic consensus and diplomatic manoeuvre rather than by American protection tended to push the political elites concerned towards social reform.

The prospective contests of the triangular balance, assuming continuance of the American detentes with both China and the Soviet Union, appeared likely to see the Russians and the Chinese engaged with each other, and the small powers concerned to maintain a prudent distance from both, as nearly equal as their particular circumstances would allow, but anxious that American power should not retire too completely from Asia, so that some reinsurance with the U.S.A. against either of the other dominant powers remained possible. The great unknown of the ultimate direction of Chinese policies after Mao's death could not altogether be provided against, but no useful options had as yet been foreclosed. By contrast with the twenty years of disaster before 1969, the reconstruction of policy in Asia appeared notably rational.[11]

CHAPTER 8

Cyprus: The Scope for Local Intransigence

Detente redistributes diplomatic leverage in rather varied and subtle ways, and though on balance I would argue this redistribution has been useful to Western purposes and also to the preservation of peace, Cyprus presents a case where the opposite seemed to be true, at least over the short term. It was easier to restrain the conflict between Greece and Turkey below the level of active hostilities during the Cold War years than it has been since the detente. The general reason for this is clear enough: the central tensions of a cold war period give small powers like Cyprus and Greece, or middle powers like Turkey, a strong sense of their own vulnerability, and therefore a reason for keeping local tensions reasonably low. Detente reduces the sense of threat, and thereby reduces the sense of need for their alliances on the part of those who are in an alliance structure. They can, as it were, defy their great and powerful friends with some *insouciance*, since their great and powerful enemies do not seem particularly menacing for the time being. They can even hope to use the putative enemy to secure leverage against the putative friend. Those outside the alliance structures may also experience a reduction in the sense of threat, and thus some reduction in caution. The scope for local intransigence may therefore appear increased. All these possibilities are illustrated in the decision-making of the Greek, Cypriot and Turkish governments in the crisis of 1974–5. But the upshot of it all illustrates a point more disconcerting for small powers than great: that in such a situation what will tend to prevail is the strongest *local* force, which in this case was of course Turkey. That is hardly novel or surprising, but it was painfully learned by the Greeks and Greek Cypriots. The great mystery of the whole episode is how they could ever have supposed anything else.

The conflict between Greece and Turkey long antedates not only the detente and the Cold War, but the present society of states. One can regard its contemporary form as a final legacy of the 'Eastern Question' that plagued Metternich in his day. Cyprus is not the only focus of this conflict, but it has been the most important one recently, so that if it could be settled the remaining issues (like the sharing of resources in the Aegean) might prove amenable. The nature of the conflict over Cyprus has always been much the same: the determined Hellenism of the seventy-eight per cent of Cypriots who are of Greek origin has made it inevitable that they should aspire to union with Greece (*enosis*). The fact that the island is located just off the coast of Turkey makes it inevitable that the Turkish government will be better able than the Greek to exert military strength there, and will always give any government in Ankara strategic reasons for wanting to do so. Moreover, the existence of the Turkish minority will give them equally an excuse and a bridgehead for intervening, and the Turkish minority was after 1963 subjected to enough ill-treatment to put an element of moral strength into the Turkish case.

Since none of these basic factors had until 1974 proved susceptible of change, the mode of suppressing the conflict over Cyprus had always involved blocking either the aspiration for *enosis*, or the exertion of Turkish military power, or both. There were *enosis* demonstrations in Cyprus as early as 1831, when Greece was just putting itself together as a sovereign state after centuries of submersion in the Ottoman Empire. But from 1878 to 1954 the British imperial presence, which replaced that of the Ottomans, in effect vitiated both Greek and Turkish power, and so stifled the conflict between them, at least in Cyprus. It was only as the British began the final winding up of the relics of empire in the early 1950s that the conflict was again able to assert its persistence.

If one may, as devil's advocate, say an occasional kind word for the Cold War, one of its modes of usefulness in the society of states was that, in concentrating attention on larger tensions, it diverted political life from traditional local feuds and vendettas. In fact it operated almost as effectively as an imperial power in stifling some local conflicts for a time. In the early Cold War years, 1945-9, both Greece and Turkey seemed more directly threatened by Soviet power, and more directly in need of American protection for survival, than almost any other of the present members of Nato. Greece was threatened by internal civil war as well as external communist military power in Yugoslavia and the Balkan states, in addition to the Soviet Union. Turkey was the target of a Soviet campaign apparently aimed at control of the Black Sea Straits. The situation of both governments was unmistakably of heavy dependence on America and Western power, and the acquisition of membership of Nato was a notable diplomatic victory for both of them, gained at the time (1952) in the teeth of covert resistance from several powers in Western Europe.[1] It was by no means a foregone conclusion to those powers that Nato should extend its military commitments to the Eastern Mediterranean and the defence of Greece and Turkey. A considerable party of Western strategists were of the opinion that Nato would prove a more defensible alliance without these vulnerable outlying members.

The peak of the Cold-War-induced suppression of the Greek–Turkish quarrel came in 1954, with the signature of a pact, which died rather swiftly but which has shown some signs of resurrection recently as a regional option conceivably useful in prospective circumstances: the Balkan Alliance or Treaty of Bled, between Greece, Turkey and Yugoslavia. The reasons for its brevity of existence were the beginnings of the Yugoslav detente with Moscow in Mr Khrushchev's time (the 1955 journey to Belgrade) and the revival of the dissension over Cyprus. That in turn was occasioned by another apparently irresistible process: the winding-up of the remaining relics of the British imperial presence in the Mediterranean and Middle East.

It was hardly to be expected that the Greeks in Cyprus, seeing Britain yield to Egypt over the Suez base in 1954, and seeing, in general, independence come the way of peoples whose level of political sophistication was markedly less than their own, should rest content with colonial status. The demand for *enosis* was revived, and an embittering campaign fought for it from 1955 to 1959, to produce the eventual constitution of 1960. Even here the Cold War was in fact the moderator of the local conflict, for it was really a change of position on the parts of the Greek and Turkish governments in 1958 that enabled the diplomatic success (such as it was) of 1959 to be achieved. And what moved Athens and Ankara in 1958 seems to have been a sense of the increasing dangers of the Cold War confrontation in the Eastern Mediterranean. That in turn arose from the crises of Lebanon, Jordan and Iraq, and a general sense that Soviet power was strengthening in the area. In effect, Athens and Ankara agreed on a *modus vivendi* over Cyprus during what seemed at the time a phase of increased general danger, and the local communities had to go along. But the Turks in Cyprus, like other minority communities in other ex-imperial situations, undoubtedly felt, and had reason to feel, that they would be less well protected by the local political arrangements than they had been by the imperial power. And though the 1955–9 campaign was mostly fought by Greek Cypriots against British troops with the Turks standing aside, there was an embryonic military encounter in 1958 between Greek and Turkish Cypriots, a foreshadowing of what might happen when the British had withdrawn to their sovereign bases. When the new and very complex constitutional arrangements came into force in August 1960, they did not please anyone much, except the British, hopeful that their troubles in the island were over. The Greeks were naturally resentful that what had been achieved was not *enosis* but independence, and the Turks were suspicious that the new constitution would be used to their detriment by the majority community. In a sense they were both right, for the developments of the subsequent fourteen years, to the attempted coup and successful invasion of July 1974, imposed considerable hardship on the Turks and will probably prove to have ruled out indefinitely *enosis* in the form that the Greeks had always wanted.

The constitution that came into force in August 1960 really only lasted three years. From August 1963 it began to break down, with the Turks withdrawing, not as yet into a physical separation but into a sort of administrative one, though the Turkish communities were still at this point widely dispersed in small enclaves throughout the island. The final break was precipitated by Makarios's presentation in November 1963 of thirteen proposals to revise the constitution. The Turkish Cypriots and the government in Ankara rejected the proposals; fighting broke out, and Nicos Sampson, an Eoka gunman with a bloody reputation from the days of the fight against the British, led his private army in a savage raid on the Turkish quarter of Nicosia. He was later to re-emerge as a figurehead of the 1974 attempted coup against Makarios, and the atrocities attributed to him on this occasion, eleven years earlier, were part of the reason for the violence of Turkish reaction to his apparent bid for power in 1974. The Turks threatened invasion in early 1964, but were dissuaded. And this was the point at which American mediators first became involved, originally with what is usually called 'the Acheson plan', though it was hardly more than a set of tentative suggestions. Two other eminent American policy-makers of the Democratic administrations, Cyrus Vance and George Ball, were concerned with the efforts at a settlement in the 1960s, and it seems to have been an unwary remark attributed to the latter that created the widespread Greek belief that the coup of 1967 in Greece itself was part of an American ploy to partition Cyprus in the interests of strategic advantage to Nato. The suspicions of American purposes, which were so notable a feature of Greek reaction to the 1974 crisis, and which inspired rejection of American efforts at mediation, thus had quite a long-established, resentful background. However, the versions current in Athens late in 1974 acquired a Byzantine elaboration: for instance, the theory that it was all part of a Kissinger 'grand design' to give the Soviet Union hegemony over the Balkans (including Greece) in return for an American free hand in the Middle East, or alternatively that it was all a plot to partition Cyprus in return for Nato bases that had been promised in the Turkish area, and that Brigadier Ioannides, the leader of the Greek junta, had been lured into arranging the coup by C.I.A. assurances that the Turks would be deterred from reprisals by American intervention. The actual influence of the C.I.A. 'station' in Athens had long been pervasive enough to lend plausible colour to such interpretations.[2]

However, a purely Greek relationship, between Ioannides, Grivas and Makarios, offers reasons enough for the initial events. The main force behind the continued Greek drive for *enosis* in the 1960s had been General Grivas, a regular officer of the Greek armed forces and a Greek (not Cypriot) citizen who had provided the military leadership of the campaign against the British, under the *nom de guerre* 'Dighenis', while Archbishop Makarios provided the political leadership. The two men parted company over the 1960 constitution, Grivas standing for a continued military drive towards *enosis*, Makarios ambiguously contriving an emotional and spiritual sponsorship of the notion of *enosis* as an eventual goal with a practical and political attachment to his own independent control of the sovereign republic of Cyprus for the time being. St Augustine is supposed to have prayed for the gift of chastity, 'but not yet'. Similarly, the Archbishop managed to combine protestations of welcome for a higher destiny at some indefinite future date with apparent enjoyment of the interim arrangements. General Grivas, a simpler man, was not up to these Byzantine subtleties. He remained determined on *enosis*, whatever tergiversations either Makarios or the Athens government might exhibit. He had command of the Greek Cypriot forces on Cyprus until the crisis of November 1967, a crisis again precipitated by the massacre of Turkish Cypriot villagers, at Ayios Theodoros. Again, the Turkish government threatened armed intervention, and again they were dissuaded by a combination of pressures, mostly American and Nato.

It undoubtedly contributed to the conspiratorial explanations involving the C.I.A. that the seizure of power by the junta in Athens in 1967 eased the resolution of this particular crisis, despite the antipathy of its leaders to Makarios. General Grivas had been appointed by the previous Greek Prime Minister, Mr Papandreou, and the leader of the junta, at this time Colonel Papadopoulos, could more readily withdraw him, as was done in December 1967, at the demand of the Ankara government. The junta were also anxious to secure restoration to American favour (and arms supplies) by showing a disposition to be co-operative allies in Nato, which meant cultivating reasonably good relations with Turkey. And, to return to the comparison of the relative manageability of the series of Cyprus crises in Cold War or detente, one might say that the junta were cold war oriented in the sense that their ostensible reason for the seizure of power was the alleged danger of a communist coup in Greece. They were thus almost obliged to profess and demonstrate attachment to the purposes of Nato, though of course this had the result of making that organization, and the American connection, an inevitable target for Greek left and liberal resentment in the post-junta period.

Despite their agreement to removing Grivas, the junta in Athens continued to regard Makarios with suspicious dislike, being especially irritated by his technique of using communist support, both domestically in the island and internationally through relations with the Soviet Union, as part of his mechanism for maintaining power. Even before the days of the junta, at least as early as the 1964 crisis, some right-wing Western opinion was inclined to describe the Archbishop as a 'cassocked Castro', creating an 'Eastern Mediterranean Cuba', though what exactly the two leaders had in common other than black beards was never entirely clear. General Grivas returned to Cyprus, though possibly without the approval of the junta, in 1971, intent on making a last bid to secure *enosis* before his death (he was over 70). But in fact death claimed him in January 1974, and the Greek Cypriot force he had created, called Eoka B, fell into even less responsible hands. Control rested, not with

Nicos Sampson (the figurehead of the 1974 coup attempt), but in Athens with Ioannides, by then the leader of the junta, a former secretary of Grivas, and the head of the Greek military police. Thus Makarios had good reason to fear for his tenure of power, and for his life, not only from Eoka B, but also from the Greek officers stationed in Cyprus under the provisions of the 1960 constitution.

It was these two sources of apprehension, or at least the Archbishop's mode of resisting them, that precipitated the threatened crisis of 1972 and the actual crisis of 1974. In 1972 Makarios had imported a supply of arms from Czechoslovakia, intending them for a presidential guard against a possible coup engineered by either Grivas or Athens. The junta were infuriated, perhaps because of the communist provenance of the arms, and delivered a sort of ultimatum, demanding that they be relinquished and the Cyprus cabinet reshuffled. But at this time, early 1972, President Nixon was preparing for his first 'detente summit' in Russia in May. The pressure from Athens on Makarios presented an unbecoming spectacle, in these circumstances, of a Nato power apparently attempting to bully a small non-aligned country that had a cordial relationship with Moscow. Whatever the view of the C.I.A., the White House and the State Department were averse to a crisis in the Eastern Mediterranean, and the American ambassador, Mr Henry Tasca, was sent to urge restraint on the then leaders of the junta. So the crisis was smoothed over with some compromises by Makarios. On this occasion at least, the detente did exert an influence towards easing the Cyprus confrontation.

By the time of the next crisis, July 1974, the decision-making mechanisms both in Athens and in Washington were out of kilter.[3] In Washington the coup against Makarios and its consequences coincided with the last three weeks of Mr Nixon's decline and fall, which absorbed Dr Kissinger's attention. In Athens the change about six months earlier in the leadership of the junta, when Ioannides had overthrown Papadopoulos, had produced growing disintegration and failure of competence. The combination of the faceless, irresponsible, anonymous leadership in Cyprus of Eoka B, the confused, inept decision-making of the decaying junta in Athens, and the distraction of Washington by the drama of Mr Nixon's final exit, produced a notably ill-considered quality in the decisions of mid-July. It was not surprising that Ioannides should have decided on a coup to remove Makarios. From his point of view, the Archbishop was behaving with great provocation in demanding the removal of the Greek Cypriot officers from the island, and he may also have seen a crisis as one way of rallying army support again to his own administration, though in fact it had the opposite effect. A more baffling question is why permit or choose Nicos Sampson as figurehead for the coup, since his name was bound to be like a red rag to a bull for the Turks. The Turks had a resentful hatred for Makarios: they would have welcomed his removal if a compromise-oriented figure had been installed in his place instead of a still more hated symbol of political murder. The cynical local answer was that, once it was known that Makarios had escaped, more respectable politicos refused to serve as proxy for the junta. But the decision-making of Ioannides at this point is the central mystery of the crisis, and one on which even his own statements do not necessarily shed much light, for they must be self-serving. A man in jail on a life sentence is hardly likely to be dispassionate about the events that put him there, especially when his only prospect of remission at some future date is to create political sympathy for himself as a victim of outsiders' plots.

The C.I.A. apparently reported to Washington on 14 July (the day before the intended coup) that Ioannides had been dissuaded from attempting it.[4] Who was deceived, and who deceiving? It is possible that Ioannides believed that the warnings from Washington, which came to him only via the C.I.A., since the ambassador, despite direct instructions from the State Department, did not see him personally (on the ground that an ambassador should not be required to see 'a cop'[5]), were talking for the record, and that they would have to go along with his decisions, since he had them 'over a barrel'. Relations between Athens and Washington had deteriorated in the previous few months, with the junta refusing to provide some facilities that the Pentagon wanted for the Sixth Fleet. It seems possible that Ioannides misconstrued this as meaning that he had something Washington stood in great need of, and that therefore he could afford to be intransigent with the Americans: they would have to go along. British military intelligence, according to later reports,[6] also took the view at this point that Ioannides had been induced by diplomatic pressures to abandon his plans for a coup against Makarios, which strengthens the reasons for supposing that the C.I.A. was deceived rather than deceiving, and that Ioannides in fact believed himself to have enough diplomatic leverage to induce Washington to restrain the Turks, just as they had done in the crises of 1964 and 1967, even if he defied their warnings and went ahead with the coup, as he did.

This would clearly indicate poor political and strategic judgement on his part, since the American and Nato facilities in Turkey were vastly more important to Washington than those in Greece, as was demonstrated in the rest of the crisis. But then the evidence is that the Brigadier's strategic and political judgement were never up to running any system more complex than a military prison, since he seems to have seriously proposed to the rest of the junta an attack on Turkey in reprisal for the invasion of Cyprus. Even his colleagues knew better than to believe that feasible, and the proposal, along with realization of the magnitude of the disaster brought about by the Cyprus miscalculation, caused the junta to put themselves into voluntary liquidation, as it were. The regime simply crumbled, sending for Mr Karamanlis, a former Conservative leader, as its last coherent decision.

Thus the Cyprus crisis did have one positive result, in the exit of the junta and the re-emergence of constitutional government in Greece, though many aspects of the crisis-management remain subject to conflicting interpretations, especially the role of the C.I.A. The Athens station of the agency was an old and powerful one, dating from the earliest days of the Cold War, and some of its more eminent members had been of Greek-

American origin, rather close to many Greek decision-makers and close also to other Greek-Americans, who had in turn been close to Mr Nixon or his original Vice-President, Mr Agnew (like the Greek-American millionaire, Mr Thomas Pappas, who was said to be a large contributor to campaign funds). Obviously there is a good deal that has yet to be divulged concerning the policy-making between the ambassador, the C.I.A. station, the Pentagon and the State Department during the years of the junta, as well as during the fortnight or so that determined the outcome of the crisis. But if the choices of the decision-maker in Athens were irrationally reckless, and of those in Washington somewhat distracted,[7] those of Ankara were entirely clear and candid, if ruthlessly opportunist. As they saw it, the Turkish government had been obliged to watch the situation of their lieges in Cyprus go from bad to worse for fourteen years under the governance of the Archbishop. For eleven years there had not even been a pretence that the 1960 constitution was being observed. In the crises of 1964 and 1967 they had been prevented by America from going to the rescue of the Turkish Cypriots, and precisely because of that they were determined to push through the action of 1974, when the detente had made the diplomatic circumstances more propitious. As one Turk said, 'We could no longer be scared off by threats that the Soviet Union would intercede'. The Turkish Prime Minister at the time, Mr Ecevit, told the American ambassador in Ankara, Mr William Macomber, 'We listened to you ten years ago [in the 1964 crisis]. You stopped us doing this then: that was your mistake. It was our mistake for listening to you. I refuse to compound that mistake.'[8] Once the Turkish army was established in the island, the opportunity to use it to force a population transfer, and a Turkish Cypriot territorial base large enough to allow scope for bargaining, was obviously found irresistible.

Thus I think one may say that for the Turks the scope for intransigence was real as well as apparent; for the Greeks it was only apparent. The pressures for restraint exerted from Washington were ineffectual at the decisive stages of the crisis. The policy-makers tried first to persuade the Archbishop not to push his quarrel with Athens too far, but the Archbishop nevertheless sent his letter demanding the removal of the Greek officers. Then they tried to persuade Ioannides not to attempt his coup (and the C.I.A. reported and presumably believed they had succeeded), but nevertheless the coup was mounted. Then they tried to persuade the Turks not to invade, but the Turks went ahead. One may of course maintain that there should have been much heavier Washington pressure against the junta to stop the coup in the first place and, if that failed, against the Turkish invasion in the second place. This argument would not, however, undermine the point I want to make: that the local decision-makers in Cyprus, Greece and Turkey believed themselves able to defy the advice from their great and powerful friends, in a way that would have been unlikely during the Cold War years. It cannot of course be shown conclusively that heavier American pressure would still have failed to deter the local decision-makers from the choices that they saw (at the time) as in the best interests of their respective political societies. But diplomatic pressure, to be effective, requires a rational decision-maker at the other end to receive the pressure and to weigh up what he has to gain against what he has to lose. It is difficult to see any such rational interlocutor in either Athens or Cyprus in the immediate aftermath of 15 July. There was, of course, a rational interlocutor in Ankara, but here the changed distribution of political leverage exerted its effect. 'What is the "or else" we have to put to them?' Dr Kissinger once demanded, in another crisis. There was not really much of an 'or else' to be put to the Turks in the circumstances of 1974: only the American arms aid, against which they could and did bargain the U.S. bases. So the widespread assumption that the American pressures on the Turks, which worked in 1964 and 1967, could have been made to work again in 1974, seems rather questionable.

Though much of the detail of decision-making is still obscure and subject to speculation, at least the general lines of national interest, for the powers involved in the situation, are clear enough to indicate what their objectives and their diplomatic leverage (or lack of it) were likely to be, and this is what most concerns us in examination of the influence of detente. Looking first at the Soviet role, one might say that their strategic interest rested primarily on maintaining the tension between Greece and Turkey, since this did more than anything else to paralyse Nato's effectiveness in the Eastern Mediterranean, and was also a source of potential embarrassment to America in the event of another Middle East campaign. Moreover, it provided an entering wedge for Soviet influence over either Greece or Turkey. But of those two, Turkey must be the rationally preferred objective for Soviet efforts, since it is strategically the more important, for Russia as for Nato. One would assume the interest vis-à-vis either Turkey or Greece must be more important than the interest vis-à-vis Cyprus itself, whose limitations as a base became amply apparent during the late British period, especially in the 1956 Suez crisis. It has no harbour of any value for naval use, and is too vulnerable for troop concentrations of any size. It can be useful for staging aircraft to the Middle East and the Persian Gulf area or for reconnaissance operations (there was a request by America for U-2 flights during the October 1973 crisis), but even here its facilities are substitutable by other airfields and by satellites. The radar installations on Mount Olympus are very useful for monitoring traffic and communications in the Eastern Mediterranean, but again the facilities in Turkey are of far more importance.

These Soviet objectives made Moscow originally a natural ally for the Archbishop: opposed to *enosis* since that would incorporate the island in a Nato member, Greece, and still more to 'double *enosis*', since that would partition it between two Nato members, Greece and Turkey. The combination of resistance (especially after 1967) to actual *enosis* with the keeping alive of the aspiration or sentiment for *enosis* (which preserved the suspicions and resentments of the Turkish community, and thus the tension between Greece and Turkey) was from the Soviet point of view quite a favourable situation. Thus they had every reason for endorsing the Archbishop's policy of Cyprus as a non-aligned independent republic. The main communist party on the island, Akel, which is recruited mostly from Greek Cypriots, has been among the Archbishop's most faithful supporters from the days of the *enosis* campaign in the British period, though the party has had, like the Archbishop, to practise a good deal of ambiguity on the question in order to avoid losing support to the nationalists. Because of their opposition to *enosis* the Soviet Union was also looked on with some favour by the Turkish Cypriots, and by Turkey itself, though the Turkish Cypriot Communist party is very weak compared to Akel, which can command about forty per cent of Greek Cypriot votes. How the change from the junta to the Karamanlis government in Greece will affect Cypriot communist attitudes is not yet clear, but in any case the developments of 1974 have probably made *enosis* (as against 'double *enosis*') a dead issue for the foreseeable future. Considering these sources of diplomatic or political leverage, what was striking about Soviet policy throughout the crisis was how little advantage they managed to take of some rather handsome opportunities. Greek Cypriot left-wing opinion did constantly urge a journey to Moscow on the Archbishop, with apparent faith that deliverance from the Turks would somehow be found there. But in fact the Russians seem to have taken few serious initiatives at all, either on the international plane or through the left-wing parties in Greece or Cyprus in the confused aftermath of the invasion and the fall of the junta. One might of course argue that Greek resentments at the policy of the American administration, and Turkish resentments later at the arms ban imposed by Congress, were in any case doing so good a job of disrupting Nato or American power in the Eastern Mediterranean that there was no reason for the Russians to exert themselves, but actually some of the apparent disruption seems to have been declaratory rather than operational. Greece announced its withdrawal from the military wing of Nato in August 1974, but only began its slow-motion gestures to this effect in September 1975, and Greek officers have to date remained at the Brussels headquarters. Turkey announced that it was closing the American monitoring bases, but the American officers and equipment remained, with Turkish officers in titular command. No attempt was made to disrupt the British bases, though this can easily be done by withdrawing Greek Cypriot labour. In fact, in the upshot of the crisis the Greeks seem rather more reconciled to the presence of the British bases (both are in the Greek zone of the island) since they are some kind of military offset to the Turkish army presence, and also represent an element of income for the Archbishop's government. So the point in general may be sustained that though the projects of disruption for Nato were made much of by journalists and government spokesmen on both sides, they were thinner in actual fact than in nationalist oratory, and this was no doubt apparent to the Soviet Union.

Nevertheless, the Russians maintained a relatively low profile, hardly encouraging to the far left in Greece itself or to the Archbishop in Cyprus. One may argue that they were deterred from much wooing of Greek opinion by the potentially greater strategic hopes that could be pinned to the prospective cultivation of influence with Turkey. But though one must give some weight to this factor and to Soviet reluctance to see serious hostilities in an area used by a lot of Russian ships, it still seems reasonable to put Soviet caution down partly to the influence of the detente – the consciousness that anything they could pick up in Cyprus (a base had sometimes been mentioned) or in Greece itself was not worth the potential cost in terms of damage to their hopes of America, via the detente. Even Soviet polemics concentrated on the vague and safe target of 'Nato aggression' and on demands for U.N. intervention, rather than on real efforts to embarrass American policy.

Insofar as the Soviet Union did make temporary strategic gains during the crisis, it was by the fringe-effects of Congress's ban on arms supply to Turkey, which caused some restriction of the activities of the American monitoring bases in Turkey, though to what actual extent and for how long is not quite clear. There are twenty-six bases involved: the most important being at Belbasi, Pirinclip, Sinop and Karamursel. These bases do a variety of monitoring work: checking communications and troop movements in the south of the Soviet Union, tracking missile launches, recording underground nuclear tests. Though some of them are useful locally to the Turkish armed forces and to Nato command in the Eastern Mediterranean, their most vital function is undoubtedly related rather to the true central strategic balance, that is relative nuclear strike capacity as between the United States and the Soviet Union. They monitor the growth and alert status of Soviet missile forces; they are an important element in the vast invisible net of mutual surveillance on which, for instance, the maintenance of the SALT agreements, existing and prospective, depends. Congress's action in imposing the ban that moved the Turks to reduce their effectiveness and threaten their future was obviously some strategic bonus or 'windfall gain' for the Soviet Union: the conversations of Russian aircrews and such were no longer being listened-in to from Turkey. But in larger calculations, since the Russians also value the arms-control measures and tacitly acquiesce in the surveillance system that makes them possible, the congressional action had a backhanded quality for the Soviet Union. It may even have contributed to the reasons for delay over a new SALT agreement.

American interests in the Eastern Mediterranean are bound up with whatever solution of the Cyprus problem will most nearly reconcile Greece and Turkey, thus permitting them to resume co-operation in Nato and allowing the use of American bases in both countries. Of the two sets of facilities, the Turkish bases must remain the more important to any American government, not only because Turkey sits astride the Black Sea Straits and is a substantial conventional military power, but because the monitoring devices in Turkey are part of the intrinsically more important balance, the overall nuclear relationship. The Greek facilities are convenient rather than vital to the Sixth Fleet, which is supplied by fleet-train from the American west coast and fuelled from Italy. The use of Greek facilities for 'home-porting' some destroyers permitted American families to live in Athens, and there were an anchorage and range for Nato exercises in Crete. In view of the intensity of left-wing

Greek feeling against the Nato connection, it was obviously injudicious to allow any great reliance on these arrangements: the choice had to be for phasing down their use and a general 'low profile' by both Nato and the United States in Greek affairs. As to the alleged American demand for a base in Cyprus itself, on which some machiavellian interpretations of the crisis depend, it is difficult to see much plausibility in the assumption that this could provide any adequate motivation for U.S. intrigue. Since there is no harbour good enough to be of interest to the U.S. navy, it would have to be an air-base that was envisaged and why this should improve seriously on existing U.S. use of the British base at Akrotiri is not clear. It was an open secret that U-2 reconnaissance aircraft were already able to use this airfield, the Archbishop's government duly receiving payment.[9] More to the point, since any secretary of state must be conscious that America's strategic interests lie predominantly with Turkey, whereas Congress's political interests lie predominantly with Greece, the only Cyprus solution that can keep the island from being a thorn in his side is one that helps reconcile Turkey and Greece. Logically it would be justifiable to sacrifice any strategic facilities in Cyprus itself to that end.

The shape of a prospective settlement had emerged by 1976: a northern province, which will be almost wholly Turkish Cypriot in population, and a southern province, which will be wholly Greek Cypriot since all the Turks have moved north. The remaining bargaining was essentially about where the line of demarcation should run, and what the powers of the central government would be. Greek Cypriot efforts were concentrated on reducing the Turkish province from the third of the island seized militarily towards a quarter, which would allow the Greeks to retrieve some vital areas round Famagusta and Morphou. But no prospective settlement seems likely to reverse the population exchange enforced by the Turkish army. The human cost in death and grief and loss by those operations was, of course, enormous and irreparable. But since the communities are now divided into two ethnic provinces or cantons, a federal system in which each community could live under the protection

Cyprus: The Scope for Local Intransigence

of police and administrators of its own culture has become possible. The 1960 constitution did not work well enough for many people to want its revival; a new one, when ultimately it is agreed, may produce a more viable mode of coexistence. The economy of the island has recovered surprisingly well, especially the Greek southern province.[10] Greek–Turkish relations have not yet recovered, nor as yet has the relationship of either Greece or Turkey with the United States fully done so, though the formal mechanism of diplomacy has worked to produce a remeshing at least on the government-to-government level. There have been new agreements to cover the U.S. bases in both Greece and Turkey, providing for a potential resumption of their usefulness to the Western alliance, though on a colder and more uncertain basis.[11]

Of the episodes of diplomacy in the detente period examined in this book, the Cyprus crisis was perhaps the least reassuring in its final outcome. The basic tendency that it appeared to illustrate, the loss of diplomatic leverage by the great powers against middle-power allies (and the consequent probability that the strongest local force would determine the outcome of such conflicts), was not necessarily one to be deplored in principle, but these events showed it operating harshly against the vital interests of the least powerful of the communities involved, the Cypriots. (The same point was illustrated in a smaller and more obscure case, East Timor, which will be glanced at in the next chapter.) Yet if the detente operated in this case to diminish American diplomatic leverage, it also operated to limit the capacity or will of the Soviet Union to secure advantage from the resulting situation. No doubt the effectiveness of the Western alliance in the Eastern Mediterranean was reduced by these events, and may yet be further damaged by their consequences in Turkish policy, but no dramatic gains were made by Soviet power. In early 1977 the prospect of the eventual patching-up of a constitutional settlement under American auspices appeared reasonable.

CHAPTER 9

Portugal and Southern Africa: Setback and Rebound

'They are helping their friends: why should we not help ours?' That remark, attributed in Washington to the anonymous senior official who was Dr Kissinger's *alter ego*, appears to have been the central doctrine of both sides – or rather the several sides – in the process of competitive diplomacy that sought to influence the outcomes of the sequence of crises stemming from the revolution in Portugal in 1974. I use the phrase 'sought to influence' because local social and political forces were probably the predominant ones in all the territories chiefly concerned: Portugal itself, the ex-colonies of Mozambique and Angola, and the other southern African territories – Rhodesia, Namibia, South Africa – whose strategic and political situations were in due course affected by this confluence of events. Quite possibly the manoeuvring of the Powers vis-à-vis each other affected the outcomes only marginally if at all; that must be left for later histories to prove or disprove. All that is clear at this stage is that the Powers were engaged in the situation, and that it was widely alleged in the United States and elsewhere at the time that detente operated to facilitate Soviet gains, or embolden Soviet activities, particularly over Angola. Alexander Solzhenitsyn, for instance, was reported as saying that he did not know how any tongue could utter the word detente after Angola. Dr Kissinger was publicly and vehemently exhorted to impose various kinds of penalties (usually economic) on the Soviet Union until it desisted from its policies, and the alleged Soviet gains in southern Africa were cited with much frequency in the 1976 presidential campaign claims that detente had proved a 'one way street' for the advance of Soviet power.

If detente had actually perished over the Angola crisis, its demise would have been rather that of one who is despatched by the ricochet of an opportunist sling-shot after surviving the attentions of massed machine-guns, for the degree to which United States and Soviet interests were engaged in the combat over Angola was initially quite marginal. Nor was that a surprising state of affairs, for the susceptibility of either the West or the Russians to damage or advantage by the political complexion of the government there is relatively slight. There were, however, complex symbolic issues involved in the use of Cuban troops, and in the mode whereby the Angolan regime was established, which offered some insights into the way detente diplomacy might develop over the years, and into the respective strengths and weaknesses of the Powers.

The dominant points of interest in this story as a whole are in the waxing and waning of local forces. But for the purposes of analysis of the diplomacy of detente, the primary question must be in what way events would have worked out differently if the context had been cold war instead, and whether these differences would have been to the advantage or disadvantage of the prospects of peace, the prospects of the peoples concerned, and the interests of the West. Tentatively I think it can be established that the maintenance of a detente strategy worked out better than the possible alternative on all three counts, even allowing for the assumed Soviet political benefits in Angola.

In Portugal itself, the sequence of events from the peaceable revolution of April 1974 to the settling into power more than two years later of General Ramalho Eanes as president and Dr Mario Soares as prime minister may be seen as a series of dangers improbably well survived, from the point of view of the Western interest. The interim outcome was so compatible with what Western decision-makers had hoped that it is inevitable one should suspect a degree of backstage management at various points. Ample motive for intervention certainly existed. The strategic situation of Portugal is vital to the control of the Atlantic shipping-lanes. The Lajes air-base in the Azores is also vital to U.S. policy in the Middle East, since it forms part of the military resupply route to Israel, as during the 1973 war. Portugal was also, just after the onset of the revolution, due to become a temporary member of the Nuclear Planning Group of Nato, and thus its decision-makers would have had access to the most important military secrets and contingency planning of the alliance. Further, the sight of so historically significant a member of the Western society of states as Portugal opting voluntarily to instal, as at one time seemed possible, a social and political regime similar to that of an East European or Third World 'people's democracy' would have been a devastating vote of 'no confidence' in the Western system, and would certainly have affected developments in Spain and probably also those in southern Europe as a whole. So the likelihood of intervention was always high, whatever moral qualms such an operation might entail, at least in the West. It is difficult to see how the Powers could have failed to interest themselves in the evolution of Portuguese events. Talleyrand's famous definition of non-intervention as a political and metaphysical term meaning much the same as intervention is almost a statement of plain fact in some cases. The models and potentialities the Powers present, even if their policy-makers do not intentionally manipulate events, are a form of intervention. They can no more opt out completely than a magnet can opt out of creating a field of force. The question, therefore, was not whether they would refrain from competition, but whether the modes of competition would be inhibited by the conventions of detente, and if so which Power would be the more affected. On the evidence as it appeared at the time of writing, one would be inclined to say that such inhibitions affected Soviet policy at least as much as American, possibly more.

What happened in Portugal in April 1974 was the first actual revolution (as against coup d'état) in a Nato country, and on its origins it seemed inherently threatening to the existing interpretation of Western interests. The moving force in the revolution against Caetano's regime was a junior officer corps – mostly captains and majors – radicalized (as it apparently proved, only temporarily) by the experience of fighting long and hopeless colonial wars. The cadre of officers who organized the Armed Forces Movement and its capture of power included several vivid and charismatic personalities who seemed at the time likely to provide effective leadership in a sharp left direction. General Spinola was adopted by them as a suitable figurehead: he did not control them. The one political party that had maintained its organization through the almost fifty years of the dictatorship was the Communist party, and its leader, Dr Alvaro Cunhal, initially looked tougher and more sophisticated than the other party and armed forces leaders on the scene. At the best of times, earlier, the Portuguese economy had remained viable only by a large tourist trade and overseas remittances, both sources very vulnerable to the revolutionary upheaval. The economy was also affected by the general world recession of 1974–5, and burdened by the need to assimilate the 'retornados' from ex-colonies. It did have a cushion to fall on in the very large reserves of gold and foreign currency accumulated in Dr Salazar's time, but possible economic distress and its political consequences were a constant factor in calculations.

During the first year of the revolution, from the overthrow of the old regime to the Constituent Assembly elections of April 1975, the possibility of a Portuguese departure (voluntary or forced) from the Western camp was a constant subject of speculation. The elections themselves, however, showed only seventeen per cent of support for the Communists and their allies, and allowed the Socialists to establish a claim on legitimacy as commanding the largest single segment of the electorate, thirty-eight per cent. The four months from May to September 1975 were the period during which the Portuguese revolution was steered from its initial apparent sharp left course towards its later moderate or even conservative social democracy. The central enigma of the episode as a whole is precisely what confluence of forces secured that turn-about, and (for the purpose of this book) what part the manoeuvrings of the Powers played in it. By the evidence of the later elections, the outcome did indeed seem to be what a majority of Portuguese voters wanted, but their wishes would not necessarily have been conclusive in a situation in which coups of the right or the left were freely forecast, and quite possible.

The decisive 'constituency' – the group that determined the choices of the leaders, and their rise and fall – was the cadre of young officers who had originally organized the revolution. That is, primarily the 240 members of the Armed Forces Movement General Assembly, and 29 members of the Supreme Revolutionary Council. During the summer of 1975 their assumptions or attitudes seemed to change. There was a decline in the prestige and influence of the radical members who had previously been in the ascendant – the Prime Minister, General Vasco Gonçalves, the security chief, Brigadier Otelo Saraiva de Carvalho, and Admiral Rosa Coutinho – and a rise in influence of a more moderate group, whose chief spokesman was Major Ernesto Melo Antunes (a marxist though not a communist). Early in August this group issued a proclamation known as the 'Manifesto of the Nine', which crystallized the change of mood. The President, General Costa Gomes, was enabled to manoeuvre the Prime Minister, Vasco Gonçalves, out of office (reportedly by promising him the post of Commander-in-Chief) and to replace him by a more moderate figure, Admiral de Azevado. The army officers later refused acceptance of Gonçalves as Commander-in-Chief, so that he was left without any power base. In early September a process of reinstituting discipline in the revolutionary army got under way. By mid-September it was said in Lisbon that defeat for the radicals could already be smelt in the air. The attempted left-wing coup of late November, in which Saraiva de Carvalho was implicated, may therefore be seen as a kind of counter-offensive on behalf of what was already becoming a lost cause. It was easily put down, in forty-eight hours, and the then-unknown lieutenant-colonel who suppressed it, Ramalho Eanes, promoted General, was elected

President by a large majority of Portuguese voters about seven months afterwards.

We are left with the problem of what precisely produced the change of mood among the group of young officers who had to make the decisive choices that summer in Lisbon. A study of the rise and fall among them of faith in radical doctrines (communism, Maoism, and the 'revolutionary surrealism' associated with Saraiva de Carvalho) will make an interesting study some day. One might perhaps see a parallel between the (apparently) temporary radicalization of this group by the experience of interminable, unwinnable wars in Africa, and the temporary radicalization of a good deal of the youthful middle class (university students) in America by a similar hopeless war in the Third World, Vietnam. As in the American case, so perhaps in the Portuguese, the political shift leftwards seems to have proved temporary or superficial once its root cause, the hopeless and resented war, was removed. Probably also the young officers, along with the Portuguese electorate as a whole, became disenchanted with the effects of the revolutionary process, after seeing it in operation for a year or so. The personal duel between Dr Cunhal, for the Communists, and Dr Soares, for the Socialists, was fought out in this period by demonstrations and speeches, and (somewhat to the surprise of some Western commentators) victory went to Dr Soares.

Western journalists reporting from Lisbon in the first year of the revolution had made a good deal of the alleged zeal and skill the Soviet Union was devoting to the effort to secure that Dr Cunhal and the Communist party should come to power by the side or on the backs of the radical officer corps. The figure of $4 million a month was freely ascribed to Soviet generosity in support of the party cause.[1] But retrospectively, neither skill nor zeal seems to have been demonstrated, and certainly not any such generosity with funds. Later observers noted that the Communists seemed quite poverty-stricken in contrast to other parties, especially on the far left, which were reported as 'suspiciously rich'. In view of the wrecking role of the far left to the Communist party's chances, through the November coup and in other respects, a subsidy for them would have been a judicious investment of the C.I.A.'s budget for Portugal, though of course the Chinese were also interested in that sector of opinion. The Socialists were well endowed with fraternal funds from social democratic parties in Western Europe, especially West Germany. (Whether these also included 'laundered' C.I.A. funds was a matter of speculation.)

Nor does skill seem more apparent than generosity if Soviet advice is deduced from the actual events. The militancy of the Communists, in their efforts to secure nationalization of resources and the silencing of other sectors of opinion, especially the Socialists, clearly proved to be counterproductive. The crises over the attempted suppression of the Socialist newspaper, *Republica*, and the Catholic Church's broadcasting station *Radio Renascenca* alienated a good deal of opinion. So did the attempted expropriations of land in the basically conservative north. The anti-communist demonstrations there, the burnings of Communist offices and the breakings-up of meetings, provided a sharp warning to the armed forces leadership that civil war or partition were among the possibilities consequent on a forced march leftward under the guidance of radical theory. For a few weeks the memories of Spain in the 1930s hung thick in the air.

One must not, of course, attribute the errors of Communist strategy and tactics in Portugal necessarily to Soviet guidance, even though Dr Cunhal was strongly Moscow-oriented. Very probably he was left to make his own mistakes: it was said in Lisbon at the time that he had been too long in Russia or in jail to understand the situation in Portugal. Some very small scraps of evidence seem to indicate that the Russians advised caution and were disregarded. So on the whole, considering the outcome, one might say there was as little evidence of Soviet zeal for the Portuguese revolution, or strategic skill in forwarding the interests of the Communist party, as of the lavish budget at one stage attributed to them. The West, by contrast, apparently served its friends a good deal better and more generously. The sequence of events in Portugal may in fact be interpreted (though the evidence is not yet available to prove the case) as quite a skilful exercise in joint crisis-management, with most of the initiative coming from Washington, but a conscious division of labour between the Americans and the West Europeans, and some measure of acquiescence (diplomatically induced) on the part of the Russians.

That was not the way it was interpreted at the time. Dr Kissinger's policies incurred a good deal of criticism,[2] especially in the first phase of these events, from American and European liberal and left opinion on the ground of his alleged undue pessimism or alarmism, and from the American right for his failing to denounce and resist the assumed Soviet plots for a take-over of Portugal. But though he frequently talked as if Portugal might be a lost cause, this seems to have been an element in a discreet but assiduous effort towards preventing it actually being one. The very well-publicized stories of his viewing the situation with alarm and despondency, which 'leaked' every week from the Department of State and hinted that he was contemplating everything from the detachment of the Azores to full-scale destabilization, were possibly part of his highly characteristic crisis-signalling technique.

When the revolution occurred, the American ambassador in Lisbon was an elderly political appointee, Mr Stuart Scott, a sixty-nine-year-old lawyer who had been added to the Department in Mr Rogers' time, and sent to Lisbon when it was one of the quieter and less demanding posts in the president's gift. After the fall of President Spinola, Dr Kissinger retired Mr Scott somewhat abruptly from his post (incurring pointed press comment and Departmental murmuring) and replaced him by a much younger former State Department 'trouble shooter', Mr Frank Carlucci, a career man who had been in the Congo, spoke Portuguese and had a reputation for toughness and vigour. Of course it is very possible that Mr Scott would have proved an effective ambassador, even in the circumstances of Lisbon in 1975–6, but it is certain that Mr Carlucci was one. Brigadier Saraiva de Carvalho in fact is said to have regarded him as so powerful an influence that he wanted him thrown out in March 1975, but the ambassador had made enough friends within the junta to avoid that fate.

The Portuguese revolutionary leadership (including Costa Gomes and Soares) were invited to Washington for what seems to have been an undiplomatically candid but effective set of discussions in October 1974. (Kissinger to Soares: 'You may be the Kerensky of the Portuguese revolution.' Soares: 'I don't want to be a Kerensky.' Kissinger: 'Neither did Kerensky.') In general one can say that the small political elite in Lisbon were provided with a steady (and decidedly loud and insistent) stream of signals that communist participation in the Portuguese government was viewed with disfavour in Washington, and that American disfavour carried with it some serious disadvantages. This stream of signals may be judged to have been carefully tuned to the crucial 'target audience', the young officer corps able to make and unmake the leadership. For instance, Portugal was persuaded to opt out of the Nuclear Planning Group of Nato, of which it would normally at this time have been a temporary member, a device that reduced prospective dangers and frictions in that very sensitive area and also offered a rather pointed hint of the possibility of larger exclusions. (It was restored to the Nuclear Planning Group after the political change of direction, in early 1976.) Discussions had been begun before the revolution about the American bases in Portugal: they also were quietly shelved during the sharp left phase, to be resumed later. President Ford was prompted to say, apparently rather gratuitously, in May, that the time was coming when Nato might have to decide whether Portugal was still acceptable as a member: again a pointed hint, of particular interest to a young officer corps not unconscious of the advantages of Nato membership from the point of view of the supply of weaponry and their own professional futures. One may regard this as a system of long-distance persuasion, and though it was frequently denounced by critics in America as likely to prove counterproductive, on the evidence of the outcome this can hardly have been the case. Only a very secure and self-confident political elite, in a prosperous economy (like the

Portugal and Southern Africa: Setback and Rebound 165

French) are readily able to shrug off the consequences of loss of American cordiality. For countries in economic trouble (like Italy or Portugal) it is an unattractive option, even for the left.

In a curious way, the myth of the infinite capacity of the C.I.A. for mischief, a subject much debated during the period, might also have conceivably been an asset to American policy-making in such circumstances. The agency was keeping a low profile from early 1975, being much harassed by congressmen, and there have been as yet no disclosures of its role. General Vernon Walters, its Deputy Director, paid a quiet visit to Lisbon in August 1974, and was said to be pessimistic. The 'Forty Committee', which among other things authorizes covert operations, met several times during the period of these events. One would assume there was scope for C.I.A. funds to help along tactically useful factors like the anti-communist demonstrations in the north (there was speculation that this might be done via Church connections) and by subsidizing the activities of far left groups, which were the Communists' most effective competitors for a segment of the vote, as was shown in the presidential elections of 1976. The left's own assumptions as to what was feasible to American policy-makers – denial of economic aid, exclusion from Nato, the detachment of the Azores (where separatist feeling was real enough among a predominantly right-wing electorate, and there was strong pro-American feeling because of the large Azorean emigrant population that sends home remittances from the U.S.A.), even 'destabilization' in the Chilean manner – made actual explicit threat unnecessary.

At the level of summit diplomacy, there seem to have been some behind-the-scenes 'warning-off' efforts. Direct discussions between American and Russian policy-makers took place at Vladivostok in November 1974 during the first Ford–Brezhnev meeting, and though these were mostly devoted to the SALT negotiations, the Americans were reported as making strongly the point that they regarded Portugal as an essential area of Western interest. During the months between then and the Helsinki meeting in July 1975, which happened to include the decisive period for the turn-around in Portugal, the Russians were according high priority to avoidance of anything that might damage detente in advance of the conference, so they had good reasons for restraint in help or advice to the Portuguese party. At Helsinki itself, and in its immediate aftermath, there seemed to develop a concerted 'midwifery' operation for the social democratic embryo government by then emerging in Portugal, with a conscious division of functions between Dr Kissinger on the one hand and the West Europeans, especially Mr Callaghan and Chancellor Schmidt, on the other. The European social democratic governments and parties appeared in general agreement on support of Dr Soares in his combat with the communists, and his determination to exclude them from the Portuguese government. These fellow-Europeans clearly had a better moral claim and more diplomatic leverage on this point than Washington, in that they were able to define the permissible limits of eligibility for membership of the European Community, which Portugal wished to join. In effect the Community posted a sign over the door, 'pluralist democracies only'. Conceivably a communist party may take part on some occasions in the government of a pluralist democracy, but in 1975–6 the American assumption (for both Portugal and Italy) was that such participation must for the moment be discouraged. In Spain, which also had aspirations towards the E.E.C., the bar to eligibility for membership was by contrast at this point that the regime was still too much of a right-wing dictatorship. Those who control the entrance to an advantageous and sought-after economic club clearly have a powerful instrument of diplomatic and political influence in their hands.

So have those who can facilitate access to aid funds. Dr Kissinger promised a small sum in aid ($20 million) quite early in the revolutionary period, in December 1974, but it became clear by summer 1975 that Portugal would need a great deal more economic help in the aftermath of revolution to reconstruct the shattered economy or entirely remake it in a post-colonial form. A larger amount of aid was offered by the U.S.A., and further sums by the Community after the decisive political turn of late 1975, but the actual provision of these funds seems to have been delayed until the new government was securely in office. In the last few weeks of the Ford administration a loan of $300 million was approved, and the possibility forecast of U.S. participation in a consortium that would provide Portugal with $1,500 million for economic reconstruction.[3]

Though many American voices were raised against alleged Soviet machinations in Portugal, Dr Kissinger's own was initially restrained, even emollient, until August 1975. In July for instance, at Helsinki, he even put in a kind of exculpatory plea for the Soviet Union: 'We should keep in mind that detente cannot be used as a means of asking the Soviet Union to take care of all our problems ... many problems in Portugal have indigenous roots.' On the other hand, in a speech in Alabama a fortnight later, he issued a sharp warning against Soviet action in Portugal, pointedly invoking European security (the Helsinki conference was just over), and offering aid to Portugal on condition that a pluralistic democracy survived.[4] It was reported that he had been asked to provide a strong signal by President Costa Gomes: this was the delicate period during which Vasco Gonçalves was being edged out of office as Prime Minister and the critical moment of the turn away from the left. An indication of Washington's constant preoccupation with the situation was presumably reassuring or helpful to the pro-Western party in Lisbon. President Ford reiterated the warning to the Russians about a week later, remarking that detente was 'not a licence to fish in troubled water'. The November attempted coup completed the ruin of the left. How far Saraiva de Carvalho was its strategist will presumably become apparent at his trial, but it was clearly an ill-judged and forlorn enterprise, and one would say that the continuance of Portugal in the Western camp had been fairly well determined in August and September.

As the government of General Eanes as President and Dr Soares as Prime Minister settled into office in July 1976, the new Foreign Minister, Jose Medeiros Ferreira emphasized the Portuguese choice of a Western identity:

> The defence of our land borders commences at the frontier of Western Germany, and the Atlantic Pact guarantees our security ... There is an effective link between Nato's containment of Soviet influence and defending the transformation of Western European societies in the direction of democratic socialism ... The theory that Portugal is a country of the Third World isolated from Europe has been a failure ... The government now in office believes it should take the European option...[5]

The phrase about the tentative 'Third World orientation' of Portugal having proved a failure offers a neat illustration of the change in the political climate of Portugal between the summer of 1975 and the summer of 1976. The 'Third World' identity had been particularly associated with Major Melo Antunes, who in the revolutionary Lisbon of mid-1975 seemed a force for moderation or even for the right. In post-revolutionary Portugal, in mid-1976, the moderates of the earlier period found themselves on the far left of the political spectrum. The 'Nine' who had played the leading role in the edging of Vasco Gonçalves out of power, were in their turn being edged out, though Major Antunes himself retained an office of some significance.

The social democratic government that had settled into power by late 1976 in Portugal (with Spinola permitted to return) faced formidable economic and social problems, needing to make a new economy from such remaining assets as tourism and agriculture. Nor could it be regarded as safe from coups of either the right or left. Nevertheless, the dangers avoided looked greater than those remaining. There was no civil war between north and south, no partition, no loss of the Azores, no general drift downward into economic decline and political anarchy, no dictatorship of either left or right, no Red Terror or White Terror (not a great deal of bloodshed at all, in fact), no serious harm to the strategic interests of the Nato powers, at least in the European and North Atlantic theatres of operations, no disruption of the political evolution next door in Spain, not much rise in tension in the central balance. Considering the episode as a revolutionary transition from long-established authoritarian rule to social democracy, in a country of major strategic importance to the central balance, one might reasonably say it was accomplished at relatively low damage and risk, and may be judged a success story. How much this success owed to behind-the-scenes management on the part of the Western alliance, and how far it was the product of purely indigenous forces in Portugal, is difficult as yet to be certain. Dr Kissinger has been cryptic about it:

> My position has been that without a systematic effort to encourage the pluralistic forces in Portugal, they would be defeated. For a while there was a disagreement between us and the West Europeans who thought that the forces of the government that was in office earlier this year [1975] would over a period of time produce pluralism. I was skeptical about this. During the summer the West Europeans came to the same conclusion we had earlier reached; namely that pluralism had to be actively encouraged. And that has always been my position ... Recent trends are more encouraging.[6]

Whatever 'active encouragement' to pluralist forces was undertaken by the Americans or the West Europeans may have been unnecessary, but can hardly be said to have been counter-productive, though that *was* in fact said by a good many commentators at the time.[7] If the overall diplomatic context had been cold war rather than detente – if, for instance, the revolution had happened in 1964 instead of 1974 – it would, one may argue, have been vastly more dangerous to the society of states as a whole, threatening even general war, as well as full of dangers to Portugal itself. There is certainly no plausible case, on the outcome, for any supposition that detente inhibited Western diplomatic manoeuvre or operated to the disadvantage of Western power.

It might, however, be argued that success for the preservation of the Western power sphere as regards Portugal itself was bought at the cost of Soviet advantage in the ex-Portuguese colonies. (There have been occasional hints that this was the Soviet interpretation of a reasonable bargain.) The revolution has already proved to have larger and longer-lasting effects in the spheres of the 'overseas provinces' than in Europe itself. In early 1974 Portugal still held sovereignty in Angola, Mozambique, Guinea-Bissau, the Cape Verde Islands, Sao Tome and Principe, East Timor and Maçao. Ironically, only the last and most vulnerable of all these, Maçao, the tiny fragment of titular Portugal on the coast of China, remained unchanged in formal status. Portuguese Timor became the twenty-seventh province of Indonesia, at the cost of considerable fighting in the area itself and some diplomatic friction with Australia. The rest graduated suddenly towards independence, most of them without any serious tension between the Powers. Mozambique and Guinea-Bissau had already so far crystallized into their present political identities that the situation was one of no real contest. But Angola was still in 1974 debatable ground, and so the establishment of the new regime there became the occasion of a major crisis of the detente. One other point on which it differed from the rest of the Portuguese territories, it may not be unduly cynical to note, was in being a potentially rich country, an exporter of oil, diamonds, iron and coffee, and geographically important to the control of strategic shipping routes in the South Atlantic.

The struggle between the Powers in Africa had been of relatively low visibility, especially as far as the United States was concerned, for the ten years from the fading away of the Congo crisis in the middle 1960s until the Angola crisis in the middle 1970s. When the Nixon administration arrived in power in 1969, African policy was reviewed in a National Security Council memorandum,[8] and a decision was taken for an option based on the premise that the white regimes in southern Africa would persist for the foreseeable future, and that any constructive change was more likely to come about through change in their domestic policies (as conceivably in the South African case) or in their colonial policies (as at that time in the Portuguese case), rather than through guerrilla action by black nationalists or through military initiatives by African governments. Policy should therefore be directed towards persuading the white regimes towards concessions and moderate black governments that they could look to some advantage from dealings even with white-dominance political elites like that of South Africa. The choice of this option was sharply contested by some radical opinion among the 'Africa desk' at the State

Department, on the grounds that it constituted an undue tilt towards the white regimes.

The South African government's own policy of detente with black African states, however, allowed scope at least for temporary and tactical accommodation in the early seventies. The general definition of detente suggested earlier, that it should be regarded as a mode of management of adversary power, fits the South African case as well as that of other powers, though South Africa is of course concerned primarily with the local rather than the central balance and Mr Vorster, the Prime Minister who sponsored the policy, would probably not have adopted that phrase for his hopes or intentions. But clearly, in the prospective balance of power in Africa he was faced with an increase in strength of adversaries or potential adversaries in much the same way as (on a far larger scale) American policy-makers were with regard to the central balance of power. And, again as in the central balance, those adversaries might in some cases have strategic or tactical reasons of their own for finding detente useful as a *modus vivendi* for the time being. In the South African case, only a few members of the O.A.U. could be induced to shrug off even for temporary and tactical reasons the offence to racial feeling inherent in South Africa's domestic politics: Malawi, Liberia and the Ivory Coast, for instance. On the other hand, even a radical African regime like Samora Machel's government in Mozambique could be impelled into an operational (though not declaratory) policy of some cooperation with South Africa by the hard facts of economic dependence. The sale of electric power from the vast dam at Cabora Bassa had to be to South Africa; the remittances home of the Mozambican migrant workers in South African mines continued to be necessary, and also the port revenues from South African exports through Maputo (formerly Lorenço Marques). So perforce, the level of tolerance by black African governments, especially neighbouring ones, of dealings with the government of South Africa was considerably greater in practice than in theory. One might make a parallel between the ideological repudiation by African nationalists of detente dealings with South Africa, as a government whose domestic politics put it outside the moral pale, and the similar repudiation by right-wing Americans of detente dealings with the Soviet Union, as a government whose domestic practices put it outside the moral pale. In both cases, moral qualms could sometimes be overborne by economic necessity or advantage.

The American policy option defined in the 1969 N.S.C. study and adopted in early 1970 was undoubtedly overdue for revision by mid-1974, but the summer of that year was a bad time in Washington for detached consideration of policy options in less than immediate crises. Watergate, Cyprus, and Portugal itself rather pre-empted the agenda. The Russians were less pre-occupied, and had in fact been engaged in something of a drive for enhanced influence in Africa since about 1972-3. There had been some successes, for instance in Somalia, permitting the Berbera base to be constructed, in Uganda, where they had supplied arms, including Mig aircraft to President Amin, and in Congo-Brazzaville, which was to serve as an arms supply route for Angola.

These Russian efforts may possibly have been inspired almost as much by the need to compete with the growth of Chinese influence in Africa as by the wish to out-do the Western powers.[9] China had been engaged with African developments since the early 1960s, and by the early 1970s the most notable of its aid projects, the Tanzam railway (formally handed over in 1976), was approaching completion and generating a good deal of prestige. China had thus attained considerable influence temporarily at least in East Africa, particularly Tanzania, Zambia and Mozambique, and was also providing training and arms to guerrillas in Angola and elsewhere. Comparing the operations of the three Powers in Africa, and their respective diplomatic assets in political manoeuvring there, one might say the Chinese had proved best adapted, in their modes of living and their labour-intensive technology, to fitting into the human and economic landscape without frictions. The Americans were most able to supply funds and high-technology goods. But the Russians had very large built-in advantages: no ties to existing white regimes, no problem over the possible sacrifice of investments, no scruples about arming regimes like that of President Amin, no shortage of the sort of weapons, like the rockets used in Angola, that were becoming obsolescent in the Soviet forces themselves but were still very effective on an African battlefield, and, as it proved, the ability to supply a considerable number of well-trained proxy troops at a crucial stage of the battle.

In Angola, three factions, divided by leadership and tribal affiliations rather than by really decisive differences in political complexions, were in contention for power during the final stage of colonial abdication by Portugal. The FNLA (National Front for the Liberation of Angola) was based on the Bakongo tribe who extend across the border into Zaire (their leader, Holden Roberto, was the brother-in-law of the President of Zaire). They were also supported by northern Protestants and black and white coffee farmers. The MPLA (Popular Front for the Liberation of Angola) was based on the Mbundu tribe, but was less tribally oriented than the others: it was led by marxist and Catholic left intellectuals, including many of mixed race, and supported by trade unionists in the towns and cotton farmers in the central regions of the country. The third group, UNITA (National Union for the Total Independence of Angola), was based on the Ovimbundu tribe, strong in the south and east of the country, and was led by southern Protestants. The remaining white settlers (most had fled before Independence Day) tended towards FNLA or UNITA rather than the MPLA, though all three were radical–nationalist in outlook.

The American choice of the FNLA as the faction with most prospect of proving compatible with Western purposes seems to have been motivated largely by the connection with Zaire, where the U.S.A. had had close and equable relations ever since President Mobutu established his authority in the days of the Congo crisis in the middle 1960s. (The country was formerly known as the Belgian Congo.) A very small C.I.A. operation to channel funds (about $300,000) to the FNLA via Zaire seems to have got under way about the beginning of 1975, at which point Soviet aid to the MPLA was already of long standing. In

April 1975, however, much heavier deliveries of arms from Russian and East European sources (often carried in Yugoslav ships) began to arrive in Angola for the MPLA (which held the port of Luanda), and the military tide rapidly turned in their favour. The Portuguese, organizing the relinquishment of sovereignty, had arranged that it should be transferred early in November to a transitional government representing all three factions. The O.A.U. at the time also favoured that arrangement, but it became clear by mid-year that the verdict of the battlefield was likely to pre-empt the envisaged coalition. American arms and funds were hastily increased to the FNLA and UNITA to sustain their resistance in the hope of military stalemate and political compromise. For a time, between August and October, the military tide was reversed, but from August Cuban technicians began to appear among the MPLA, and from October Cuban troops (at their peak reported to be about 15,000) were deployed on the battlefield to stiffen MPLA forces. They proved rapidly decisive against the ill-trained levies of the other two factions, which were reduced to guerrilla warfare in about three months. The MPLA was therefore able to secure recognition for itself as the government of Angola (though its writ did not yet run in the whole country) early in 1976. A South African expeditionary column had also entered the south of the country in October, at the behest of UNITA, but it withdrew when the ascendancy of the MPLA became clear.[10]

This interim outcome in Angola may be interpreted as having been determined almost as much by the political infighting in Washington as by the operations on the Angolan battlefields. Congress was by late 1975 sharply at odds with the administration over the operations of the C.I.A. The memory of the final debacle in Vietnam was also still vivid. Moreover, the Democratic majority in Congress was already warming up for the presidential fight with the Republicans in 1976. In the circumstances, the request for approval of a C.I.A. operation (however limited) in support of one faction in a civil war was bound to evoke parallels (sufficiently plausible to be politically effective) with Vietnam. Congress therefore, despite intensive efforts at

Portugal and Southern Africa: Setback and Rebound 175

persuasion by the administration, insisted at the end of the year on a ban on any further funds for Angola, the Senate voting 54–22 against in December and the House of Representatives 323–99 against in January 1976. Dr Kissinger, in a speech in San Francisco early in February, implied that the congressional refusal of aid for Angola provided a green light or 'all-clear' signal to the Russians, whereas previously they had been made at least to hesitate:

> At first it was feared that the Soviet-backed faction, because of massive Soviet aid and Cuban mercenaries, would totally dominate by Independence Day, November 11. Our assistance prevented that ... On December 9 the President warned Moscow of the consequence of continued meddling and offered to co-operate in encouraging a peaceful outcome that removed foreign influence.
>
> The Soviet Union appeared to have second thoughts. It halted its airlift from December 9 to December 24. At that point, the impact of our domestic debate overwhelmed the possibilities of diplomacy. Our effort was cut off.[11]

After the vote Cuba more than doubled its forces to reach the peak of 15,000 by about April and the Soviet arms supply was resumed on a heavy scale.

It was inevitable that the prospective or apparent Soviet gains in diplomatic influence in Africa through this particular episode should be cited by those distrustful of detente as proving that it worked solely to Russian advantage. Certainly, of all the diplomatic crises of the detente period, it was the one that provided most ammunition against the concept in the routine 1976 battles of electoral politics for the Senate and the House of Representatives, as well as in the pursuit of the presidential nominations, though not to any great degree in the final Ford–Carter campaign itself. However, what happened in Angola was not that detente *itself* created the opportunity for Soviet advantage, but that the particular conditions of the time in Washington (Vietnam trauma, the C.I.A. revelations, and the beginnings of the presidential battle) created a situation in which the normal capacity of America to play an effective hand in the competitive diplomacy of detente was temporarily suspended, and so the Russians got a victory by default.

Dr Kissinger's primary preoccupation was not with which faction inherited power in Angola – he said at one point that he had no objection to the MPLA, or a marxist government there – but with the conventions of detente diplomacy, and still more the signals as to the state of American will and purpose that would inevitably be read into the outcome of the election year foreign-policy debate in Washington, and that are the subject of a permanent running 'trial balance', kept most importantly in Moscow and Peking though also of course in other capitals. It might be argued that since he was likely to lose the policy contest at home (which was in fact fairly clear, given the known state of congressional opinion almost from the beginning of the episode) it would have been better to avoid it altogether: never to have put the arms request to Congress. On the other hand, one may also argue that it was preferable that the signals coming from Washington over Angola should convey temporary paralysis of will (because of division between Congress and administration during the election run-up) than that they should convey indifference to or acquiescence in an extension of the Soviet sphere of influence in southern Africa. The foreign offices of even the remotest Third World capitals are well-endowed with young diplomatists who did their graduate work in American universities and are acquainted with the U.S. electoral process and with the likelihood that such arguments between president and Congress would be resolved in a few months by a new president with a new mandate and a Congress of his own party. There was therefore some advantage, even if the day was likely to be lost, in making clear the reasons why, and dramatizing them a little.

A kind of diplomatic fringe-benefit may be derived from such a defeat. Reactions to it may be used as a mode of signalling to the adversary that the limits of domestic tolerance are being approached: in effect, using the arguments to convey to the Russians that a few more such victories for them would damage the detente beyond repair. In such signalling Mr Reagan, Senator Jackson and Admiral Zumwalt might be regarded as among Dr Kissinger's chief aides at the time.

The third phase in this complex diplomatic evolution was still under way at the end of 1976: it was the process of retrieval of American influence and diplomatic initiative in Africa after the setback that Angola must be held to represent, along with a sort of 'damage-limiting operation' directed at Cuba and the Soviet Union. This second operation was concerned primarily with preventing the extension or transfer of the Cuban troops from Angola to Rhodesia or Namibia, both of which had in being guerrilla forces and embryo governments that might plausibly be applicants for Cuban military benefits. Beyond that, the American objective was to see the Cuban forces sent home as soon as possible. And in general it was desired to demonstrate to African governments that the securing of reasonable political objectives, like majority rule in Namibia and Rhodesia, was possible without reliance on Soviet or Cuban help, and might in fact be more rapidly advanced through American diplomatic and economic leverage. Since the only way the situations in Rhodesia and Namibia could be changed in relatively short order was by securing the acquiescence of South Africa to large political transformations in both those territories, this meant that South Africa must be persuaded that its own long-term interests continued to lie in restored detente with the black nationalists who were bound to inherit power, even though the immediate sympathies of the South African electorate were with the white settler community in Rhodesia who were at the time still determined on a strong military defence of their privileged lives.

American efforts towards these ends dominated events after Angola. They were aided by the fact that Mr Vorster, the South African Prime Minister, appears to have been alerted by the crumbling of the Portuguese position in Africa to the necessity of a new effort at detente with his black African neighbours, and the possibility that that would entail drawing in his defensive lines, giving up the idea of sustaining a white minority regime in Namibia, and reassessing the usefulness of Mr Smith's regime in Rhodesia or its viability in the new circumstances. That regime had itself begun to show some increased consciousness of vulnerability by mid-1976, with higher levels of emigration by white families and an acknowledgment of the necessity of forbidding its young men to go abroad until they had completed their military service. The pressures to which it had been subject for more than ten years, including U.N. sanctions, general international disapproval, and more recently the beginnings of a successful guerrilla campaign from forces based in Mozambique and Zambia, might nevertheless have been sustained by the Rhodesian political elite for a further five or ten years but for the vulnerability built into the Rhodesian situation by total dependence on South African support for its economic and military survival.

Dr Kissinger's essential role in the diplomatic process that secured the capitulation (at least temporary or ostensible) of the Rhodesian leadership was in effect to convince them that the game was lost as far as the maintenance of white ascendancy was concerned, and that they might as well settle for what they could get in the way of a 'safety net' against loss of the value of their farms and businesses, if they could not adjust to the expectation or the arrival of a black government and had in the event to restart their lives elsewhere. His African 'shuttle' diplomacy of September 1976 was directed to that end, and his characteristic technique of arranging the 'orchestration' of signals has seldom seemed to produce more dramatic effects. The decisive moment however, one would say, was during the conversations with Mr Vorster in Bavaria and Zurich, and until someone leaks a transcript of those meetings it will not be possible to say precisely how the arguments went, or how Mr Vorster's co-operation was secured. Not, it would seem, by an assurance that South African society could itself be protected from social and economic change. On the contrary, Dr Kissinger said publicly and candidly at the time that the South African political system, apartheid, was in his view incompatible with human dignity. One should not assume, of course, that intellectual arguments were the only signals of which Mr Vorster had to take note. Dr Kissinger himself called this diplomatic venture an exercise in the politics of power, and that may well have been as true of his pressure on Mr Vorster as of their joint pressures on Mr Smith. There were several possible levers accessible to American hands: the price of gold, for instance, already forced down by the I.M.F. auctions, the prospects that South Africa would shortly need American help to avert U.N. sanctions over Namibia, even perhaps the hint that the Shah of Iran might be prompted in some circumstances to join an oil blockade against South Africa. The coincident rioting in the black South African townships like Soweto may have been organized by far left forces opposed to the Kissinger mission: certainly some of the demonstrators carried banners proclaiming that stance. But whether accidentally or not, the demonstrations would also tend to remind Mr Vorster that the day appeared to be arriving quite rapidly when the South African government might need its resources at home to defend its own interests, and might further need Western friends, if only to secure time to put its own house in order. The black African presidents and nationalist leaders in the surrounding 'confrontation' states (Tanzania, Zambia, Botswana and Mozambique) may be regarded not only as recipients of U.S. signals of their own, but as elements used in the pattern of signalling to the white regimes. And, as in the Middle East case, the process of involvement in Dr Kissinger's diplomacy had its impact on individual attitudes, as noticeably Dr Kaunda's. After the first Kissinger–Vorster meetings, the South Africans themselves seem to have provided strong hints to the Rhodesian political leadership of a change in attitude through, for instance, the withdrawal of helicopter crews, which had been helping the anti-guerrilla operations, and the permitting of 'congestion' on the South Africa railways to delay Rhodesian cargoes. Thus, by the time the Kissinger–Vorster meeting with the Rhodesian leaders took place in Pretoria, the latter had already had time to prepare themselves and their party supporters for apparent capitulation to diplomatic *force majeure*.

The long-term American objective, of seeing that power in southern Africa passed to moderate black governments by a rapid political evolution, rather than to radical black governments after long and atrocity-ridden racial wars was still a relatively distant prospect at the time of writing.[12] A more short-term American objective was to limit the operations and influence of the Cuban troops in Angola, and if possible persuade the Russian and Cuban governments that they ought to be taken home as soon as possible. A brisk campaign to this end began in March with a speech by Dr Kissinger in Dallas:

> The United States will not accept further Cuban military interventions abroad. We are not the world's policeman, but we cannot permit the Soviet Union or its surrogates to become the world's policeman either, if we care anything about our security and the fate and freedom of the world.[13]

This blunt message was backed up by intensive signalling of possible penalties that might be applied either against Cuba or against the Soviet Union. There was a spate of 'unattributable' stories out of Washington, leaking details of alleged contingency planning for operations against Cuba. One of the Democratic presidential candidates, Mr Fred Harris, provided colour, consciously or unconsciously, for an otherwise rather implausible story by charging the Ford administration with 'planning an act of war against Cuba' and by writing to the Senate Foreign Relations Committee to demand hearings on this supposed project. The chairman of the Senate Africa Subcommittee was invited to a briefing and was quoted as declaring his conviction that the Secretary was not bluffing. Among the options mentioned by well-informed journalists as being under consideration were a new blockade against Cuba, on the model of 1962, or a reinforcing of the Guantanamo base with troops that could be used to push out its perimeter, or even an invasion or airstrike at Cuba itself. These heavy hints may have seemed rather unconvincing in the context of American politics in mid-1976, but they would not necessarily seem so as a possibility for 1977, even or especially assuming a change of administration. Dr Castro had good reason to remember what happened a few months after the last time a Democratic president, inexperienced in foreign affairs, succeeded a Republican, in 1961. Even well short of invasion, a new president, with a strong mandate, might not have had much trouble arranging reasons for Cuba to need its forces close to home. At the time of writing, however, the Carter administration appeared hopeful of securing the removal of the Cuban troops by way of renewal of the earlier movement towards detente with Dr Castro's government.

The American signals to the Soviet Union were relatively restrained, but clear enough. A long-projected ceremony involving Mr Ford and Mr Brezhnev in the signature of a new agreement on the inspection of peaceful nuclear explosions was postponed, and so were meetings at the official level on energy, economic relations and housing. A good deal of American press comment on Angola demanded much stronger action: the refusal of supply of grain, for instance, or even the repudiation of the SALT agreements. But one might argue that weakening such central components of the detente because of so marginal an area of Western strategic interest as Angola would be in the class of using the roof-beams of the house to mend a rather obscure corner of the back fence. At any rate, Dr Kissinger showed no inclination towards it, and by April or May there were indications that Soviet and Cuban policies were beginning to respond to the milder existing signals. Assurances were apparently received quite early (possibly when Dr Kissinger was in Moscow in January) that no extension of Cuban activities to Mozambique or Rhodesia or Namibia was contemplated. And in May, the Swedish Prime Minister, Olof Palme, received a letter from Castro with a message for Dr Kissinger (who was visiting Sweden at the time) that Cuban troops would be withdrawn from Angola at the rate of 200 a month. By late 1976 the numbers were said to be down to about 10,000.[14]

Looking back over this very complex confluence of events and forces, it is striking how large a transformation in the world seemed (perhaps deceptively) to arise from trivial beginnings. The temporary radicalization of the Portuguese junior officer corps (partly, it was said, by conscripts from the universities being mixed with professionals from the army training schools) produced the revolution. That produced the precipitate decolonization of the former Portuguese territories in Africa. That in turn produced the strategic transformation in the situations of Rhodesia and Namibia, and in the South African assessment of how its own interests were affected. It likewise produced, over Angola, a temporary shock to the central detente relationship, affecting the United States, the Soviet Union, Cuba and even China. But far more importantly, it transformed American policy in Africa, changing a role that had been rather passive for ten years to one of vigorous competitiveness with the other powers. That transformation might conceivably result in due course in America becoming the decisive extra-continental power in Africa, as had happened a little earlier in the Middle East, even though the African powers were acutely sensitive to any hint of encroachment on their independence.

It is ironic that this congeries of events stemming from the revolution in Portugal did more damage (even outside America) to the detente than any other crisis-sequence. (It was, for instance, cited as the chief evidence of Soviet bad faith and imperialist intentions in the speech made by the British leader of the Opposition, Margaret Thatcher, on the first anniversary of Helsinki.)[15] In reality the case against detente deducible from these developments was very thin or non-existent. It is difficult to see how the Western powers, or anyone else, would have been advantaged if the context had instead been cold war. The first round of competitive detente diplomacy, over Portugal itself, very clearly went to the Western powers. The second round, over Angola, did go to the Russians, admittedly, but that was less because of detente itself than because of the temporarily intense level of rivalry and distrust between Republican administration and Democratic Congress at the opening of the 1976 electoral battle. The third round, the general competition for influence in southern Africa, was still undetermined at the time of writing. The catalyst injected into the politics of that area by Dr Kissinger's diplomatic initiative continued to work, but its outcome remained uncertain, as did the influence of the change in the American administration, and the more radical views of President Carter's apparent chief aide in this field, Mr

Portugal and Southern Africa: Setback and Rebound 183

Andrew Young.[16] The phenomenon of 'Afrocommunism' had just begun to define itself, with the claim of Samora Machel's government in Mozambique to be following the marxist-leninist path after the model of East Germany. Obviously the Soviet Union had considerable advantages in the sharpening diplomatic competition in the area, but after the initial setback the American rebound seemed determined and resourceful. Even the outcome in Angola was not necessarily as ill-boding for the West as it was represented: it had a certain convenience to it, though not of the sort that could be officially proclaimed. The presence of the Cubans supplied a form of pressure on the governments in Rhodesia and South Africa that America and Britain had no other means of effecting, and that seemed already (in Rhodesia at least) to be helping induce change of the sort the Western powers had been urging to meet the racial and strategic realities of the late twentieth century.

Still more important as a bonus from the detente was the fact that these diplomatic manoeuvres, affecting the future of an entire subcontinent as well as the whole Iberian peninsula in Europe, involved far less chance of hostilities between the Powers than would have been the case if the general context had been cold war. Portugal and southern Africa may thus in due course be classed as among the major evidences of benefit of the diplomacy of detente. Certainly if one compared the great-power rivalry over southern Africa in the mid-1970s, in the context of detente, with the great-power rivalry in South East Asia in the mid-1960s, in the context of the Cold War, there seemed little doubt as to which sequence of events was the less dangerous and damaging to human happiness, both for the people in the areas concerned, and for the citizens of the Powers and other countries affected.

CHAPTER 10

Australia: The Range of Middle-Power Manoeuvre

As a case study in a middle power's adaption to change in great-power relationships, Australian policy in the years under consideration illustrates how the international context may help magnify and dramatize domestic political argument, in this instance rather with the effect of a fire-cracker happening to be set off inside an empty barrel. Initially and essentially it was the American detente with China that had the most real significance for the world within which Australia can act effectively, but the detente with the Soviet Union was preoccupying the Australian Prime Minister a good deal by the end of the period, and even being used in his relationship with China. To put it in the most general terms, one might say that Australian policy choices in the period of the full Cold War in Asia, 1949–69, were dominated by a sense of threat (mostly from China) and a sense of the necessities of alliance. In the period of Mr Whitlam's government, from late 1972 to late 1975, they were notable for a kind of detente euphoria. After his fall, the successor government reverted to more dour and traditional policies, but with threat assumed to stem from the Soviet Union rather than China. Looking back over the episode as a whole, one might say that detente originally helped make acceptable changes seen at the time as rather radical, though in fact marginal and overdue, but that later it was seen as multiplying a number of ambiguities, in a way that threatened to impose future discomforts.

Let us look first at the sense of threat that, as I said, was the dominant factor in Australian policy in the 1949–69 period. This sense of threat generated a strategy to meet it, and that strategy was essentially to rely on the protection of what Sir Robert Menzies, the Prime Minister for most of the period, used to call 'our great and powerful friends' (meaning America and Britain). A prompt and cheerful performance of the duties of alliance was the obvious way of, as it were, keeping up payment of the premiums on the insurance policies that these alliances were assumed to represent. It would, however, be quite misleading to imply that the Cold War in Asia suddenly in 1949 imposed this concept on Australian foreign policy. It simply led to an existing tradition being adapted to contemporary circumstances. Australians as a political community had a long and well-protected national adolescence in the tolerant nursery of the British Raj, throughout the nineteenth century, and the sense that imperial protection ought to be requited by participation in the protector's wars was perfectly visible even then, in for instance Australia's insistence on sending contingents to fight in the Sudan campaign and the Boer War. These expeditionary forces were not conscripts whose services were exacted by British pressure: they were volunteers originating a rather exuberant Australian military tradition in a world and time that did not suffer much doubt or misgiving about the benefit of white imperial presences in the non-European world.

But though the Cold War was not the first origin of the sense of threat in Australian policy (it was quite audible through most of the nineteenth century, and all of the twentieth), it did focus it on one particular power, China. Or perhaps one should rather say *re*-focus it on China, for that country had certainly been a centre of Australian defensive preoccupations of a sort in a much earlier incarnation, long before the communist consolidation of power. Australians have always been essentially rather open-minded in casting the role of chief menace in the national future: the French in the Napoleonic war period, the Russians (improbable though it seemed, then as now) in the late nineteenth century, the Japanese from the beginning of the twentieth century, the Indonesians for a while in the 1960s. But though the Chinese never remotely looked militarily formidable until after the communist victory, they had looked sociologically and economically like a threat to a good many Australians as early as the 1850s. The gold-rushes then had brought many Chinese to the 'diggings': their presence generated prejudice and even riots, and the feelings so aroused found legislative form in Chinese exclusion acts that in time were extrapolated into the White Australia policy. The consciousness of Australian identity, as it crystallized in the nineteenth century, incorporated a sharp sense of difference from Asia, and among the Asian peoples it was the Chinese who, despite their governments, formed the most visible Asian communities overseas. So that long before 1949 one can see a sense of the potential Chinese future as a faintly threatening though remote question-mark over Australia's destiny in a good deal of the Australian popular nationalist journalism that defined the new country's image of itself.

But for the half-century up to 1951, these feelings were in general overlaid by apprehensions concerning Japan's much more immediate military and naval strength. The fact that Japan was Britain's ally from 1902 till the 1920s did not do much to relieve this feeling: in some ways it exacerbated it, with fears that Australian interests might be sacrificed to the necessities of the alliance with Japan. And since American policy before and after the First World War was also suspicious of the growth of Japanese military power, one can date from this time the sense (which was much stronger after 1941) that America rather than Britain was the most useful and natural strategic fellow-traveller for Australia in the Pacific.

Thus there was a phase of sharp tension in Australian policy between 1949 and 1951, as the strategic landscape of the Pacific was redefined in the early Cold War period. On the one hand, Australian fears and resentments were still directed primarily against Japan, as was inevitable only four years after a war in which many Australians had suffered acutely at Japanese hands, and during which a Japanese invasion fleet had been widely believed to be prepared for Australian shores. Moreover, there was a Labor government in power in Australia (as in Britain) at the time the question of recognition of the new communist government in Peking came up, in October 1949. And that government was intellectually dominated by a relatively radical figure, the then Minister for External Affairs, Dr Evatt, who was bent on following the choice made by Britain and India for a rapid recognition of the new government in Peking and an effort at a *modus vivendi* with communist power in Asia. But an election intervened at the end of 1949 and the government changed: the new Prime Minister, Mr Menzies, decided to follow instead the American policy of postponing recognition for the time being. Within six months the outbreak of the Korean War was to begin a chain of events ensuring that temporary postponement should actually last for twenty-two years.

If Australian policy-makers suffered discomfort at this decision, however, it was at the time not America's alienation from China but its rapprochement with Japan that was seen as the danger to Australian interests. The outbreak of the Korean War had determined Truman and Acheson to move rapidly to a non-punitive, reconciliatory peace treaty with Japan, at a time when Australian opinion was by no means convinced that Japanese militarism had actually been overcome. There was not much Australia could do about this, except barter its acquiescence in the American-designed treaty with Japan against as good a mutual security treaty for itself as it could exact from Mr Dulles, who was conducting the negotiations. And because of the Australian ambivalence as to whether the menace in its future might not be a revived Japan rather than China, there is nothing in the treaty that restricts its operation to 'communist aggression', as the American protocol to the Seato treaty for instance does. The Anzus agreement (Australia–New Zealand–U.S.) was thus designed as an open-ended pact of indefinite duration that could as readily be invoked against an expansionist autocracy in Indonesia, or Japan, or the Soviet Union, or even India, as against anything that was likely to emerge from China. From the vantage point of the detente, the Australian negotiators of the time seem commendably prescient.

However, during the later years of the Vietnam War, the

question of whether American protection was not being bought at far too high a price came into active debate in Australia. The moral duties of alliance were interpreted by the governments of the fifties and sixties not only as including participation in the Korean and Vietnam wars but as requiring loyal endorsement of every act of American policy in Asia, including the continued recognition of Tapei rather than Peking as the seat of the government of China. 'All the way with L.B.J.', as a prime minister of the Vietnam War period used to put it, and that unenterprising formula was to redound against its sponsors in due course. The Liberal–Country Party coalition, which was in power for the whole period from 1949 till the end of 1972, appeared incapable of adjusting itself to the changes in American policy with the advent of Mr Nixon and Dr Kissinger, and this was illustrated with rather comic effect at the time of Dr Kissinger's first visit to Peking. The then Australian leader of the Opposition, Mr Whitlam, had been paying a first visit to Peking in the week or so just before the announcement of Dr Kissinger's secret journey, and had been publicly reprimanded by the then Prime Minister, Mr McMahon, for this exhibition of disloyalty to Australia's vital American ally. So Mr Nixon's announcement of his own envoy to Peking left Mr McMahon rather cruelly and visibly stranded on the rocks of an outmoded policy. In fairness to the policy-makers of the Liberal–Country Party coalition in power in Australia at the time, one might say that their slowness of adaptation in the early Nixon–Kissinger period, 1969–71, was not entirely due to intellectual fossilization, though the government of Mr McMahon did rather give that impression. Beneath the surface, efforts to modify policy were stirring, especially among the professional diplomats at External Affairs, but the response of government decision-makers was made sluggish by the fact that their twenty-three years tenure of office had depended largely on the votes of the Democratic Labor party, a small splinter group that sponsored a strong anti-communist ideology in foreign policy, was highly suspicious of detente with both China and Russia, and would gladly have persisted in fighting the battles of containment in Asia long after the Americans ceased to be willing to do so. In effect, the Australian government of the time could not move from its cold war stance without depriving itself of this vital element in its electoral base.

Whatever one may say in explanation of its choices, the impression created on the voters by the Australian governments of the 1969-72 period was of incapacity to adapt, intellectual blankness, and psychological paralysis at a time when the strategic landscapes of the Pacific and Indian oceans and South East Asia were in rapid change. It seems to have partly been this image that ensured the success of the Labor party in December 1972. Elections in Australia are not usually won or lost on foreign policy, and there were some domestic reasons also for discontent, but actually the Australian economy at that time had been in a state of continuous and rather spectacular boom for about twenty years, inflation was still distinctly low (about 4 per cent), unemployment very low (about 1.6 per cent), the foreign exchange reserves were impressively high (about $A 5,000 million) and in general the outgoing government, as far as material prosperity was concerned, might well have campaigned on Mr Macmillan's old slogan, 'you never had it so good'.

However, the effect of the immobility of twenty-three years in foreign policy was to make it possible for the new Prime Minister, Mr Gough Whitlam, to achieve the impression of considerable radicalism by effecting the overdue changes with notable speed in his first hundred or so days of office. In that time he recognized the communist government in China and withdrew representation from Taiwan, recognized East Germany (and later North Vietnam, North Korea, and the P.R.G. in South Vietnam), ended conscription, cancelled defence aid to South Vietnam and Cambodia, announced that he would take Australian forces out of Malaysia (though some air forces in fact remained), ratified the non-proliferation treaty, took the French to the World Court over their nuclear tests in the Pacific, rebuked the U.S.A. for the bombing in North Vietnam and Cambodia, changed the Australian voting pattern at the

U.N. (giving it a 'Third World' orientation with stands against apartheid and such) and further speeded existing moves towards independence for Papua–New Guinea.

These gestures were seen at the time (and not only in Australia) as representing a sharp left turn in Australian foreign policy, but it may be argued that they represented a change of image rather than a change of substance. Putting it cynically, one might say Mr Whitlam had observed that Australian policy created a rather militarist, racialist, colonialist impression (participation in the Vietnam War, Seato, the Five Power Pact, friendliness with South Africa, the retention of authority in Papua–New Guinea) and that this image was ill-received in the neighbourhood and could be remedied at very little cost in real security by a few changes in what were essentially 'declaratory' policies rather than 'operational' ones: recognitions of communist governments, voting at the U.N., disapproving for the record of those activities of which his neighbours were likely to disapprove. Thus one might ask whether the change of image was any more significant than that of the 'square' young man deciding to discard his business suit for blue jeans and grow his hair longer, in order to conform with a new *zeitgeist*.

The change of image in itself may not have been necessarily all that significant (or, as it turned out, permanent), but the point of interest is indeed the influence of the *zeitgeist* (in this case detente) on the flexibility of policy choices. Mr Whitlam expressed it himself: 'It is a great thing for me and my colleagues not to have to waste time pushing against the wind on matters like China and Vietnam ... what a relief it is, what an exhilaration it is, what a help it is to be moving on the wave of great events rather than swimming against the tide.'[1] If attention is transferred from image and rhetoric to the real substance of security policy, it is difficult to see much change in either the basic question or the basic answer. The basic question for Canberra's policy-makers has always been how Australia can ensure the preservation of its territory and identity though located within the possible orbit of any one of several Asian great powers: China, Japan, India, Indonesia, or Russia (which also is a great power in Asia, and prospectively in the Indian Ocean as well). And the answer continued to be what it had been since 1941: that Australia was part of the U.S. protectorate in the Pacific, a situation given treaty form since 1951 by the Anzus pact, and still substantiated by several directly strategic connections, such as the U.S. installations in Australia.

One might go on to maintain that a major effect of detente was to lower the cost to Australia of this situation in the American protectorate, without necessarily reducing its reassurance. In the Cold War period the cost to Australia of the alliance with America must be interpreted as relatively high. Australia participated as an American lieutenant in two wars, Korea and Vietnam, both of which cost casualties (about 300 in Korea and 500 in Vietnam) and the second of which also cost a good deal in terms of the Australian political consensus. It was obliged to accept a Japan peace treaty that it did not at the time like much, and to help prop up the Seato organization (which Australian policy-makers at the time did rather like, but which Australian intellectual opinion had always disparaged). It even had to accept some unwelcome fraying of its relationship with Britain: Churchill, who became Prime Minister a little later, considerably resented Britain's exclusion from the Anzus agreement, an exclusion necessitated by American fears of involvement with British territories like Hong Kong. (Mr Attlee's government, in power at the time, had not resisted this decision.) And in the process of going along with American policy on non-recognition of Peking and the preservation of diplomatic links with Taiwan, Australia was put considerably at odds on various occasions with British and especially Indian and Commonwealth policy. To these counts one might add a somewhat unassessable item: 'opportunity-cost'. Every foreign policy has an opportunity cost, in the sense that it requires abandonment of the alternative foreign policy that could have been pursued in the same period. In the Australian case, for this period such an alternative would presumably have been some variant of a non-aligned or neutralist policy in the Swedish style, and though it is questionable whether this would have been to Australia's advantage, an argument could be made for it on either a moral or a power-political basis.

The point of interest in considering the fringe-effects of detente involves a 'cost–benefit' analysis of the Australian–American alliance as representative of alliances between small or middling powers and great powers. One may look at the relationship in terms of costs imposed and advantages conferred on either party, in both cold war and detente. From the American point of view, the alliance with Australia was a very low-cost one, under either condition. It did not add appreciably to American risks vis-à-vis either the Soviet Union or China. It did not claim either American forces (like Europe) or American aid funds (like Israel and a great many other places). It provided useful facilities in return for a nuclear protectorate very unlikely to come into operation save during general war. In general it was among the least demanding of America's overseas commitments.

On the other hand, the costs to Australia of the American alliance were clearly determined by the character of the period rather than by the fact of alliance itself: high in cold war, much lower in detente. If America is not engaged in combat in South East Asia, it is not going to require its allies to show their flags alongside its own; if it no longer sees much diplomatic or strategic *raison d'être* for Seato, its allies can cheerfully describe that organization as moribund, as Mr Whitlam did. If it has accepted China as a useful element in the balance of power, rather than an ideological danger to be contained, its allies need no longer sacrifice such advantages or opportunities as they see for themselves in the cultivation of relations with Peking. Thus in a perfectly real sense detente widened the area of diplomatic manoeuvre not only for America itself but for assorted allies, including Australia. Ironically, the two chief parties of resistance to the cultivation of better relations with China were India, once the most ardent friend to the idea, and Indonesia, which once seemed likely to be Peking's closest fellow-traveller.

The main costs that remained were the American bases in Australia, which were predominantly oriented to the strategic nuclear balance vis-à-vis the Soviet Union, not to the balance

Australia: The Range of Middle-Power Manoeuvre 193

vis-à-vis China, which hardly required anything of the sort.[2] In fact, China ought quite logically to be a friend to their maintenance and even extension, since it is sedulously concerned with the central balance in general and the strengthening Soviet grip in South Asia and the Indian Ocean in particular. The Australian intellectual left, though on balance more sympathetic to China than to the Soviet Union, appeared not to appreciate this point and campaigned quite fervently against the bases. Probably they were of less moment to America in detente than in cold war. At any rate the State Department conceded a change in the regime of the best known of them, the one at North West Cape (a communications station geared chiefly to the requirements of Polaris submarines), with no great struggle in 1974, and the U.S. Chiefs of Staff seem not noticeably to have objected, though at the time the base was negotiated in 1963 they were alleged to be adamant that only sovereign status would do. There were a number of other U.S. installations that continued to attract left-wing protest in Australia, but on the whole one would say that the spurt of radicalism in foreign policy exhausted itself in 1972–5 and the bases were probably not in much danger unless and until a new head of steam built up in the protest movements.

There remained the question of what range of manoeuvre a middle power like Australia can expect to have, assuming a continuance of the detente. The official assessment until the end of the Whitlam administration was of such a continuance: no new threat of importance was envisaged by the political interpreters of the intelligence estimates for fifteen years or so. A striking contrast is to be noted between this assessment, in the early 1970s, and the situation about ten years earlier, 1964–5, which probably represented the peak point for the sense of threat in Australia's post-war consciousness. The reason then was the short-lived 'Peking–Djakarta axis', the combination of an apparent wave of enthusiasm in China for promoting revolutionary prospects in the Third World generally with a government in Indonesia that was conducting a military campaign against Malaysia by guerrilla action, and that looked likely to be taken over by the Indonesian Communist party. In fact, if that party did organize the coup attempt in 1965, it was quickly overwhelmed by a military counter-coup, and more or less wiped out in a subsequent bloodbath. So one might argue that the largest single factor in the reduction of officially estimated threat as far as Australia was concerned depended on domestic political change in its nearest neighbour, Indonesia, rather than on the general international climate.

Ironically enough, a sort of spin-off or side-effect of the 1965 attempted coup and effective counter-coup in Indonesia proved the major limitation on Australia's most ambitious effort at a detente initiative of its own. The Indonesian junta of President Suharto, the leader of the 1965 counter-coup, retained a sharp suspicion of China because of belief in Chinese complicity in the 1965 coup attempt, allegedly through the Indonesian communists. It was thus the least inclined of the governments of South East Asia to move towards easier relations with Peking. In an expansive moment soon after taking office Mr Whitlam committed himself to promoting a regional association for Asia and the Pacific – something free from the great-power rivalries that he always cited as having bedevilled the area. The membership he had in mind included Japan and China and Indonesia, but not Russia or India. But when he broached the notion in Indonesia he got rather a snubbing because of the inclusion of China; the Indians and the Russians were similarly suspicious of something that would include China but not themselves; the small powers were dubious about taking sides and reluctant to see their own organization, ASEAN, overshadowed; Japan was hesitant about involving itself. So the idea came to nothing much, save as an illustration that it does not necessarily take great-power ideologies to preclude international cordiality: local allergies and resentments can as readily manage to do so.

There was also a built-in limitation, in terms of the Australian national interest, on its range of manoeuvre in what Mr Whitlam called 'resources diplomacy'. Australia is uncommonly well-endowed with exportable resources like iron-ore, bauxite, tin, zinc, lead and uranium, and economic nationalism had been among the sharpest and most persistent of Labor party traditions. It was probably inevitable that there should be resentment at the level of overseas holdings in these fields (over 60 per cent) and a determination to 'buy back the mineral farm'. But the efforts to do so by borrowing 'petrodollars' from Middle Eastern interests provided their own case study in the difficulties of financing this enterprise, and indeed contributed very substantially to the downfall of the Whitlam government in 1975. Australia cannot be converted into a member of the 'Third World' merely by changing its voting at the U.N.: it may be geographically southern but it is culturally and socially Western, part of the rich, consumer-oriented, self-indulgent advanced world. Its chief economic partners are North America, Japan and the E.E.C., and it fares well or ill economically as they do. So any vision of Australia as the leading member of several Opec-style producer cartels in the commodities it exports was always rather unrealistic. In any case, there were domestic political inhibitions on the international company Australia could opt to keep. Australian political parties need to win elections at very close intervals: three years normally, though Mr Whitlam had to face one every eighteen months. The electorate was by no means as radical, internationalist or determinedly 'colour blind' as some of the Labor leadership or the bright young intellectuals of its 'brains trusts'. The wave of post-war migration to Australia, though it had fallen to low tide at the time, had brought in substantial ethnic minorities, which like those in America were learning how to make themselves into pressure groups. They are predominantly anti-communist because a good many were refugees from Eastern Europe. In fact, the first wave of migrants from the displaced people's camps were generally known as 'Balts' because so many were from the old Baltic states of Estonia, Latvia and Lithuania. They could not be expected to be enthusiastic about detente with either communist power, especially the Russians. It was in deference to opinion among this group that the government of Mr Fraser, succeeding Mr Whitlam in 1975, withdrew recognition of the incorporation of the Baltic states into the Soviet Union, though it was a purely symbolic gesture, amounting in fact only to instructions to the Australian ambassador in Moscow not to visit the Baltic Soviet Republics. One might expect that, as in the United States, the strongest anti-detente feeling as far as the Soviet Union is concerned will persist among the members, and even the children and grandchildren, of the East European *diasporas*.

There are thus a number of permanent domestic factors limiting the freedom of manoeuvre of Australian governments, even assuming continuance of detente. The more important limits however will probably be those of the international context, including the ambiguities of the balance of power as it now operates in the great arc from Japan round to the Indian Ocean. I argued earlier that what has been emerging in Asia since the end of the Vietnam War has been something surprisingly like the old concept of the 'heartlands' and 'rimlands' dichotomy, and that Australia belongs obviously to the 'rimlands' element in this system, along with Japan, Indonesia and the Philippines, all countries having (and being likely to maintain) ties with the maritime great power, the United States.

This on the whole seems likely to prove an acceptable outcome for Australia, since it aligns with each other the two powers most important to its own security and prosperity – Indonesia and Japan – and links them, via America, to the world most important to its past tradition and present identity, that of Britain and Europe. The growth of Soviet naval power in the Pacific obviously makes the American connection still more essential to China, Japan and Indonesia as well as to Australia, and may help keep the residual tensions between them under control. Soviet overtures to Tonga about facilities for Russian fishing boats (which are usually assumed to have other duties as well) caused a ripple of alarm from Japan to New Zealand.

There are more uncertainties in the strategic landscape of the Indian Ocean, and along the East African littoral. And again there was a link between domestic and international policies, because the two alternating possible governments in Australia take more diverse views on Indian Ocean issues than on most areas of foreign policy. Mr Whitlam, in consonance with the general Fabian socialist angle to his political stance, put a good deal of stress on arms-control measures, and committed himself early in his prime ministership to a notion originally proposed by Ceylon, of the Indian Ocean as a nuclear-free 'zone of peace'. That concept seemed more feasible when it was first proposed than it did by late 1976, with the Canal reopened, the Soviet base at Berbera in operation and the Indian Ocean, with the growth of the Soviet mercantile fleet, increasing in importance to the Russians as (among other things) the natural highway from the Pacific coast of the Soviet Union to its Black Sea and northern ports. The Indian Ocean is also, of course, the central concourse for all the sea lanes of the vast tanker trade to the Persian Gulf ports for oil, not only for Europe but for Japan and the United States. The interest of the world's navies in the area seemed hardly likely to diminish therefore: in fact the prospects of keeping the naval and air forces of the Powers out of it appeared negligible. Nor did the futures of the littoral powers – Iran, India, Indonesia, Pakistan, the East African states – seem so predictable, or so reassuring to Australian eyes, as to make a conclusive case for the exclusion, even if it were possible, of the outside Powers. After the withdrawal of Britain, the main Western strength was that of France, for whom the security of the tanker routes was particularly important in view of its heavy dependence on oil for energy. The American navy's interest in the area was relatively slight until the late 1960s, but grew rapidly with the increase in American dependence on Middle Eastern oil, and with a felt need to match the Soviet navy. Most especially it grew after the 1973 Middle East War because of perception that a 'west-about' route might conceivably be needed someday for resupply to Israel (the normal 'east-about' route having shown considerable difficulties on that occasion) and with the build-up, from 1976, of American interest in East Africa (especially Kenya) and southern Africa. Moreover, the possibility of an American military operation in the Persian Gulf itself could not altogether be ruled out of contingency planning after the experience of the 1973–4 oil embargo, distant and desperate though such an operation might seem.

For it to be even remotely feasible, control of the Indian Ocean approach lanes would be the first requirement.

Thus the importance of the Indian Ocean rose steadily in the 1970s, and with it the importance of British islands like Diego Garcia and Australian facilities or potential facilities like those at Cockburn Sound,[3] near Perth. In the early days of the U.S. navy's interest in building up a presence on Diego Garcia, to match that of the Soviet forces at Berbera, the idea was rather discountenanced not only by liberal congressional opinion (voiced by Senator Edward Kennedy and others) but by the State Department. Mr Whitlam in his time as Prime Minister was also strongly opposed to the project, *on* the record; perhaps rather less so *off* the record, as time went on. The successor government of Mr Fraser (a coalition of the Liberal and National Country parties, both of which are quite strongly oriented to defence) was committed during its election campaign to the proposition that Australian and general Western defensive strength in the area was in dangerous decline and ought to be reconstituted. It therefore favoured the build-up of the facilities on Diego Garcia, among other measures.

Indeed the government of Mr Fraser was initially as much committed to the rhetoric of the cold war and Australia's traditional alliances as Mr Whitlam had been to the rhetoric of detente and Third World internationalism. I am not implying that the differences in the foreign-policy lines of the two governments were purely rhetorical: just that the substance of difference in security policy looked rather less if one examined what was actually done than if one listened to what apparently was said. Early in his tenure of office, Mr Fraser incurred as many difficulties from overselling his distrust of the Soviet Union as Mr Whitlam had from detente euphoria. This was particularly the case during his first visit overseas, to Japan and China in June 1976. (The fact that these *were* his first visits to foreign capitals as Prime Minister in itself indicates how much of Mr Whitlam's reorientation of foreign policy he had retained. Australian prime ministers, especially conservative ones, used always to go first to London and Washington.)

Ironically, by the time Mr Fraser reached Peking, the mood there was such that his views, especially on the Soviet Union and the American detente with that power, were more welcome than the milder and more optimistic assumptions of Mr Whitlam would have been. Possibly by error, a transcript of his conversation with the Chinese Prime Minister was delivered to the Australian press corps accompanying his tour, and naturally published, making it embarrassingly clear that Mr Fraser regarded with suspicion not only the purposes of the Soviet Union and India but the stability of Singapore, Malaysia and Indonesia, and might even look favourably on an anti-Soviet four-power informal understanding (U.S.A.–China–Japan–Australia).[4] While these views did him no harm in Peking, they were less welcome elsewhere, including some senior bureaucratic circles in Canberra, who have their own modes of arranging the discomfort of politicians. As in Washington so in Canberra, the leak may attain the status of an art-form.

One might argue that the anti-detente rhetoric of Mr Fraser and his Defence Minister, Mr Killen, was an over-reaction to the detente euphoria of Mr Whitlam. And as Mr Whitlam's style had been rather flamboyant and emphatic, calculated to make his attitudes and views rather more different in appearance from those of his predecessors than they were in actual substance, so the same technique was practised (less skilfully) by his successors. Discreet diplomacy is no longer an Australian tradition, if indeed it ever was. Yet the substance of policy was probably not unlike what the Labor government might have chosen. The defence of northern and western Australia, which had been somewhat neglected by governments of both parties in earlier years, because most of the population lives in the south-eastern corner of the continent, began to receive more attention. The oil and mineral resources that are Australia's great assets for the future lie there, and the direction of threat is now assumed to be from the Indian Ocean rather than the Pacific, with the Soviet build-up and other factors. Even the final phase of the Portuguese empire provided an equal lesson for both governments, since it happened at the moment of transition between them, late 1975. The territory of Portuguese Timor, which is within striking distance of the Australian city of Darwin, and was involved in Australian defence against the Japanese in the Second World War, was absorbed by Indonesia, despite the military resistance of its one articulate political movement, Fretilin, just at the time of the election. Both the Australian alternative governments had decided not to resist Indonesian plans for the take-over, and Mr Whitlam appears to have reached the decision sometime before his own domestic crisis, so his lack of inclination to take action cannot be put down to the election. Some Australians (mostly on the far left but with a few on the right who had sentimental memories from the Second World War) would have wished a different decision to be made. But if either government had contemplated an effort to resist Indonesian plans for East Timor, they would hardly have had the military capacity to do so. And the Indonesian objection to the alleged communist danger of an independent East Timor might quite logically be extended to the political colour of some future government in independent Papua–New Guinea, where Australia has much more real moral obligations and national interests.

The general lesson of the story was that, for a middle power, detente is no reason to assume that its local environment will hold no dangers, or that its defences can be happily neglected. There sometimes seems to be a 'law of the conservation of tension' in international politics. As tension is reduced at the centre, it increases at the periphery. As the great powers are easier in their relations with each other, they have less reason to involve themselves in the management of such peripheral tensions, unless the particular area is of strategic interest: Portugal or southern Africa as against East Timor. So the local issue may be determined by the will of the strongest local power, and middling powers may need to remember that diplomatic leverage usually has something to do with local military strength.

CHAPTER 11

The Enemies and Sceptics of Detente

Very few people, even during the 1976 U.S. election campaign, described themselves candidly as enemies of detente. Since the word was associated in the public mind with peace, to proclaim oneself against it was rather in the category of announcing a dislike of mother-love or apple-pie: it seems to cut one off from the normal value systems of mankind. Yet the policy did have (objectively speaking) many enemies; most of them disguised as what might be called 'improving friends'. By that I mean those who in effect said 'Certainly I am not against detente as such – but let us improve it. Let us make it detente with a human face, or with better moral values, or dependent on the Soviet Union (or the United States) making this or that reasonable concession.'

It may well seem a crude oversimplification on my part even to use the word 'enemy' in connection with such reservations. Yet in the ordinary bargaining of daily life, over for instance the sale of a house or a car or setting the level of a salary or fee, if one found that the price proposed to the would-be buyer was consistently and ascertainedly beyond the level he was likely to pay, one would be entitled to conclude that whoever was proposing that price was an enemy to a bargain's actually being struck. Something of the sort is possible with detente, and this is made more feasible as a technique by the fact that the 'price' normally asked for detente by those who are no friends to the idea consists only of the mildest and most ordinary conventions of Western liberal societies – freedom of communication and movement within the country, free emigration, the most common-place political liberties. Nothing could be more reasonable and desirable; the only difficulty is that to institute such changes would mean not only dismantling the standard practice of the Soviet or Chinese state, but discarding most of its theory as well.

Stipulations as to improvements on the other side before detente becomes acceptable have usually been directed, as far as Western liberals and conservatives are concerned, to the detente with Russia. No doubt the detente with China had its enemies, but they were far less audible. At first sight this may appear odd, since China is undoubtedly, judged by Western liberal values, a more whole-hearted party autocracy than the Soviet Union has now become. Its control over the lives of its citizens is far more total: the possibility of dissent in the present Russian manner has not appeared since the 'hundred flowers' campaign of the 1950s. The extremes of the cult of personality are more recent: there was no Russian equivalent to the Maoist 'little red book' demonstrations of the mid-sixties, even during the worst days of the Stalin personality cult. In terms of revolutionary theory, both as to domestic transformation and as to transformation of the society of states, Maoism is far more radical in its proposals than orthodox Moscow-oriented communism. And when occasionally in the Third World the local political situation allows Maoist political elites, as against orthodox communists, to assert their values for the moment, they seem to try and live up to their proclaimed theories.

All this ought to mean, if ideological incompatibility were the determining factor, that for both liberals and conservatives the detente with China ought to have aroused more alarm and resistance than that with Russia. Yet it did not: only an occasional voice has been raised against it in America, and in Europe it has been universally accepted as the most wholly welcome of all the changes in American policy in Dr Kissinger's time. Even in Asia and Australia there has not so far been much articulate dissent from it. Mr Lee Kuan Yew in Singapore, a few grumbles from Indonesia, and notes of protest from the political and intellectual right in Australia are about the most that can be cited as indicating resistance or misgivings.

I will later suggest reasons for this highly differential reception of detente in the two instances. But for the moment let us concentrate on those voices that, for one reason or another, have been raised against the detente between America and Russia, manifesting doubt, distrust or suspicion. And since, as I said, many of the people concerned would resist the imputation of being enemies of the concept, let us regard them merely as sceptical of its value, either to peace or to the power interests of the party to which they adhere.

The first thing that might be said is that scepticism of the detente has produced an interesting set of bedfellows, from Ronald Reagan, Henry Jackson, George Wallace, Clare Luce and Melvin Laird on the right wing of American politics through Russian dissidents like Solzhenitsyn and Amalrik, to some communist party leaders in Europe and Latin America on the left. One might say that the single blanket that covers them all is distrust of the power of the Russian state, and a belief that diplomacy in the mode of cold war rather than in the mode of detente is the more likely to check that power. But this would clearly not provide for the case of a few of the left-wing enemies of the concept, for whom the motive is distrust of American power and a fear that detente will enable it to be stabilized or even extended.

Since this is very much the less familiar group, at least as far as Western attention is concerned, let us look at it first. The true 'radicals' among its members are the leaders of communist parties, in Western Europe or in Latin America, who maintain that the wish to get on with the Americans has vitiated Soviet and/or Chinese revolutionary ardour in the Third World. This also used to be a Chinese line of attack on the Soviet Union before their own detente with the Americans got under way. However, with the emergence of 'Eurocommunism' and the conspicuous influence of the Italian Communist party on those of France and Spain, one might say that this strand of opinion has been in rapid decline since the early 1970s, and the orthodoxy is now that detente allows a useful basis for communist co-operation with socialists and social democrats, and thus an increase in their influence by parliamentary means.[1]

The issue of whether the detente, especially through its economic aspects, actually helped the capitalist world to survive during what, in 1974–6, was by some left-wing theorists being interpreted as 'the final crisis of capitalism' has clearly been a major point of 'undercover' intellectual controversy within the communist world, and probably continues to be one. One might expect it to reach a crescendo when the succession to Mr Brezhnev is being determined, but there have already been audible echoes of it on Party occasions, for instance the fortieth anniversary celebration of the last congress of the Comintern, in July 1975, in the speech of Mikhail Suslov, a senior Party ideologist. The main lines of intellectual dispute are clear enough, since the general issue is not new. The recurrent crises of the capitalist world offer two possibilities of interpretation for the Party faithful. On any given occasion it may be argued, as by some theorists in the period concerned, that this at last is the 'final crisis of capitalism', allowing and requiring the Party to 'ignite the revolutionary energy of the working masses'. However, the crisis may in capitalist societies produce either a 'Hitler' figure or a 'Roosevelt' figure, and it may either cause the reactionary regimes to seek a way out of crisis through international war, or offer opportunities for the military support of revolutionary movements. Either of the two latter possibilities may be advanced as a reason for increased military preparedness by the Soviet Union. Thus an acute 'crisis of capitalism' does not call for military relaxation on the Soviet part, but on the contrary increased vigilance and preparedness and higher arms budgets. And so interpretations of the 1974–6 crisis of capitalism that laid stress on its severity and its potentially cataclysmic quality for the capitalist world as a whole, or even for a weak link in the capitalist chain like Portugal, would be more congenial to the hawks than the doves in the Kremlin, and an argument weakening to detente.

Contrarywise, interpretations that played down the severity

of the crisis, treating it as just another of the normal cyclical crises of the capitalist world, and still more policies that actually helped to mitigate it, were indications that the friends of the detente still had the upper hand. At the time of writing this had been the predominant stance. The Soviet Defence Ministry newspaper, *Red Star*, asserted on 29 October 1974 that capitalism would probably be able to overcome its existing crisis. Mr Shelepin, then still a Politburo member, told the Bureau of the World Federation of Trade Unions in January 1975 that Soviet orders were helping maintain workers in employment in the West. Mr Brezhnev similarly stressed the value of Soviet trade to floundering Western economies during the visit of the British prime minister in February 1975. Soviet oil exports, which the Russians could, if they had chosen, have used to reinforce the effects of the 1974 Arab blockade on Western economies, were instead administered with an eminently profit-minded drive to increase markets and raise prices towards the new world level despite the anti-Soviet resentments this aroused in Eastern Europe, the main Soviet market.

So on the whole it appeared that whatever opportunities for revolutionary change some party theoreticians had seen in this particular capitalist crisis (the most severe for forty years), the orthodoxy among actual policy-makers remained to play it down and pursue rather the non-revolutionary benefits of detente-fostered trade with the capitalist world. The more revolutionary-oriented theorists were not silenced, however, and continued apparently to be led by Suslov, with Timofeyev and Zaradov prominent among those arguing, by implication, that official policy was ignoring or refusing to recognize the depth of the capitalist troubles and the favourable conditions prevailing for revolutionary upsurge in Western Europe.[2] An endorsement by Brezhnev of a *Pravda* article by Zaradov on revolutionary violence may be regarded as a sop cast in the direction of the dissenters. One could also regard as a concession to them Brezhnev's insistence, during the visit of the French president in October 1975 and on subsequent occasions, that there could be no detente in the ideological field.

Despite the Soviet rejection of the U.S. Trade Bill on account of the Jackson amendment, Soviet–American trade grew rapidly in the detente period, including the recession. American exports to Russia increased about ten-fold, a highly favourable ratio compared with imports, and one that may be interpreted as indicating that a good deal more dependency was being generated on the Soviet than on the American side. (One of the arguments against detente by some analysts had been that the opposite would be the case.)[3] The Russians imported grain and advanced industrial goods, both of critical importance to their economy. The Americans imported some raw materials, a token amount of oil, and diamonds and furs, which were readily dispensable or substitutable elsewhere. The deals actually held up by the Jackson amendment, or at least by the restriction on Export–Import credits associated with it, were large development projects, like that for Siberian natural gas, which involved such enormous sums that even very powerful capitalist enterprises were chary of proceeding without adequate government credits.

Assessments would differ as to how valuable trade with the Soviet bloc was to Western economies, either in general or particularly in recovery from the recession. The judgement would no doubt be different for each Western economy, and probably for each Western economist. As far as the *political* impact of the economic side of detente was concerned, however, one might say that initially it made some damaging enemies, but later probably some useful friends. The enemies were made mostly by the 1972 grain deal, which was not in fact part of any official detente arrangement, but was a successful coup by astute Russian negotiators, exploiting American market possibilities on the best capitalist principles. It was, however, unfairly but effectively attributed to the detente, especially by Mr George Meany, the American trade union leader, and a myth was fostered that the rapid rise in American food prices during 1973 was attributable primarily to this cause, and that the Russian buying coup was in some way generated by detente. These legends constituted almost the only way in which the average American consumer could construe detente as having an adverse effect on his day-to-day interests, and thus probably did it a good deal of damage in popular estimation. However, the actual official grain deal, concluded in 1975, by which the Russians agreed to buy at least six million tons of grain in each crop year from 1976, for six years, but were required to enter diplomatic negotiations if they wanted more than eight million tons, probably created a bloc of electorally influential friends of the concept in the Mid-west, where they were important to any presidential candidate. The deal guaranteed the corn-belt farmer a market worth at least a thousand million dollars a year, and though some farm leaders resented *any* limit being put on the amount they could sell the Russians, undoubtedly the sense of benefit was widespread. To find the foreign exchange to buy the grain, the Russians were obliged to contemplate selling more oil to the Americans, again a benefit to the Western hand, especially against Opec.

As to advanced technological products, it is difficult to see a compact voting bloc of either friends or enemies. Senator Jackson's constituency (Washington State) and the Pacific Coast in general are heavily dependent on contracts for advanced armaments, and thus might be adversely affected by the SALT agreements. But the American arms trade in any case boomed spectacularly after 1975, partly because of the markets in the Middle East among new-rich oil states, and these sales owed a good deal to Dr Kissinger's diplomatic success there, which in turn owed a good deal to detente. So the arms industry as a whole probably made up on the Middle East swings more than it lost on the SALT roundabouts, and of course there were many other high-technology goods (excluding armaments) that could be sold to Eastern Europe, provided the detente continued. China, with its foreign exchange reserves plumped out by oil, was also prospectively a market for high-technology goods (perhaps including defensive armaments) and again the commercial prospects depended a good deal on the diplomatic ambiance. So there was on balance very little reason for Dr Kissinger's policies to be unpopular with businessmen. Before the Angola complication the embryonic detente with Cuba also held some prospect of recreating economic opportunities, and this prospect seemed to be reappearing in early 1977.

The instance of Cuba brings up a point whose influence is difficult to assess, but that would prove important if detente were to survive over a long period. One might call it the 'disappointed expectations' factor: the reaction against the basic concept when the most hopeful interpretations of it prove disappointing. It had obviously some influence on Western opinion, in reaction against initially over-optimistic expectations, but it also, in another form, seems to apply to a good deal of *radical* opinion outside the communist states in attitudes to the Russian and Chinese leadership, which in the eyes of the hopeful young revolutionary became a good deal compromised by American embraces. In a sense, Russian leadership claims in the Party's world may need the cohesion provided by belief in a monolithic, determined and dangerous enemy even more than the non-communist leadership in the West does. If one looks at the attitudes of the Party in France or Italy, for instance, and the difficulties of the Russians in convening a European communist summit in 1975, or even at the attitudes of the student left in English and American universities, it is clear that Moscow loses a good deal of prestige and emotional appeal when it ceases to look like the endangered fortress of a universalist doctrine. It is no longer a place that inspires protective feeling, much less crusades, and this affects what may be called its informal alliance structure with communist parties and other left parties in or out of power in the rest of the world.

In fact one can see the disruptive effect of detente on the Soviet alliance structure at its earliest in the original breach in the Sino-Soviet alliance, 1958–9. The conflict had quite a number of causes, but the Soviet efforts to promote detente with the United States in the two crises of 1958, and in Mr Khrushchev's journey to America in 1959, were undoubtedly major factors, perhaps *the* major factor. So, contrary to the usual assumptions, one might argue that adding up China, Eastern Europe and parties elsewhere, detente has proved more damaging over the years to the formal and informal alliance structures of the Soviet Union than to those of the West. Neither the American relation with Japan nor that with the European members of Nato suffered equivalent adverse effects, despite apprehensions that this would be the case.

Latin America is especially an area where the detente has been adverse to the hopes of the local revolutionary left, since it diminished their prospects not only from Russia and China but from Cuba, and conspicuously failed to prevent the overthrow of the Allende government in Chile. Mr Brezhnev visited Cuba in January 1974, some months after that event, but the main drive of his counsel to Dr Castro seems still to have been in favour of rapprochement with Washington. The Cuban signals to America were more conciliatory after his visit than earlier. (This was of course well before the Angola complication, which temporarily appeared to dispose of the prospective rapprochement between Cuba and Washington in late 1975.) Possibly Mr Brezhnev found it necessary on this occasion to defend himself against charges of appeasement of the U.S.A. In one of his speeches he protested that the Russians 'were not for peace at any price'.[4] The guerrilla groups of Latin America still adhere to the doctrines of Che Guevara, but actual material help from Cuba had become quite sparse, in contrast with their more ambitious efforts in Africa and the Middle East. One may interpret this as a reasonable Cuban assumption that revolutionary prospects are better elsewhere, but that is hardly much consolation to a Latin American revolutionary. The disenchantment of the Latin American far left with all three of their possible sources of help did not necessarily mean much reduction of local social ferment, which has predominantly local causes and dynamics, but it did deprive it of what once seemed to be its strategically organized character.

One could conceivably include with the group of those whose opposition to detente is based on fear of its stifling the revolutionary struggle of the left, or dulling the edge of Russian or Chinese power, the obvious category of those whose professional duty is the care of that power, the Russian or Chinese military.

However, it would be incongruous to equate these with radicals or dissidents, so I will look at them rather in conjunction with military groups in the United States, professional interests and attitudes having interesting similarities and differences on the three sides.

Though the left-wing group of the opponents of detente is very much the less audible party in the West, one may plausibly argue that they have the better case against it. That is, it seems likely that detente cannot over the long term be an ally of radical causes: that it does on the whole vitiate the drives for change theoretically characteristic of China and the Soviet Union and of protest movements elsewhere, rather more than it vitiates the will to conserve the existing world characteristic of the prosperous West and its fellow-travellers. If you give someone a reasonable share of the apples, it will usually tend to undermine his urge to upset the apple-cart: he will begin to see advantages in maintaining the situation, even though no doubt with the *arrière-pensée* of taking over the cart and the orchard for himself in due course. The Chinese used to employ a phrase about the prospects of world revolution riding the winds of high international conflict as the seagull rides the rainstorm. In calmer times, its flights tend to be less spectacular.

Let us turn now to the better-known group of the enemies and sceptics of detente, those whose misgivings are motivated by distrust of Russian power, and who are mostly to be found on the right and at the liberal centre of Western political systems. The American members of this clan are the most articulate, with the West Europeans on the whole more hesitant or ambivalent. The useful dividing line to be drawn between them is not geographic, but divides those whose opposition is moral and emotional from those for whom it is strategic or even tactical. The two groups are not exclusive of each other, and sometimes one will find that a position that is really based on moral feeling is presented in strategic terms, and a position with strategic or even tactical reasoning behind it is presented in moral terms. But working out the overlap of reasons offers a useful vantage-point for examining the complexity of motives.

The Enemies and Sceptics of Detente 211

The most morally sympathetic of the enemies of detente are the members and children of the East European *diasporas*. By that I mean those whose origins are Russian Jewish, Polish, Czech, Hungarian or otherwise rooted in Eastern Europe, in the sphere of what is now Soviet domination. These are people for whom distrust of the power of the Russian state seems built into the very bones of their minds. And I want to stress that I mean the *Russian* state, not necessarily the *Soviet* state, since those who feel most strongly on this point in Britain and America or Australia are as often the children of those who fled from the Czarist Russian pogroms of the turn of the century as of those who fled the Soviet Russian invasion of Eastern Europe during the Second World War or just after. Their deep-rooted aversion to the power system centred on Moscow is not dependent on its mutation into a revolutionary form. The exiles produced by later flights from the face of Russian power, up to the most recent Jewish émigrés, have a newer sense of grievance, but not necessarily a more bitter or irremovable one. Many of the exiles and their children are now American or British or Australian citizens, and quite a number are successful journalists and academics, able to make their emotions articulate.

The existence of this quite large group of people, who do in fact have an excellent moral and emotional case against Soviet or Russian power, seems to me one of the two main reasons for the differential reception, which I mentioned earlier, of the detente with Russia as against that with China. There is no Chinese *diaspora* of this sort. There are, of course, plenty of ethnic Chinese living overseas, and some of them left China for political as against commercial reasons. But they are not integrated into the scholarly and journalistic establishment of the West in the same way as the children of the East European *diasporas*.

One might say also that there has been an intellectual as well as a geographical exile from Russian communism, which as yet is almost absent in the case of Maoism: the ex-faithful of 'the god that failed', the one-time converts to marxism who deserted the party at various points from the Nazi-Soviet pact in 1939 to the invasion of Czechoslovakia in 1968. Koestler once remarked that the last battle will be between the marxists and the ex-marxists. There is something about the situation of the disillusioned lover that naturally results in special suspicion (one might agree well-justified by experience) of the ex-beloved. It is too soon for Maoism to have a similar legion of ex-converts.

I have described this group (the *diasporas* from Eastern Europe and the analogous though not identical *diasporas* from the moral and intellectual lost territory of communism) as the most morally sympathetic of the assorted clans of enemies of detente, because of recognition that their disillusionment with (and distrust of) Soviet power and practice has often been achieved at the cost of personal anguish, and reflects a judgement, on the basis of personal experience, of what Soviet policy and practice feels like to those beneath its power. This also applied of course to the Russian dissidents, at home or in exile, like Solzhenitsyn, Sakharov, Amalrik and the brothers Medvedev. One might add to their testimony the evidence of the dead, and the writing they or their wives or children have produced concerning life in the Russian camps or prisons.

Of all the Russian dissidents, the most forthright, articulate and well-publicized has of course been Alexander Solzhenitsyn, who since his forced exile from the Soviet Union in early 1974 has denounced Soviet policy and the society that Russian revolutionary leaders from Lenin on have created in speeches of an eloquence and fervour not heard in the West even in the heyday of the Cold War. He is averse not only to detente diplomacy with the Soviet Union, but to all diplomatic dealings with that power; even the 1933 recognition by the U.S.A. was an error. The whole period since the Second World War must be regarded as World War III in which the West has gone down to defeat (a view that appears to imply that the Western powers did little better during the Cold War than during the detente). World War IV is just beginning.[5]

On first analysis, the Solzhenitsyn episode appeared to have been the largest single public relations disaster for detente in the whole period since 1969. Many commentators presented, in particular, the original decision that Mr Ford should not meet him as proof of the moral squalor of the concept: Dr Kissinger was heavily reproached for his advice that a meeting would not be of advantage to American foreign policy. ('Giving the Kremlin a veto over the engagement-book at the White House.')[6]

Yet over a slightly longer perspective, the episode began to seem rather more ambivalent in its effects. Solzhenitsyn's influence is chiefly on intellectual opinion rather than at the grass-roots level. His chilling picture of Soviet reality as he had experienced it was perhaps the most damning and effective evidence against the system and its creators since Khrushchev's de-Stalinization speech of 1956, or perhaps even since the great disillusion of the late 1930s. Thus for the young intellectuals of the mid-1970s it possibly had the 'conversion therapy' effect that their elders had experienced in 1939 or 1948 or 1956 or 1968, and provided a similar inhibition against an unduly sentimental view of Soviet purposes. Further, Solzhenitsyn's denunciation was not merely of Stalin and his successors among the Soviet leadership, but particularly of Lenin, and hence of party structures based on Leninist principles. Moreover, as he developed his views in exile, it became clear that he saw the origins of the catastrophic evils of Soviet society as implicit in the Western traditions of humanism, liberalism and socialism. Insofar as he had a determinable political influence on the Western societies that listened respectfully to his denunciations (amplified by the mass media) of their *mores*, the effect thus seemed likely to be an intellectual climate, in universities and elsewhere, less inclined to idealistic illusions about communist systems than, for instance, the student generation of the 1930s. Over the long term, as I argued earlier, a viable detente requires a stable balance of power and a capacity by the West to hold not only its strategic ground but what one may call its political and moral ground as well, especially in societies like France and Italy where communism is a more fashionable intellectual position than it is in northern Europe. So on the whole one might argue that though the Solzhenitsyn speeches initially appeared deeply damaging to the detente, he might well prove a long-term psychological prop to the necessary infrastructure of the policy: a sort of one-man moral rearmament campaign of considerable long-term impact on the willingness of Western intellectuals to concede the necessity of a balance of power.

Not all Russian dissenters, or their equivalents in other East European countries, shared Solzhenitsyn's views on detente. Some of them, like Roy Medvedev, represent a sort of 'loyal opposition', in that they remain marxists and adherents of the system, only maintaining that the present leadership had misused it. The position of the eminent physicist and Nobel prize-winner Andrei Sakharov appeared to be about half way between the 'loyal opposition' and the 'revolutionary opposition' standpoints, wanting large changes to promote human rights in the Soviet system and a sort of convergence with the West, but not regarding the regime as evil incarnate or wanting its total overthrow, like Solzhenitsyn. His view on the detente maintained that its arms-control aspect should be pursued, but that on other matters a better price should be exacted by the West. By implication, this Russian group as a whole argued that the West, particularly the Americans, should use foreign and trade policy as leverage to secure change in Soviet domestic policy, and the area in which they hoped to force change was not merely the relatively small and peripheral one of the issue of visas for Jewish emigration, but the whole central issue of the Soviet Union's treatment of its own citizens. Yet with all due sympathy, it was certainly not the case that the situation of Russian dissidents was better in the Cold War period: if their pain was more audible during the detente, it was because the system was somewhat less efficiently stifling. A reversion to cold war policies on the part of the West seemed likely to extinguish such glimmers of intellectual liberty as had appeared rather than to promote their extension.[7]

To revert to the reasons why anti-detente feeling in the West has been almost exclusively directed against relations with Russia, and why there is no equivalent groundswell of Western resistance to the detente with China, the absence of any group of equal articulacy and influence in the Chinese case seems to me the most important factor, but one ought to acknowledge that the reason China has had a 'better press' than the Soviet Union may be that the Chinese government has actually behaved better than the Soviet government, both to its own people and to those round its borders. There is no real Chinese equivalent to the satellization of Eastern Europe (the case of Tibet is more like that of Kazakhstan and similar long-established Russian territories) or the Nazi-Soviet pact, and probably not to the system described by Solzhenitsyn in *The Gulag Archipelago*. Anyone familiar with the two literatures must be struck by the similarities between the writings of those who returned from China in the seventies and those who returned from Russia in the thirties. Yet the fact that the thirties' travellers were wrong about the Soviet Union is not necessarily proof that the seventies' travellers are wrong about China, though it may offer grounds for suspicion.

There is however another very vital factor involved in comparisons of the two rapprochements, and it is one that brings us to another clan of enemies or sceptics, those whose doubts I would describe as strategic or tactical. The Soviet Union is a power formidable even to the United States, and growing regularly more so in terms of military capacity. China is not as yet anywhere near the same class: its military capacities are certainly growing[8] but they are not for the time being formidable to America, and barely so to the Soviet Union. Thus there is clearly less case, or at any rate less *immediate* case, for alarms on the purely strategic level about Chinese than about Russian military capacity. This is undoubtedly the main reason why, for instance, Senator Henry Jackson or Mr Melvin Laird (the former U.S. Secretary of Defense) would speak up strongly *against* the detente with Russia but warmly *for* that with China. Strategically speaking, China had become widely regarded as a fellow-traveller of Nato, since the primary military interest of both was the containment, and if possible outmatching, of Soviet military capacity. One could even write some rather implausible scenarios that made China an actual cobelligerent of the West, in the event for instance of a Russian attack directed at both Yugoslavia and Albania.

I have dealt elsewhere with the actual and prospective military balance (both on the nuclear and the conventional level) between America and the Soviet Union, and have argued that there was no reason why the detente, or specific agreements formulated in association with it, should necessarily be disadvantageous to the West. Indeed I would argue that the real edge of Western strategic advantage normally had to be underrated in the reports of official spokesmen and their allies among defence journalists, for reason of the domestic political resistance to arms budgets among Nato powers. It is obviously no help to the American defense secretary, for instance, in his efforts to prevent Congress from cutting his budget if he presents a rosy picture of the balance of forces, and there are techniques by which any *couleur de rose* may be somewhat artificially drained from the defence scene. But before considering the strategic debate proper, as exemplified in the case of Dr Schlesinger, let us look at some tactical aspects, as in the case of Senator Jackson and Mr Reagan, for whom they amounted in essence to the tactics of their respective fights for the presidential nomination. Taking first Senator Jackson, all the potential Democratic candidates looking to 1976 were, of course, faced with the problem of constructing a platform from which to convince the party machine of their promise as 'the best available man' to do combat with President Ford. Since by universal acknowledgement the only substantial successes that the Republican administrations of 1969–76 could demonstrate, and thus the chief claim to four more years of power, were in the field of foreign policy, it was necessary for would-be Democratic presidential candidates to concentrate their fire in that quarter. And of all the Kissinger policy innovations, the detente with Russia looked the one most vulnerable to attack. No one could make a plausible case for reversion to the old hostile relationship with China or for reinvolvement in South East Asia; Cyprus was too small an issue, save for the Greek lobby, and the

Middle East too much an agreed success story to be tempting targets. A tougher line on Latin America, especially the Panama treaty, was a natural for the hard-line Republican right like Mr Reagan, but not for a liberal Democrat from a far North-West state. That really left only the detente with Russia, and it fitted very naturally with Senator Jackson's other interests. A 'cold-war liberal' of the Acheson generation, with strong connections with the union leadership (which is, as Solzhenitsyn observed, the most consistently anti-communist force in American life, far more so than big business), strong connections with the 'friends of Israel' lobby, and with a state constituency heavily dependent on contracts for advanced weapons systems ('the Senator from Boeing'), he was a natural spokesman for those wary of limitations such as have been negotiated in the SALT treaties, and of the detente generally.[9]

Mr Reagan's tactical need for an anti-detente banner in the fight for the presidential nomination was even clearer. His natural constituency was on the far right of the Republican party and, as Barry Goldwater's campaign had shown earlier, that territory alone was not large enough to produce anything but electoral disaster. There were not many domestic issues on which he could outbid President Ford for the Republican faithful. But the Nixon–Kissinger foreign policy, as accepted and sustained by Ford, did genuinely represent a large deviation from Republican tradition. So it was logical to concentrate his fire there: against the proposed Panama treaty, the abortive rapprochement with Cuba, and above all the detente with Russia. One point of interest here is to note that earlier right-wing Republican Californian politicians, Senator William Knowland for instance, might have been much more ardent against the detente with China. The relative playing-down of any such *motif* in Mr Reagan's campaign was among the evidence that the old China lobby was in severe decline and unlikely to offer effective opposition to a full normalization of relations with China after the election.

Anti-detente feeling, in the event, proved of course inadequate to securing either candidate the nomination, though it contributed fairly substantially to Mr Reagan's near-success. Its high-water mark as an electoral influence was to be seen on the Republican foreign-policy platform adopted in August, pointedly praising Solzhenitsyn rather than Kissinger. But even in Mr Reagan's case, it may well have been on balance an uncertain asset. While it recommended him to the right of the party, it also contributed to the assumption, reflected in many editorials, that his would be a dangerous and unpredictable hand in crisis-management from the White House. The Republicans had ultimately to rely for their hopes of success on an image of reassurance and predictability, not of adventure, and it secured them at least a close presidential result through Mr Ford's candidature.

That account of the tactical political reasons why the anti-detente banner seemed potentially useful to Senator Jackson and Mr Reagan should not be taken as necessarily indicating doubt of their preoccupation with the actual strategic balance between the Soviet Union and the U.S.A. But we may see this issue in a form less alloyed by assumed political interest by looking at the involvement of Dr Schlesinger in the arguments. The obvious differences between him and Dr Kissinger in the period of the SALT I and SALT II treaties must be related to their specific professional preoccupations, with the balance of *power* and the balance of *forces* respectively. The balance of forces constitutes a large element in the balance of power, and undeniably some military opinion has been inclined to confuse the two. I would not attribute any such tendency to Dr Schlesinger, but he had to speak for his constituency, the Pentagon, and reflect its arguments. On the other hand, economic and diplomatic leverage, and power over opinion, are vital elements in the larger balance (the balance of power), especially if one is preoccupied with using it in the service of building a concert of powers, as in Dr Kissinger's case. There is no evidence of any major differences between Kissinger and Schlesinger over the basic proposition that a stable balance of power is the necessary infrastructure of detente, or over the proposition that detente may be a useful stratagem in the management of adversary power. Schlesinger's final speech to Pentagon staff outlined his essential position on this point: 'Whether we are successful in pursuing detente or we hedge against the possible failure of detente, a military balance remains necessary. Though we should pursue detente – vigorously – we should pursue it without illusion. Detente rests upon an underlying equilibrium of force, the maintenance of a military balance.'[10] There was nothing in this incompatible with Kissinger's views. There was however an underlying intellectual difference of emphasis, in that Kissinger has been concerned with arms-control measures as they affect diplomatic relations in general, and Schlesinger with them as they might affect the prospective balance of forces at a defined period, as much as five or ten years ahead. One might say that the secretary of state must be oriented to *preventing* the battle, and the secretary of defense to winning it if it should, nevertheless, take place. In this each was speaking for his constituency, and this conscious division of labour, given a strong and capable president to adjudicate between them, could have continued to be productive. But Mr Ford was not well suited to such a role, since he had no electoral mandate, and in intellectual powers appeared no match for either of his lieutenants. As he found discomfort in trying to run them in tandem, he had to make a choice. Dr Schlesinger, though the more popular with the right wing of the Republican party (and right-wing Democrats like Senator Jackson), was considerably at odds with Congress at the time over the arms budget, and not necessarily an asset in the 1976 election, whereas Dr Kissinger seemed still likely to be.

Whatever the personal elements and political ambitions behind the episode (which involved others than Schlesinger and Kissinger), it illuminated what one might call the almost necessary clash between the professional military and their allies (among whom one would normally classify secretaries of defense) and the overall policy-maker, in this case probably Kissinger rather than Ford. Military men are not necessarily militarists, in the usual pejorative sense of that word: that is, persons excessively apt to believe that military action is the right solution to political problems, or eager for military adventures. Historically, in looking at crises, one quite often finds the Chiefs of Staff more sceptical of the case for military action than the civilians, more cautious of commitment, more conscious of the limitations of their forces. On the other hand, it is the professional tendency, and no doubt the professional duty, of the military to make a 'worst case' analysis of any given situation: that is, to make contingency plans for the worst outcome their respective societies may have to face, rather than the most probable, much less the most favourable.

As regards detente, the 'worst case' analysis requires planning for the situation of its breaking down, into either resumed cold war or actual hostilities. I would assume that the professional need to make plans for this contingency is present among Chiefs of Staff and defence ministers of all of the powers with which we are concerned, though the process is only open to inspection in the West. In the case of China there was nevertheless a very dramatic illustration of a plausibly parallel process in the sudden fall of the then Chinese Defence Minister, Lin Piao, just after the beginning of the America–China detente. Lin, who had been until then Mao's heir-apparent, fell from favour and was killed fleeing towards the Soviet Union by air, along with the air force Chief of Staff and the other high military planners, in September 1971, a few weeks after Dr Kissinger's first visit to Peking. The usual Western interpretation of this episode is that Lin and his party represented a faction of the military who were opposed to the stratagem of detente with the United States, and favoured rather a detente with the Soviet Union, as the more immediately dangerous of China's two enemies. Some analysts maintain rather that he was concerned with the air force budget, and averse to detente with both potential adversaries. If either of these Western interpretations is sound, the episode represented a level of resistance to detente that would make the efforts of defence ministers and 'top brass' in the West and the Soviet Union pale into insignificance, but there were obviously factors of domestic policy and party rivalry involved as well. It may seem rather far-fetched to propose a parallel between the fall (temporary) of Dr Schlesinger and the fall (much more permanent) of Lin Piao, but in each case we have a defence minister who apparently argued his strategic misgivings too long against the judgement of his political chief. No such instance was demonstrable in the case of the Soviet military planners, and in one respect it might be argued that they had better reasons for acquiescing in the detente, and less reason for resisting it, than their Western equivalents. This is, to oversimplify, that the major restriction on Soviet military capacity was the low general productivity of the Soviet economy, and that the 'import-led growth' hoped for from the import of Western technologies, in expanding general Soviet economic capacity, would expand its capacity to produce military goods among others. This is a factor in the Soviet and to a lesser extent the Chinese situations that has no precise equivalent in the American case. On the other hand, the benefits from this source to the Soviet military are distant and theoretical, whereas the restrictions on missile-forces growth, for instance, may be immediate and practical. If one thinks of the difference between strategic and tactical interests as bound up with planning for the longer and shorter term, one might say they have strategic reasons for welcoming the economic advantages assumed to lie in detente, but tactical reasons for resisting, for instance, a SALT agreement that might affect the prospects of the 'Backfire' bomber or other weapon systems.

There is thus a case for saying with respect to both sides that a detente *without* arms-control measures may be much easier to sustain than a detente *with* arms control, because it is this small strategic heart of the relationship that creates its most powerful enemies, rather than the economic rapprochement or the diplomatic junketings. Furthermore, once arms-control agreements are signed, the rumour or the reality of their being breached, even in rather insignificant ways, has very explosive implications for the detente relationship as a whole. One would not wish the effort at arms control abandoned, no matter how many enemies it may create, but if it came to a choice between sacrificing the prospect of new arms-control measures or sacrificing the detente as a whole, there would clearly be a case for the former.

The most dangerous enemies of the detente are, however, not those who differ on the technicalities of trade-offs between weapon systems, or the importance of a few percentage points up or down for arms budgets. They are those who expect too much of it, either from a right-wing or a left-wing stance. On the right, excess expectation runs to an assumption, or at any rate an argument, that the Russians can and should be made to pay for detente by a remodelling of their entire behaviour, international and domestic: that they can be made to refrain from competing in areas whose future is ambiguous, like Angola, to relax their grip on their buffer-zone in Eastern Europe, and to behave with more liberalism towards their own citizenry, all for the sake of detente. No doubt all these things are desirable, and not just from a Western point of view. But from the point of view of the Soviet political elite it might seem less dangerous and embarrassing simply to return to the full cold war, and that might logically be their preferred option if the bargain were presented solely on those terms. On the left, excess expectation assumes that in a detente situation the normal modes of conserving the Western power base can and should be neglected or abandoned: that arms budgets should be cut, the capacity for covert operations dismantled and in general the security necessities of international politics disregarded. These are, in my view, equal and opposite errors. They confuse a strategy with the end towards which it is directed. Detente does not mean that the power contest has ended: it only proposes a mode by which it may be made less dangerous and pointed in a more creative direction.

CHAPTER 12

A Balance of Ambivalences

The survival of detente as an American strategy seemed very doubtful on a good many occasions during the eight years of the Republican administration, yet after the 1976 electoral battle had been decided, the moment did not seem to have arrived for writing its obituary, regretfully or otherwise. The omens were ambivalent: a new lease of life in the new administration, or an erosion into insignificance. In missile systems, a demonstrated sturdiness under test is the main indicator of 'survivability', and by that criterion detente seemed still to have a future. It had seen out the Middle East War, the American defeat in Indo-China, the Portuguese revolution, the Angola crisis, the Spanish succession, the Italian elections, the ignominious dismissal from power of its original sponsor, Mr Nixon, the assorted attacks from intellectual opinion (both left and right) on its chief architect and manager, Dr Kissinger, the storms within Nato, the polemics of the Chinese, the eloquence of Solzhenitsyn, the presidential campaigns of Senator Jackson and Mr Reagan, and a variety of other dangers and assaults. If in early 1977 it appeared somewhat paralysed by recent batterings, there were nevertheless indications that such paralysis might (with care) prove temporary.

Of all these reprieves from threatened extinction, the most significant for the long term may prove to be that represented by the defeat in Indo-China. From the point of view of crisis-management within the central balance, the most dangerous moment must be the one at which a dominant power is faced with a fair-sized defeat, since there must be uncertainty as to whether that power will be able to accept the setback or will resort to general war. This doubt existed rather more as regards the United States than as regards the Soviet Union or China, since defeat has played little part in American historical experience, in contrast to that of the other two powers. Indeed, one may say that the prolongation of the American anguish in Vietnam arose from the fact that neither Kennedy nor Johnson nor even Nixon was prepared to be the first president under whose aegis the country must experience the bitter taste of undisguised defeat. History so arranged matters that in fact President Ford had practically no decision to take, nor power to act at the time, given his weakness vis-à-vis Congress. But the comparative placidity with which the country accepted the defeat – positively with a shrug of indifference it seemed to me, in Washington during the final debacle – makes one wonder how much basis the previous agonizing about the impossibility of such acceptance ever had. And while one would not wish America to cultivate too much proclivity towards a placid acceptance of defeat, a certain minimum of such resignation – a spirit of 'you can't win 'em all' – is obviously necessary on the part of the Powers of the central balance if the detente is to have prospects of long-term survival. For crises will continue to arise during any such detente, as they already have; they will be more or less adroitly managed; their outcomes will redound more or less to the damage or benefit of one or other of the three (or perhaps ultimately five or more) chief actors in the central drama. It is undoubtedly a major advantage of Leninist states like China and the Soviet Union that their doctrines allow for equable acceptance of this pattern of diplomatic life. If you lose one round of the diplomatic battle (or for that matter if you win) it is simply, to a good Leninist, a signal to prepare for the next. I would tend to argue that this attitude is not only a strength to them (one that the West ought also to cultivate) but a factor making for the stability of the system. One might compare them to the bare-knuckle fighters of pugilism in the days before the Marquess of Queensberry rules, when the fight might persist beyond a hundred rounds, and a necessary element in the combatant's art was the determination not to commit too much of his resources in any one round. Acceptance of the near-permanence of conflict is a disincentive to pushing conclusions too far in any particular crisis. That may prove important in the two recent and prospective succession crises, China and Yugoslavia, which may in due course severely test the capacity of the Powers to take long views and exercise restraint when large changes in the balance appear threatened or promised.

The detente has already, of course, survived an earlier succession crisis in the downfall of Mr Nixon, but in that case Dr Kissinger was present to maintain the element of continuity, and the world balance was not at stake, only the possible future of a particular strategy. To concentrate attention on succession crises may seem to imply that the element of personal policy – the particular views of individual decision-makers – is especially important in detente, and it may be asked why this should be so, since for all three Powers the detente may, as the Russians say, 'correspond to objective reality'. But as always, those are objective realities as assessed by a particular mind, and in fact there *is* a reason why the personal element is likely to be larger in detente diplomacy than in some other aspects of policy. I argued earlier that detente is to be seen chiefly as a strategy for the management of adversary power, and I have maintained that this is its primary function for the decision-makers of China and the Soviet Union as well as the United States. But it is one of the characteristics of strategies (as against interests or objectives or value judgements) that even those who come from within the same system, and would in general have almost identical views about interests and objectives and value judgements, might differ quite sharply about the probability of success for a strategy. One may illustrate this by the persons of Dr Kissinger and Dr Schlesinger, who came out of the same kind of family and educational background (German-Jewish families settled in America, and Harvard in the 1950s) and possessed similar intellectual experience and equipment, and had access to precisely the same intelligence assessments. It would be unconvincing to argue that they differed much about interests, objectives, values or threats, but it would not be surprising that they should differ, as they obviously did, about some aspects of detente, since it is the kind of intellectual construct in which, even with precisely the same information, differences of temperament produce differences of calculation. And one must suppose that the same kind of analysis would hold good for Russian and Chinese decision-makers, if one knew as much about the personalities involved as in the American case. Thus it is not unreasonable to maintain that succession crises, which change individual policy-makers, even coming in the constitutional form as with the Americans, or a quasi-constitutional one as now with the Russians, must be of major significance.

The case of Yugoslavia is somewhat different, in that what is at issue there is not just a choice among strategies on the part of the successor decision-makers as they emerge, but the estimates by policy-makers in the United States and the Soviet Union of what the chances and changes mean to the power bases of their own respective systems. It is obvious that either Power could come out of the two succession crises either a large net winner or a large net loser, in terms of the balance in central Europe and the Mediterranean and in Asia.

At the time of writing, not long after Mao's death and with Tito reported from time to time to be suffering from assorted illnesses, the value of detente in restraining the contest for power appeared to be possibly approaching its most severe tests. There had been as yet no indication from the Chinese side that Mao's successors were more inclined to reconciliation with the Russians than Mao himself. Detente with the Soviet Union offers a *domestic* danger to China, so long as it remains Maoist, in a way detente with the Americans cannot. It offers the possibility of ideological contamination with revisionism. But even though Mao's heirs may continue to feel this as ardently as the Chairman himself did, there had been enough indication of internal differences in the purging of the 'gang of four' to produce an uneasy feeling of obscure dangers, such as also appear inherent in the analogous situation after Tito.

There was a mild variant of the same problem of potential change in the balance of power in the cases of Portugal and Italy. Given that detente supposes the acceptance of a *modus vivendi* with a significant power whose political values you dislike and think ultimately threatening to your own (which is the case for Russia and China as well as America), does the fact of that acceptance undermine your reasons for resisting the establishment of those political values elsewhere, in less powerful countries? Does the fact that you have decided that you can, after all, live with a communist great power in Peking mean that you can have no logical base for resisting a communist small power in Saigon? Does the fact that you have decided you can live comfortably enough with a communist super-power in Moscow mean that you should logically be indifferent to a Moscow-oriented party in government in Lisbon or Rome?

This may be the recurring policy problem of the forthcoming period of detente, if it survives through to the eighties. For there is an implied statement by the central balance powers to each other in the present phase: 'I can live with you on your present power-base: I can even tolerate marginal increases, perhaps. But we must agree together against *radical* changes in the power balance between us, for if they changed to the degree to which I felt the threat to myself seriously increased, I should be obliged to reconsider my strategy.'

The field in which fast and radical change in the power balance is most plausible is the field of strategic arms, and the conventions to govern that field of potential change are being worked out. But the other field in which fast change in the power base of the two alliances is also possible is the gain or loss of allies and fellow-travellers. There are as yet no agreed conventions to guide action in this field. It is the most urgent area of intellectual endeavour for the policy-makers concerned. But it will be a very difficult and delicate one, because the principle reason why allies are lost (or come to be assumed lost) are sudden domestic political mutations, by revolutionary means, as in Portugal (and conceivably elsewhere), or by parliamentary means, as potentially in Italy or even France. Thus the prevention of instability in the international balance may seem to impose limits on 'legitimate' change, even by legitimate means, in domestic political complexions. It is the contemporary version of Metternich's dilemma, and must carry temptations for U.S. policy-makers to subvert the popular will in a left-inclining ally by covert and illegitimate means.

The heart of the problem for Western policy-makers has been the cold war assumption that a domestic success for communism is equivalent to an increase in the power base of the Soviet Union, and should be read as such in strategic calculations. But even the most extreme right-wing opinion would, I think, now concede that this is not necessarily the case. The 1949 domestic success of communism in China, which appeared at the time as the most radical swing of the balance in favour of the Soviet Union in the entire period since 1917 (and was described as such by Soviet policy-makers as late as 1954), is now very clearly the origin of the essential strategic dilemma of the Soviet Union, the fact that it could face a two-front war and has to ration out its military resources between the requirements of its Far Eastern frontier and the garrisoning of its restive allies on the Central Front in Europe. Moreover, if one looks back at the original Yugoslav situation of 1945-7, the communist success in that country also was originally interpreted as an enormous swing of the strategic balance to the Soviet Union, bringing Russian forces right to the Mediterranean and the Adriatic. Yet in fact it has been precisely the existence of an independent communist Yugoslavia that has kept Soviet power out of this area and prevented it from consolidating itself in the Balkans generally, even permitting the little Chinese-allied enclave of Albania to survive.

So, looking at these two case studies, one might say that Russian decision-makers have uncommonly good reasons to be doubtful of the benefits to themselves of the success of communist parties in areas that they cannot directly control and garrison with Russian troops, as for instance Portugal and Italy. Conversely, Western decision-makers can certainly say, looking at China and Yugoslavia, that these two countries have proved, despite their communist complexions, very useful strategic fellow-travellers of the Western powers in view of the common need of all three – the West, the Chinese and the Yugoslavs – to contain Soviet military power and offset its growth where possible. And this interest will certainly remain vividly present to Western minds as they react to any adventurism or opportunism in the two cases.

Thus, if one is thinking of the nature and function of Nato over a long period of detente, it could prospectively be defined, at least in policy-makers' minds, not as an alliance against *communist* power (since Yugoslavia and China must be regarded as potential co-belligerents) but as a precautionary coalition to inhibit possible Soviet military adventurism. Yet inescapably it still has overtones of missionary anti-communism, the official cold war ideology attached to its origins. It is difficult to envisage a time, at least in the near future, when a government including communist participation, for instance in Italy, would not be regarded as possibly a Trojan horse within the Nato camp. And it is almost impossible to see right-wing Republican congressmen tolerating for long a situation in which American servicemen were stationed in Europe to protect communist-dominated governments against potential attack by a communist great power. Thus European voters are obliged to weigh any domestic political advantage they see as stemming from communists in government against the benefits of the American protectorate. Anything gained in political efficiency at home has to be assessed against losses arising from damage to the painfully achieved stability of the central balance.

When the problem arose with regard to Italy in 1976, the American and West European signals intended to discourage participation by the Communist party in the Italian government were in effect successful, though resented. Possibly the success owed as much to the Italian Communist party itself as to the Christian Democrats: an American election year would have been an ill-considered one for trying the experiment, since many of the American opponents of detente had campaigned against it on the basis that it made West European communist parties look more respectable. Seeing that assumed threat apparently substantiated in Italy might have been the last straw for some wavering American liberals. The success of the American signals of 1976 postponed the problem, which was probably all that could have been done at the time, but leaves it for future solution.

(Incidentally, if Nato is defined as a counterweight to *Soviet* power rather than to *communist* power, there arises the issue of whether it should exercise this function only for Europe or for the world balance in general. From a Chinese point of view, the latter would be the more useful since Europe is not the most likely area of contest. But the European members of Nato have tended strongly to resist any extension of its concerns beyond the actual European area, even to a region as vital to Europe's own survival as the Middle East. The present Chinese wooing of Europe, the fervently expressed concern for its interests vis-à-vis the Soviet Union, seems intended to modify this European parochialism.)

If one had to construct a general defence of detente as a strategy to forward the interests of the West, it might be done on the basis of comparing the overall situation of the Western camp 'before and after using', as the advertisers say, contrasting the situations at the end of 1968 and the end of 1976. In late 1968 the United States seemed to be politically shaking itself to pieces as a consequence of its unwinnable war in Asia, and diplomatically alienating both its Western allies and Third World neutrals in the process. Its relations with China had hardly moved from the rut of pointless hostility in which they had been stuck since 1949. Its relations with the Soviet Union were also quite bad at this point, in the aftermath of the Soviet invasion of Czechoslovakia. Western Europe was tense, jittery, disillusioned and resentful of American inaction in that episode. Eastern Europe was in a state of trauma. No significant move had been made towards the control of either nuclear or conventional armaments. The two Iberian dictatorships were wearing out with their incumbents' lives, and the succession process in either seemed to offer formidable prospective dangers for Western strategic interests or even for the general peace. The Middle East appeared as far from any kind of settlement as it had been for twenty years, and the Arab world seemed positively eager for the status of a Soviet protectorate. Latin America was on a rising tide of anti-American sentiment and apparently strong revolutionary prospects. Japan was caught in a crunch between the need for some rapprochement with China and an inability to move until the Americans did. The political temperature in southern Africa was simmering up towards the point at which it would sustain a race war in which the Western powers would become involved with the fate of their delinquent fellow-travellers in Rhodesia and South Africa.

Eight years of a strategy of detente saw change in every element in that situation, and in each case to the net advantage of the Western camp. It eased the process of American disinvolvement from Vietnam, both in the treaty negotiations and the final American acceptance of the end. The change in the relationship with China, from apparently interminable hostility to something like the status of potential co-belligerent, was made at astonishingly little cost: not even full sacrifice of the connection with Taiwan. The relationship with Russia has been 'mutated' to a degree that has made significant co-operation in crisis-management possible, and has brought the beginning of control of armaments (nuclear and conventional) at least into distant prospect. The Middle East is not only closer to an overall settlement than it has been since 1948, it has been astonishingly converted from an area of Soviet diplomatic paramountcy to an area of American diplomatic paramountcy – and with Soviet acquiescence, all in the name of detente. Latin America has seen some harsh enough manoeuvres, but a measure of detente has been accomplished over Panama and (after setbacks) is being tried again on Cuba. The succession crises in Portugal and Spain have been survived with results surprisingly satisfactory to the West. Southern Africa has at least been manoeuvred towards a course that seems to hold some prospect that the great race war (which had earlier seemed inevitable) might with luck be avoided, and that its relations with the West might be reconstructed. Japan's difficulties in reconciling her economic and diplomatic situation as a member of the advanced capitalist club and an American fellow-traveller with her cultural and political need to be on good terms with China had been greatly eased.

These seem very substantial gains for the Western camp, but one might regard them with doubt if they had been secured at undue cost, either in power advantage to the Russians or in moral terms. Looking at the plane of *realpolitik* first, no such excess costs can be demonstrated. The arms-control agreements do little to prevent America maintaining its still considerable edge, in warhead numbers, in accuracy, in invulnerability and in general technological sophistication for its nuclear strike-force. On the Central Front in Nato, Western forces and the American contingent within them have actually *increased* and been given a higher proportion of combat troops in the past few years. The Mansfield amendment, which used to seem so threatening to their stability, appears to have been successfully robbed of steam: it was not even presented in 1976. The American army has been brought back up to strength and repaired in morale after the damage of Vietnam. The German army has grown formidable in numbers and equipment for the first time since 1945. To speak, as Nato officials often find it convenient to do, as if a cut in the armed forces of Denmark or the Netherlands was a serious offset to these larger gains is an exercise in public relations rather than military analysis. Soviet naval forces, it is true, have made a marked advance in strength, and the once-unchallenged ascendancy of the West in that particular form of power has been lost, unless the Western allies decide on a drive to retrieve it. But even here the change is not as dramatic as ship numbers can be made apparently to show.[1] The balance of forces is complex and asymmetrical, with Western advantage in some fields and theatres, and Soviet advantage in others. But as *The Military Balance* for 1976–7 pointed out, it was still of a nature to make aggression unattractive.[2] And provided the balance of *forces* does that, the larger balance of *power*, of which it is part, will favour the West, since its economic productivity and intellectual vitality remain the stronger.

It is not surprising that Western defence analysts should regard as sinister the Soviet failure to cut arms spending, and ask for what reason it continues to improve its military capabilities, despite the climate of detente. Such capabilities must inevitably be construed as signalling a hope of ultimately effecting the 'Finlandization' of Western Europe, by some mixture of overweening military power and diplomatic or political manoeuvre. It is not necessary to doubt that there are long-term strategic planners in the Kremlin inspired by such a happy ideological vision, but even if one is prepared to assume that this is what they are planning, that does not mean it need happen. Western Europe is not actually much like Finland: one might as well argue that because a boaconstrictor will readily swallow a squirrel it can be regarded as successfully rehearsing to swallow a Clydesdale.

There are possible explanations other than imperialist ambition for the size of the Soviet military establishments. Firstly, the three most formidable forces that the Russians must take into account in contingency planning have all increased their capabilities lately: the Americans in being no longer obliged to divert their resources to Vietnam, the Germans in at last resuming their old levels of military efficiency, and the Chinese in acquiring some nuclear muscle. Secondly, the officer corps is one of the most powerful lobbies within the Soviet political apparatus. Its resentments against Mr Khrushchev, for instance, seem to have played a large part in his fall. And a powerful officers' lobby is in a good position to demand and secure funds for its professional pride, advanced weapon systems. This seems to be particularly the case with the naval forces: Western admirals when sounding the alarm on this matter tend to speak with wistful admiration of the success of Admiral Gorschkov, a disciple of Mahan in geopolitical theory, whom they see as a pressure-group in himself. Pressures from the military have similar effects in most political systems, of course, but in the Soviet Union the armed forces have not much competition from other lobbies.

Despite the economic distress of the capitalist camp in 1974-6, the Russian policy-makers as they contemplated the overall changes in the world since 1969 were not much entitled to feel full satisfaction at the turn of events. They had to see as a possible contingency a two-front war, and the formidable power and ideological competitor on their Eastern frontier, China, had done well enough diplomatically since 1969. In 1967-8, at the height of the Cultural Revolution, it seemed to have not a friend or ally in the world save Albania. By 1976 it was on improved, almost cordial, terms with the United States and Japan; it had established diplomatic relations and influence in most of South East Asia; it was cultivating Western Europe as a natural and vital strategic ally. It was working hard in the Third World, despite setbacks in Africa, and competing ideologically with the Soviet Union in left politics everywhere. Moreover, on Russia's Western front the Europeans, recovering from the distresses of recession, were again asserting their economic elan by 1976 and continuing to attract the wistful regard of Eastern Europe. The Helsinki declaration, which Moscow had worked long and hard to secure, had entirely backfired against them, and far from legitimizing their situation in Eastern Europe or their repression at home, was providing extra weapons to the East Europeans in their subdued struggle for autonomy, and even to the Russian dissidents in their rising demand for human rights. In the Middle East, twenty years of cultivation of the Egyptians and 3,000 million dollars of Russian armaments had brought, by 1976, neither real military success, nor firm bases, nor secure diplomatic influence. And for all its super-power status, the Soviet government was likely to remain in many years (as in 1975) dependent on America for the very grain to feed its peoples.

This was a situation of some overall vulnerability, and as I have argued earlier, detente policies have in general in the Russian case seemed to reflect periods of conscious vulnerability. In Mr Malenkov's time the sense of vulnerability arose partly from domestic jockeying for power after Stalin's death; in Mr Khrushchev's time partly from a sudden dismayed realization of how very uncomfortable an ally China was; in Mr Brezhnev's time

A Balance of Ambivalences

apparently mostly from economic deficiencies. Economic dependence on the West, such as seemed to be increasing in 1975–6, could hardly reduce either the feeling or the actuality of such vulnerability and it thus helped to maintain the Russian case for persisting with detente policies.

The economics of detente, as against its diplomacy, is a subject clearly requiring more exploration than it can be accorded here, especially as I am not an economist. By early 1977 the level of Soviet-bloc indebtedness was estimated at $45,800 million, a striking indication of how much more rapidly communist economies became dependent on Western sources of supply than the reverse.[3] No doubt the goods supplied, insofar as they contributed to the general strength of these economies, also contributed to their military capabilities, and that is a consideration that must be taken into account in any general assessment of the pros and cons of detente. But even if it is conceded that the exchange provided more *economic* benefit to the Eastern side of the balance than the Western, that does not make a conclusive case against detente. One would have to measure whatever increased military capability was held to accrue to the Soviet bloc against the reduced motivation to adventurism, in a situation in which the West had become a crucial economic partner, remembering also that East European relations with the Soviet Union were considerably altered by the development, as was quite visible by early 1977. There is always a sense in which arguments against economic ties offer part of the truth, but to follow their logic fully would require a version of the 'no-trading-with-the-enemy' prohibition to be extended from war to peace. The process of economic exchange involves a complex set of 'pay-offs', in which any ascription of costless benefit to Soviet strength is quite misleading. The obvious case is that of the American grain sales, running in 1975 at about 20 million tons. One way of looking at this trade was that it represented 'feeding the enemy': the other way of looking at it was that permitting or even encouraging the Russians to acquire dependence on American supplies in this fashion created what might one day prove an immensely useful economic–diplomatic lever in American hands, exactly as a similar Western dependence on Arab oil put a very powerful economic–diplomatic lever into Arab hands. Certainly the economic relationship that had grown by 1977 made the Russians a lot more vulnerable than the Americans if there should ever be a case for economic warfare.[4] But that was shot that had to be kept in the locker for a really serious threat to the balance of power, as over China or Yugoslavia.

The assorted embargoes of the Cold War period, the 'Cocom' and 'Chicom' lists, did not effectively inhibit the growth of either Russian or Chinese military power. They motivated the search for autarky or for alternative sources of supply, and a general forced march towards industrialization and self-sufficiency. A siege situation, either for Russia or China, also served in itself as a justification for political repression at home, a sort of ideological spur to the Party *apparatchiki* and a rationalization of oppression for the people generally. Besides, such economic policies tend to carry the quality of self-fulfilling prophecy. If economic relations between great powers are geared wholly to the expectation of hostilities between them, neither side will be conscious of having much to lose by the actual outbreak of hostilities, at least in that respect. The defences of peace are thereby weakened, for both parties.

It is often argued by those who are suspicious of detente but not wishful to proclaim the virtues of renewed cold war that a third way might be found, intermediate between the two: the version of 'peaceful engagement' formulated by Professor Brzezinski for instance.[5] No doubt other strategies than cold war or detente are possible in the continuing contests of the central balance, but there is one measure to which all of them must be related: the level of tension between each pair of potential adversaries. If the figure 100 is assigned to the level of tension that will produce actual central war, then the figure 70 might be used to denote the characteristic tension-level of cold war and 50 to denote the characteristic tension-level of detente. On such accounts as have been published, one would say that 'peaceful engagement' in actual operation would hardly differ in tension-level from cold war, but even if one assumes that it would fall midway between that and detente (assigning the figure 60), it is not clear precisely what advantages this change would confer on the West. There may be a case for a cold war strategy when tension is necessary to put an alliance together or re-arm it, but the American alliance system was in good repair in 1977 and very massively armed. A detente strategy may 'pay off' in various ways, as this book has hoped to show, once the balance of power coalition is constructed and armed. The zone between the two strategies, presumably a chilly diplomatic correctness without cordiality, does not seem to offer the benefits of either. Middle ways are not always best: there is a case for hot coffee and a case for iced coffee but practically none for lukewarm coffee.

The most influential arguments that can be (and are) made from within the policy apparatus against detente as a strategy are those made by the military and their allies: that it tends towards the cutting of arms budgets in the Western world but apparently has no such effect within the adversary world, either because the military lobby is too strong, or because the political leaderships are imbued with military concepts to a much greater degree than in the West, where the political leadership is (and in the nature of electoral systems always must be) oriented towards welfare or 'consumerism'. And, these arguments go on, only a high degree of international tension can effect the redirection of Western leaders and electorates from this normal state to such a sense of threat as will cause them to sustain arms budgets adequate to maintain even equivalency (much less superiority) with the chief adversary. This is partly a case against arms-control measures as in SALT and MBFR, but that is rather a secondary issue, since any such restrictions are, by definition, controlled, and have not as yet shown much sign of reducing the level of arms spending, though they have probably inhibited its potential rise. (That is, the arms budgets of both sides are less high than they might have been without arms control, in that ABM systems have been almost dispensed with, but the case for other new systems like Trident and B1 and cruise missiles is in some ways actually improved by arms-control agreements. If quantities are limited, a qualitative edge becomes demonstrably more valuable.) The other military objection to detente is on the basis of an assumption about its psychological effect in the West. The threat is real, they argue, and in a situation of real threat, tension is valuable: functional, not dysfunctional. It is what keeps the system on the *qui vive* to meet the attack, a sort of political adrenalin.

There is enough substance to these arguments to justify the view that the cutting of arms budgets ought not to be stressed as a probable outcome of detente. Arms spending is required for the balance of power infrastructure on which detente rests, and without which it might produce results indistinguishable from those of appeasement, even though the latter had a very different intellectual origin. Arms budgets have to be seen as an irksome but not entirely unproductive allocation of resources towards keeping the dry-rot out of the foundations of the structure, on which its more creative possibilities depend. This line of argument has the merit not only of being realistic, but of placating what might otherwise prove the most dangerous group of enemies of detente, on either side of the balance. Defence establishments, whether in Russia or the West, do not necessarily need wars: they do need careers and weapon systems and research grants. It is hardly surprising that the officers' lobbies should resist a diplomatic strategy thought likely to snatch these *desiderata* away from them.

A further main anxiety about detente felt inside the Western foreign-policy elite has been lest it should damage the alliance system. But this has not proved the case, except for a time on the East Mediterranean fringe of Nato. The central structure, which depends on the political relationship between America, Germany and Britain, seemed in late 1976 less than normally plagued by dissension.[6] Something had been done about the self-inflicted wound of the competition in Nato weapon systems. The offset-costs controversy had dwindled with changes in the payments balance between Germany and the U.S.A. Portugal had been restored to full membership of the alliance and Spain seemed likely to be recruited within two or three years. Turkey had been somewhat mollified, and Greece appeared unlikely to

A Balance of Ambivalences

see advantage in departing while Turkey remained a beneficiary of Nato armaments. Mediterranean operations were still embarrassed by the conflict over Cyprus and the uncertainties of Italy's political future, but there had been gain through American relations with Egypt. French defence policy, in all but name and formalities, appeared conformable with Nato hopes. President Giscard d'Estaing had moved a long distance from Gaullist defence concepts, though it would not have been politically tactful for him to admit as much. His reduced emphasis on the *force de frappe*, a chief instrument of French rivalry with the United States, and concentration instead on conventional forces, were entirely in line with Nato's hopes, as was French fleet build-up in the Mediterranean, the rise in French arms budgets, and the strategic concepts outlined by the French Chief of Staff, which envisaged using French forces on the Nato forward line in the event of hostilities (even though there is no political commitment). All in all, the military structure of Nato and the Western balance of forces with the Warsaw Pact appeared at least as sound as they had been, on average, during the Cold War years.

If any case could be sustained that a detente strategy had proved detrimental to the cohesiveness of the Nato alliance, the implication would be that a return to a cold war strategy, if feasible, would be desirable. Such a return would certainly be in the simplest sense feasible. Despite what Mr Brezhnev has said about his hopes that the detente could be made irreversible, it is difficult to see what that phrase could in practice ever mean. The Powers will choose their strategies, as they historically have done, in accordance with their concepts of the state of the balance of power, the requirements of the national interest, and the imminence of threat. If judgements by the political elites concerned on these points required it, a return to cold war levels of tension could readily be contrived within three months. It would only be necessary to suspend the SALT and MBFR negotiations, cancel any impending East–West meetings, arrange difficulties in the flow of economic exchange, especially any existing grain deal, hire speechwriters with a good command of ideological rhetoric for the U.S. president, and perhaps organize a few incidents on the borders or on the Berlin autobahn. But it is difficult to see what advantage could come of the decision to follow such a strategy. The Russians would hardly see it as a reason for cutting their arms budgets, or allowing more liberty to their own people, or more freedom of emigration for those who wanted to leave, or more autonomy to the governments of Eastern Europe. Nor would they necessarily be deterred from manoeuvring for advantage in places like Angola or the Horn of Africa. There would even be a certain logic for them in stepping up the contest on the periphery in order to absorb attention that would otherwise be focused on more vital areas. Nor, and this is a major point, would such a strategy in the least suit any of the chief U.S. allies, or reinforce the cohesion and effectiveness of the military coalition. Both President Giscard and Chancellor Schmidt emphasized in mid-1976 their continued estimates that detente was useful to their respective national societies as well as to the prospects of peace: Giscard remarking cryptically that among the European powers only France could 'authenticate' the detente, because only France had an independent foreign policy.[7] Britain and Italy would obviously be even less likely to see anything but economic and political embarrassment in such a turn of events, and the same is doubly true for the smaller members of Nato, and for Japan.

If we conclude on this evidence that the case on the power–political plane against detente is not strong, ought we to concede, however, that the moral case against it is more convincing? This case has mostly been based on the charge that it abandoned to Soviet mercies the peoples of Eastern Europe, whose freedom ought to be a matter of brotherly concern for the West. Here again the charge seemed to rest on false assumptions. Insofar as Eastern Europe had been resigned into the effective hegemony of the Soviet Union, it happened in 1944–5 through military necessity, not in 1969 or 1975. It depended on the balance of forces, not any declaration like Helsinki. The fact that the West could not or would not use anything in the way of direct military or political pressure to break that hegemony was reaffirmed in 1953, 1956 and

1968, all within the Cold War period. The Cold War was fought by the West to hold what it had, not to roll back the Soviet sphere of power. In the detente period, Western policy-makers merely drew the logical moral from the earlier inaction: that if you are not prepared to pay the costs of a policy of liberation, you might as well admit the fact (which is what Helsinki did) and see what can be done in the way of amelioration of circumstances, given the existing realities of power. The prospect that this might do rather better than the Cold War to promote the interests of the peoples of Eastern Europe, at least in a mild and gradual way and over a considerable span of time, appeared quite plausible, especially in the light of the communist summit meeting of July 1976. The Soviet leaders had considerable difficulty, over a period of two years, in arranging that meeting, and got singularly little from it for their pains. The main heroes of the occasion were Marshal Tito, for whom it appeared to provide a vindication of his thirty years defiance of Soviet pressures against his independence, and Enrico Berlinguer, the Italian leader, who represented an even more dangerous model for East European communists, since his situation could hardly be contemplated without reflecting that the protection of Nato would be as essential to Italy and Yugoslavia if Berlinguer were in power as while he was out of it. One of the items of 'conventional wisdom' characteristically used against detente by conservative policy-makers has been the old parable about the wind and the sun competing to make the traveller take off his coat. The wind tries, but the harder it blows the more the traveller buttons his coat up. Then the sun beams down, and the traveller is divested of his coat in no time. This parable has always been solemnly told as if only Nato powers were susceptible to the effects of diplomatic warm weather, but there were always reasons for supposing that it might be more applicable to the Warsaw Pact, not because the Russians are likely to abandon their security blanket, but because the East Europeans who have been enfolded in it against their will are emboldened to wriggle out of it as the climate becomes notably milder.

The relation between Soviet power, American power and the

ability of the East European peoples and governments to make some space for themselves to breathe more easily, remains the most dangerous area of detente diplomacy, an area in which it was almost counterproductive to define Western purposes, and miserably easy to misrepresent them, as in the debate over the alleged 'Sonnenfeldt doctrine', which Mr Reagan interpreted as 'requiring slaves to accept their slavery'. American policy appeared rather, in the phrase of a Japanese diplomat, to be 'acquiescing in the status quo in order to change the status quo'.[8]

One particular set of moral and strategic qualms against detente held with variations on both right and left may be summed up as a general charge that a detente strategy must entail a spheres of influence policy, and that the notion of spheres of influence was un-American, immoral, and deprived the West of a useful and vital instrument in the conflict with the Soviet Union. All these assumptions are dubious, especially the first. The Monroe Doctrine, almost the oldest American foreign policy 'plank', was the unilateral assertion of an American sphere of interest in Latin America. It has been maintained with relative consistency and success for more than 150 years. (One might take the view that Chile was its most recent manifestation, even without assuming that the overthrow of Allende was entirely due to C.I.A. efforts.) As to its being immoral, the manipulation of East European hopes and forces during the Cold War (as in the rumoured 'Operation Splinter Factor' in the time of Mr Dulles) was genuinely morally horrifying: nothing in the detente period is in the same league. And as for neglecting the usefulness of East European nationalism and restiveness as a source of diplomatic leverage against the Soviet Union, one would say that the conscious restraint of American policy here (at least in Dr Kissinger's time), like the conscious restraint and prudence of American policy in the use of China, demonstrated a proper sense of the degree of risk in the alternative policy. Prudence – the weighing of consequences – is a major moral value in diplomacy.

The case for detente does not rest solely on rebutting the case against it (the argument that it on balance worsens the lot of those captive in the Soviet sphere) but on the argument that it contains within itself possibilities of actual ethical progress in international life, possibilities that would vanish in a renewed cold war. These possibilities rest in part with hopes for a more rational, just and co-operative approach to the production and distribution of food and energy, the conservation of the environment, the development of the vast resources that lie beneath the oceans. That possible human future depends on the level of general diplomatic conflict being kept so low as not seriously to impede these projects, and detente is the only available strategy likely to be helpful to it. What is required is its extension from the East–West conflict to the 'North–South conflict', the conflict between the rich industrialized world and the poverty-stricken Third World, which has allied itself with the new-rich countries of Opec. This is a sphere in which the moral obligations and the power interests of the West point in the same direction, because the communist powers – China as well as the Soviet Union – have almost disqualified themselves from operating constructively in it. Neither of them, for instance, was even represented at the Energy Conference of December 1975, which brought the Western industrial world, the Opec powers and the Third World into a joint effort at solving oil and commodity problems. Nor have the communist powers done any better (save in propaganda) vis-à-vis the Third World on the politics of food. The recurrent inability of the Soviet Union even to solve its own food problems, much less help with the problems of the rest of the world, has been quite visible to the policy-makers of the countries that live intermittently on the margin of famine: the Russians and occasionally the Chinese have been damaging competitors for the surpluses produced by the efficient capitalist agricultures of North America, Australia and Western Europe.

The more generally understood part of the moral case for detente is its importance to the preservation of peace, and with it human society. It is true that the central peace was preserved also during the Cold War years, but only at the cost of two very painful local and peripheral wars, Korea and Vietnam. Moreover, the margin of safety during those years was very low: at one stage during the early 1950s the C.I.A. were allegedly refusing to predict the avoidance of central hostilities for more than five or six weeks ahead. It is inevitable that the level of risk should be greater in a high-tension strategy than in a detente strategy. Tension begets frictions, frictions beget crises, crises beget wars.

The long-term moral content of detente did not, on the evidence, preclude a certain deviousness and even machiavellianism on the tactical level in detente diplomacy. Western assumptions that the level of Western virtue was such that it would prove impossible for democratic policy-makers to match Russian manoeuvring in spheres of competitive diplomacy, such as Portugal or the Middle East or southern Africa, do not stand up to an examination of what actually happened in those areas, or indeed to examination of the past record of relative success of the C.I.A. and the K.G.B. If there was any handicap on such Western endeavours in 1974-7 it was due less to detente than to the zeal with which American congressmen and journalists were devoting themselves to investigations of the C.I.A.,[9] and that in turn came from the disenchantment with American institutions that stemmed from Watergate, which in turn derived from Vietnam, and thus from the Cold War context. Detente has been a wary, vigilant, competitive relationship so far, and is likely to remain so. As the Vietnam-Watergate trauma receded, the rehabilitation of American intelligence services, as part of the mechanism that provides the necessary inspection and checking on the other side's capacities and intentions, appeared to be in progress.

The uncertainty with which the future of detente had to be regarded in early 1977 did not stem entirely from the election campaign or events in Angola. There was also an element of what may be called 'normal pendulum swing' in the public mood. In the late sixties Americans were strongly conscious of the moral and social wounds of the Cold War: its costs, its dangers, its human damage. Among intellectuals this consciousness was strong enough to create a whole school of 'revisionist' historians, seeing the roots of most twentieth-century disasters in American imperial drives. Students were radicalized en masse, if only temporarily. A 'lost generation' of expatriates and dissenters was created. But after eight years of detente, the moral wounds of the Cold War were almost beginning to be forgotten, and the moral bruises of the detente looked rather serious for lack of comparison. The intellectual mood swung back towards nationalism and nostalgia: the political certainties and heroic moral posturing of the Cold War years perhaps began to have a sort of period charm. Possibly the loss of a determinate external enemy – or rather the loss of two of them, the Russians and the Chinese – left a sort of blank in the soul of the mass electorate, depriving people of a focus for the resentments that most lives accumulate. A political leader wanting, either for cynical or for more-or-less idealistic reasons, to revive any sort of crusading spirit vis-à-vis the external world in American foreign-policy attitudes, almost inevitably found the anti-detente banner quite a convenient one to rally the troops. It was the only one that would appeal simultaneously to elite liberalism, popular humanitarianism, ethnic resentments and party-political advantage.

If detente had failed to survive this period, an obituary written in early 1977 would still have been able to say that its life had been a useful one: it helped the world, and particularly America, off a painful hook in Vietnam, round a dangerous corner in the Middle East, through a difficult transition in Europe and perhaps in southern Africa. The central balance of power was more flexible at the end of the period than at the beginning, adjusted into a workable triangle, and with the capacity of evolving to make the basis for a larger concert of powers. The change allowed a glimpse of a prospect that the world would gain time to cope with its more fundamental problems: food, resources, human survival and betterment.

But in fact in early 1977 no pressing need for an obituary summation appeared as yet to exist. The prospects offered on the whole more continuity than change in the essential relationships, though with some variations.

Let us, therefore, return to the question with which this book opened: who gained by detente? My case, in sum, has been that a good many people did: enough, probably, to secure its prolongation. The three dominant powers each had found some betterment, though in different areas: the Americans in their powers of diplomatic manoeuvre, the Russians in their economic development, the Chinese in their strategic situation. A good many middle powers felt its advantages as well. The East Europeans, despite the many predictions that the opposite would be the case, undoubtedly managed to secure a larger sphere of autonomy vis-à-vis the Soviet Union during the detente than had been the case during the Cold War. The West Europeans found themselves able to put a sort of safety-guard round European trigger-points like Berlin, and to ease some of the larger human problems of divided Europe. Other middle powers, like Turkey or Iran, managed to use it to forward local interests, or, like Australia, to slough off outmoded policies. Small powers were perhaps less lucky: possibly a general context of high tension enables them to exact benefits from the international system, though it also subjects them to grave dangers.

The long-term viability of the detente undoubtedly, however, rests still on the decisions of policy-makers in Moscow and Washington. As to Moscow, there remained the uncertainties of the succession to Mr Brezhnev, the unpredictability of Soviet policy in the post-Tito period in Yugoslavia, and the possibility of Soviet heavy-handedness in Eastern Europe and of Soviet policy-makers pushing their luck or their allegedly 'liberation' causes in areas like southern Africa. Above all there remained the tensions generated by their assumed drive towards strategic superiority. As was pointed out earlier, the apparent balance or even the apparent *trend* in this central strategic relationship can be as politically influential as the true balance.

In Washington the ambiguities of the new administration were still largely unresolved in early 1977. There appeared two forces inimical to the survival or development of detente: what one might call the right opposition and the left opposition, though they were frequently in such close tactical alliance as to be almost indistinguishable. The right opposition was the more straightforward, and one might describe its members predominantly as friends of the Pentagon, apprehensive that President Carter's one-time ambition to cut $5–7,000 million from the arms budget might come to something, or that the SALT II treaty might damage the chances of development and deployment of cruise missiles and other weapon systems. Their central proposition was that the Soviet Union was not only seeking strategic superiority but in sight of attaining it. The left opposition was a less coherent group, but one might say that it centred round those who held to a rather utopian proposition that diplomatic subtleties in bargaining or 'linkage' could and should be abandoned in favour of blunt exhortations that other members of the society of states (both allies and adversaries) should conform to those standards of justice and morality in the relations between governments and their peoples that are rightly cherished (though not always observed) in Western societies; and that American economic and diplomatic leverage could be used openly to this end.

Indeed the most striking change in American foreign policy with the change of administration was that the element of messianism, which had been so conspicuously absent in Dr Kissinger's time, reappeared in full force with President Carter. 'America', he said, 'is again a beacon to the world', and he seemed clearly determined that American enlightenment should prevail in quite a number of areas where local policy-makers had other views of local realities. The set of attitudes carried into decision-making by this drive looked, on early evidence, to have more in common with the original stance of the Kennedy administration, or even with Woodrow Wilson, than with Dulles, in that the latter's missionary zeal was for a negative cause, anti-communism, whereas President Carter's was for a positive one, human rights. As a diplomatic stance, being for human rights is rather like being against sin: a hard position to argue with, and therefore politically useful. But not many of the world's sovereign states would get a pass-mark in human rights as defined by Western liberal theory: certainly none of the communist powers, and hardly any Third World countries. Even those that might be held to make the grade – the Nato powers, Japan, Australia and New Zealand, Israel, India (in mid-1977) and a few others – had mostly to be conscious of a skeleton or two in the national cupboard: Australia in the treatment of Aborigines, Japan in the *eta*, Israel in the situation of its Arab citizens, Britain in Northern Ireland and so on. Moreover, however worthy the cause it served, and however much it contributed to American self-approval, messianism as such carried a freight of memories of its consequences in earlier episodes from Woodrow Wilson to John Kennedy, and this was enough to cause *frissons* of alarm in several countries. These feelings in turn had results, some counterproductive to American hopes, in local political systems. For instance, the accession to a plurality of Menachem Begin's party in Israel was attributed by many analysts to apprehensions aroused by President Carter's statements about an overall settlement and a Palestinian homeland. For the South African government, and for several Latin American ones, the fear of solutions imposed from Washington in accordance with American values and American political pressures was real enough to contribute to some hardening of positions.

As regards the detente, one may distinguish two levels of potential damage. First, a possible weakening of its infrastructure, the Western balance of power coalition. The central elements of that coalition, the Nato and Japanese alliances, should survive well enough, but the system has also been buttressed by understandings with countries such as Iran, Saudi Arabia, Indonesia, the Philippines and South Korea, none of which would come at all well out of a scrutiny of their attitudes on human rights, and any of which could be nudged into sharp nationalist resentment by American lectures, so there seemed a possibility of the local reinforcement of various balances that they had provided being eroded away, especially if a sort of 'moral qualifying test' for the supply of American arms were seriously to be imposed.

As for the main superstructure of detente, the relationship with the Soviet Union itself, especially its arms control aspects, the Russian policy-makers had some case for complaining that they were being subjected, accidentally or deliberately, to confusing or conflicting signals. Some of the signals from Washington could be interpreted as importing renewed cold war in the name of human rights: the stepping-up of the transmissions of 'Radio Free Europe' and 'Radio Liberty', both of which the Russians had long considered prime Western instrumentalities of cold war, the nomination to their board of control (at a time when Eastern Europe was already in a state of subdued ferment) of a man held to have helped incite the 1956 Hungarian uprising,[10] and the public sponsorship of Soviet dissidents like Solzhenitsyn, Sakharov and Bukhovsky, all of which events were bound to look like a set of clear signals of encouragement to the less well-known but very numerous dissidents in Eastern Europe. The arms-control proposals that Mr Vance was required to put to the Soviet decision-makers in March 1977 could readily be interpreted (and not only in Moscow) as making them an offer they were bound to refuse. That is a technique quite familiar in arms-control negotiations, and the Russians themselves have used it often enough, but SALT I had been achieved by eschewing it, and by avoiding publicity until proximate agreement was established, a course for which Mr Carter showed initially little inclination. Moreover, both on the side of conventional arms and of nuclear strike-power, the new administration, while forecasting future cuts, was in fact recruiting considerable extra armed strength. The Nato summit meeting in May 1977 agreed on an aim of real growth rate of three per cent per annum in defence spending (which, if taken seriously in conjunction with inflation rates varying from 5 to 15 per cent, would mean increases of up to 20 per cent in defence budgets for various powers). And deployment was about to begin of a new Minuteman warhead, the Mark 12A, which was reported to constitute a greater leap in counterforce capability (which is the true measure of the American strategic edge) than either the cruise missile or the M-X, both of which also remained in prospect, along with a naval build-up to 600 ships.

A 'worst case analysis' put together in the Kremlin in the

first half of 1977 might therefore plausibly (if mistakenly) hold that the human rights campaign was a sort of moral re-tooling for an effort to use the rising disaffection in Eastern Europe to jockey the Russians out of their hegemony there, and in effect to roll Soviet power back to the borders of the Soviet Union. The military build-up would certainly be necessary in that case, as a sanction against Soviet reactions. Such a policy would, of course, be markedly less cautious than Dr Kissinger's, but then a considerable amount of evidence – the pull-out of American troops from Korea, and the attitudes to 'Eurocommunism' and 'Afrocommunism' for instance – appeared to show that Mr Carter was much the more self-assured and the less cautious policy-maker of the two.

However, as the French say, the soup is never eaten as hot as it is cooked, and there were indications by mid-1977 that the initial Carter brew in foreign policy was cooling reasonably fast, and that the detente might survive to face its next bout of perils. Since all the detentes in diplomatic history have proved perishable in due course, it would be unreasonable to assume that this one will prove immortal. If its existence should be prolonged, it will face a potential danger, which Dr Kissinger noted in the century-span of its predecessor: 'a stability so pervasive that it contributed to disaster. For in the long interval of peace, the sense of the tragic was lost: it was forgotten that states could die, that disasters could be irretrievable ...'[11] One must hope the built-in dangers of the late twentieth century will immunize policy-makers against that error. For who would restore a world after nuclear war?

Notes

CHAPTER I

1. Statement to the Senate Finance Committee, *Dept. of State Bulletin*, April 1974, p. 323. 'Detente is not rooted in agreement on values: it becomes above all necessary because each side recognizes that the other is a potential adversary in a nuclear war. *To us, detente is a process of managing relations with a potentially hostile country in order to preserve peace while maintaining our vital interests.*' (Italics added.)
2. The derivation is from the French détendre, originally the archer's action in releasing the tension on his bowstring as the arrow goes on its way. Hence, in the traditional French vocabulary of diplomacy, a policy of reducing tension, by whomever pursued, with however limited an objective in mind. In the post-war period it seems first to have re-emerged into usage, by specialists, in connection with Mr Malenkov's policy after Stalin's death in 1953. Its general use as a term for Western policy seems only to have become widespread after 1970. As late as 1969 it was seen as esoteric enough to require inverted commas in many American newspapers. Possibly a good deal of the misunderstanding of its meaning arose from confusion with the quite differently derived term *entente*, which should be reserved for a close understanding based on a sense of common interest, as in *entente cordiale*. *Detente* has always conveyed a much more guarded and limited relationship.
3. Reprinted in *Soviet News*, 2 March 1976.
4. The main speeches of this Churchillian campaign are those of 11 May 1953, 9 November 1953 and 1 March 1955. See Winston Churchill, *Speeches* (ed. Randolph Churchill, Cassell, 1961).
5. See C. M. Bell, *Negotiation from Strength: a study in the politics of power* (Chatto & Windus, 1962; Knopf, 1963) ch. 4, for a more extensive study of this period.
6. Dr Kissinger is reported to have remarked that the Russians had come up with new proposals on arms control within a fortnight of his first journey to Peking.
7. Quoted in John Newhouse, *De Gaulle and the Anglo-Saxons* (Deutsch, 1970) p. 253, to whose book I am much indebted for these paragraphs. The Maurras quotation is from a book originally published in 1912, which reinforces the argument as to the somewhat archaic quality of this Gaullist vision.
8. Ibid., p. 63.
9. Ibid., p. 282.
10. Ibid., p. 292.

11. John Newhouse, *Cold Dawn: The Story of SALT* (Holt, Rinehart & Winston, 1973) p. 189.
12. *Peking Review*, 27 August 1971, published an up-dating of this essay.
13. See the *Peking Review, passim*, especially the editions of 21 December 1973 and 15 February 1974, for further Chinese development of their views of Soviet policy in this field.
14. Roger Hilsman speech, *Dept. of State Bulletin*, 8 July 1963.
15. The policy was chiefly associated with the name of Professor Zbigniew Brzezinski, at the time one of President Johnson's advisers. For a recent restatement of his views, see an interview in *Detente* (ed. G. R. Urban, London, Temple Smith, 1976) p. 262 *et seq*. His views on the moral and intellectual differences between cold war and detente are interesting: 'the Cold War was Manichean, and under a Manichean constellation all questions are sharply put, all solutions are simple, and all contrasts are stark because Manicheism is the confrontation of good and evil, of darkness and light. Everything is crystal clear. We are now moving away from that period of easy contrasts, and the price we are paying is complexity.'

CHAPTER 2

1. This chapter does not pretend to be an exhaustive exploration of Dr Kissinger's theories; merely a sketch of some elements in them that seemed to me to bear on the notion of detente. A complete bibliography of Dr Kissinger's writings before his entry into office will be found in Stephen Graubard, *Kissinger: Portrait of a Mind* (New York, Norton, 1973).
2. *The Troubled Partnership* (McGraw-Hill, 1965) p. 195.
3. Ibid., p. 198.
4. Ibid., p. 192.
5. Lippmann's views are to be found in his 1947 pamphlet, *The Cold War* (Hamish Hamilton), which was the earliest exposition of the case against the 'domestic change' thesis, written in reply to the original Kennan article on containment, which, as mutated by Acheson, became the official stand of the early Cold War.
6. The edition used is Universal Library, 1964.
7. *Pacem in Terris* speech, 1973 (United States Information Service, 9 October 1973).
8. See, for example, Kohler, Gouré and Harvey, *The Soviet Union and the October 1973 Middle East War: The Implications for Detente* (Center for International Studies, University of Miami, 1974) as an interpretation of Soviet policy in this fashion.
9. Senator Jackson's amendment of the Trade Bill of 1972 was intended to exact from Soviet policy-makers a higher rate of issue of permits for Jewish emigration from the Soviet Union. The Soviet government had previously been persuaded by behind-the-scenes diplomacy on Dr Kissinger's part to allow a rise in the rate of emigration from about 600 a year in 1969 to about 34,800 a year in 1973. At one point in his discussion

with Mr Gromyko the figure of 45,000 appears to have been agreed. But Senator Jackson demanded 60,000 a year as 'a minimum standard of compliance', and, what was worse, in late 1974 when for a few weeks the Russians appeared likely to agree, plumed himself publicly on his triumph over Soviet intransigence, and the greater success of his public toughness rather than Dr Kissinger's penchant for secrecy in dealing with the Soviet authorities. It was probably the combination of this publicity (implying for the Soviet policy-makers the admission that they had yielded to American interference in their domestic policies) with the fact that Congress also cut the proposed credits to a very disappointing level, that caused the Russians to reject the whole proposal in January 1975. The chief sufferers were the would-be Jewish emigrants, the number of permits issued being reduced to 13,000 in 1975. (*International Herald Tribune*, 28 May 1976.)

10. *A World Restored* (Universal Library, 1964) p. 325.
11. P. 47. Background briefing, New Orleans, 14 August 1970. These background briefings to the American press were theoretically 'not for attribution', but in fact many have been published in various sources, especially David Landau, *Kissinger: The Uses of Power* (Robson, 1974). The two editions of *American Foreign Policy* (Norton, 1969 and 1974) differ at some points, and the second edition also contains the text of several Kissinger speeches.
12. *A World Restored*, p. 329.
13. The concept of linkage was much debated in the early weeks of the Carter administration, with Mr Vance and Mr Carter announcing that it had been 'abandoned', by which they obviously intended to convey that they did not expect the Soviet Union to be affected in its attitude on matters of substance like the arms-control negotiations, by such gestures as Mr Carter's letter to Sakharov and other indications of support for the Soviet human rights campaigners. But other U.S. influencers of policy in fact wanted their own version of linkage (rather than Dr Kissinger's) to remain, in for instance the continued demand for Jewish emigration as a condition of increased trade. It would not be unreasonable to say that they demanded 'linkage' when it implied U.S. influence over Soviet policy and rejected it when it implied Soviet leverage over American policy. It seemed doubtful at the time of writing whether this interpretation could be made to stick: linkage probably works both ways or not at all. Dr Kissinger's concept of linkage, as propounded in this passage from a statement to the Senate Foreign Relations Committee (*Dept. of State Bulletin*, 14 October 1974, p. 508) is very different from the versions propounded by Senator Jackson and others.
14. *A World Restored*, p. 1.
15. Background briefing, San Clemente, 24 August 1970.
16. *A World Restored*, p. 1.
17. Speech in Washington on 2 August 1973 (*The Times*, 25 August 1973).
18. Statement to the Senate Foreign Relations Committee, *Dept. of State Bulletin*, 19 September 1974.
19. *A World Restored*, p. 215.
20. Ibid., p. 187.

21. 'Will the balance balance at home?' *Foreign Policy*, Summer 1972.
22. For instance, I watched in Washington an episode in a science fiction TV series, *Star Trek* (which has become something of a cult) which had the hero (an American of insufferable nobility of moral character) prescribing a balance of power system for some warring planet, and justifying this by reference to Earth's experience in South East Asia in the mid-twentieth century. If the script-writers of *Star Trek* felt that the grass-roots audience was ready for balance of power concepts, they were probably right.
23. *Newsweek*, 18 October 1976, published a poll showing still 65 per cent approval for his policies.
24. *A World Restored*, p. 153.
25. President Carter, in his first few weeks of office, seemed a moralist, a populist and a man of formidable self-confidence and some messianic drive in foreign policy. The potential of these qualities in international politics seemed ambiguous. The most recent other exponent of moralism in this field, John Foster Dulles, devised the policies that after his time produced the Vietnam involvement, but in his case moralism was allied with militant anti-communism and undifferentiated globalism. In Mr Carter's case the pattern of thought seemed closer to that of Woodrow Wilson, with much emphasis on open agreements (or disagreements) openly arrived at.

CHAPTER 3

1. Some of Dr Kissinger's views concerning Mr Nixon became unexpectedly public in October 1975 when a dinner-table microphone was accidentally left switched on after the speeches were over. See *International Herald Tribune*, 16 October 1975.
2. See Kraslow and Loory, *The Secret Search for Peace in Vietnam* (Random House, 1968).
3. Interview in *Newsweek*, 6 January 1975.
4. *International Herald Tribune*, 27 June 1974.
5. These efforts were concluded mostly via French and Romanian intermediaries, though there was also an effort in 1967 when Harold Wilson, then British prime minister, was the intending go-between.
6. William Westmoreland, *A Soldier Reports* (Doubleday, 1976). Mr Nixon, in the Frost interviews in May 1977, said he had *not* consulted Kissinger before ordering the bombing.
7. The legal proceedings stemming from this episode are not yet resolved.
8. 13 March 1973.
9. The interview, with Oriana Fallaci, was originally printed in *L'Europeo* in 1972. The sense of being a 'maverick', to stay with this Western metaphor, had a basis in intellectual as well as personal experience. His mode of analysis, traditional *realpolitik* based on historical experience, is still the dominant one in European and British universities, but it was quite unfashionable, as an academic style, in America in the fifties when Kissinger was a graduate student or beginning to look for university posts. The fashionable mode then (now somewhat in eclipse) was 'the behavioral

approach', based rather on the methods of the social sciences, particularly economics, than on those of history, and often involving game theory and other mathematical techniques. The behavioralists were far more ambitious in their claims for scientific accuracy and certainty of prediction than the traditionalists had ever been. Kissinger once wrote drily that 'Europeans, living on a continent covered with ruins testifying to the fallibility of human foresight, feel in their bones that history is more complicated than systems analysis.' His period of army service perhaps reinforced the exile's sense of being a wanderer between two worlds: an American sergeant with a German name who still spoke German better than English; a figure of authority in the most conspicuous and resented of 'outgroups', the army of occupation.

10. Particularly what Mr Carter called Dr Kissinger's 'lone ranger' style of diplomacy, possibly a reference to the indiscreet interview mentioned earlier. The decisive difference in style, as the new administration began its foreign-policy operations, seemed to be much greater influence by the President himself than in Mr Ford's time or Mr Nixon's later years, and a division of responsibility for negotiation, and perhaps for policy, between quite a number of hands: Andrew Young and Clark Clifford as well as Vance and Brzezinski.

CHAPTER 4

1. The figures I shall use are those in the International Institute of Strategic Studies' (I.I.S.S.) annual publication *The Military Balance*. See especially the section 'The theatre balance between Nato and the Warsaw Pact' in the 1976–7 edition, p. 97 *et seq*.
2. The arms-control talks of the detente period have been divided between those concerned with strategic arms (SALT) and those concerned with conventional and tactical nuclear forces in central Europe. The second set of talks are referred to as MBFR (Mutual and Balanced Force Reductions) by the Western powers and MFR (Mutual Force Reductions) by the Russians, who have some objection to the Western concept of balance. But this division of the talks, while originally convenient and helpful to SALT especially, had become less so by 1977, since technical change had blurred the initial distinction between tactical and strategic weapons.
3. This press conference in July 1974 was originally 'off the record', but was printed in *Survival*, the journal of the I.I.S.S., September–October 1974. See also Dr Kissinger's briefing of 2 December 1974, reprinted in *Survival*, July–August 1975.
4. See, for instance, C. M. Bell, *Negotiation from Strength* (Knopf, 1963) especially ch. 5.
5. *International Herald Tribune*, 21 February 1975.
6. 'U.S. forces in Europe', *Foreign Affairs*, April 1975.
7. The comparison of Western and Soviet weapons systems is a complex matter, but expert opinion is to the effect that the Russians build larger numbers of simpler systems, which are, however, sturdy, reliable and effective. Western systems, especially American, are more sophisticated,

more technologically advanced and have on the whole higher performance, but they are more expensive. Both systems have their respective advantages; but quantity for quantity the Russian numbers usually look more impressive, and this can of course be an advantage to those wishing, for political or budgetary reasons, to make a case that Western defences are being neglected or run down. On the question of the balance between tanks and anti-tank defences, General Haig was reported in March 1977 to be accelerating the re-equipment of Nato forces with anti-tank guided missiles, increasing the numbers of TOW three fold and of 'Dragon' six fold.

8. Though, of course, this would cease to be so if there were a sharp change of the political situation in France, as with participation of the Communist party in the government coalition for instance.
9. See *The Times*, 7 May 1976.
10. These problems and their possible causes are expertly discussed in two Adelphi papers: Steven Canby, *The Alliance & Europe: Part IV Military Doctrine and Technology* and Robert Lucas Fischer, *Defending the Central Front: The Balance of Forces* (I.I.S.S.).
11. Senator Mansfield's resolution was first presented in September 1973 as an amendment calling for a 40 per cent cut in U.S. forces overseas, and was initially passed by the Senate, 49–46. However, a second vote was needed on a technicality and this reversed the decision, 51–44. The amendment progressively lost support and was watered down in later years, so that the first 1973 vote at present appears the high-water mark for the feeling behind it. A new sponsor and a new surge of feeling on the question might of course revive the amendment. For a full account see P. Williams, 'Whatever happened to the Mansfield amendment?' *Survival*, July–August 1976.
12. *Daily Telegraph*, 5 October 1976, gives the figure of 805,000 as the Soviet claim. See also *The Military Balance*, 1976–7, p. 104. The reason why armed forces numbers are more arguable than might be supposed is the existence of certain categories, like civilian employees replacing soldiers in non-combat functions, whose status is not agreed.
13. One major function of these tactical nuclear weapons for the Western powers on the Central Front, in peace-time, is that they enforce dispersal on the other side, since strategic moves like massing tanks for attack in a particular sector would present a conceivable target for nuclear strike. Thus, they might in peace-time be said to secure a signalling and deterrent function, among others. In the event of hostilities, their actual use in the early days of the attack would be a matter of political rather than military decision. But whether considering their use in peace or war, Dr Schlesinger was reported to believe that their numbers had been agreed at existing levels for mostly political reasons, and that a considerable reduction would be no disadvantage to the West. Paul Warnke, President Carter's arms-control chief, had earlier argued that the numbers could be reduced as low as 1,000. See *International Herald Tribune*, 1 March 1977.

14. Though difficulties in manpower were beginning to be reported by early 1977 (*International Herald Tribune*, March 1977).
15. See *The Military Balance*, 1976–7, p. 109 *et seq.*, for a discussion of this problem.
16. *The Road to Ramadan* (Collins, 1976) p. 76.
17. See Richard Burt, *New Weapons Technologies: Debate and Direction* (I.I.S.S. Adelphi paper, Summer 1976) for a discussion of these points.
18. This argument is controversial, and obviously no firm official information is likely to be provided of the degree to which the Soviet nuclear strike-force is either targeted or targetable by American weapons. But the acknowledged number of American warheads in existence, something in excess of 8,000, is difficult to reconcile with any supposition other than that a considerable number are required for counter-force targeting. The introduction of the Mk 12A Minuteman warhead will greatly increase the U.S. advantage. See *Time*, 9 May 1977.
19. For a general discussion of Soviet naval competition with the West, see the I.I.S.S. conference papers *Power at Sea* (Adelphi papers 122, 123 and 124). The direction of American naval policy in the early months of the Carter administration appeared to be veering away from the very large nuclear powered aircraft carrier towards smaller ships with vertical take-off aircraft. The figures for comparative ship deliveries are in *International Herald Tribune*, 5 May 1976. See also *The Economist*, 15 and 21 May 1976.
20. Block obsolescence in a fleet is of course related to the date at which the relevant building programme was begun. Allowing a 'ship life' on average of about 20 years, block obsolescence in the American navy meant that ships built in the late Second World War period were judged obsolescent in the mid-1960s. The Soviet programme of the late 1950s and early 1960s, on the same basis, would produce block obsolescence towards the end of the 1970s.
21. See papers by Michael MccGwire and Johan Holst in *Power at Sea*, Part II. Also MccGwire, 'Western and Soviet Naval Building Programmes 1965–76', *Survival*, September–October 1976.
22. Very little information has been officially disclosed concerning the nuclear exporters club. It began with an initiative by Dr Kissinger in the aftermath of the first Indian nuclear test explosion, and is designed to restrain nuclear proliferation through its members exerting mutual restraint on the export of key supplies and technologies. A good deal of American time and effort has gone into persuading particularly France and West Germany against the export to South Korea, Pakistan and Brazil of equipment that might help them towards weapons capacity.
23. During the election campaign of 1976, especially during the Republican nomination struggle, a good deal of effort seemed to be being made by various interested parties to present Nato as in a state of woeful inferiority to the Warsaw Pact. The campaign was sufficiently striking to move General Haig to issue a warning against Western exaggeration of Soviet strength (*International Herald Tribune*, 17 February 1977). The new Secretary of Defense, Harold Brown, also testified in February 1977 that

American strategic forces were in a state of adequate balance with those of the Soviet Union, and could be so maintained without excessive effort (*International Herald Tribune*, 26–27 February 1977).

One of the more unexpected benefits of arms-control talks, and a considerable offset to their failure to date to produce much arms reduction, is the way they have operated as a sort of high-level seminar enabling both sides to learn how to keep the arms balance stable. In the case of the ABM, this rise in enlightenment among the policy-making elite has in effect produced a unilateral U.S. renunciation of that weapon, through its 'mothballing' by Congress.

CHAPTER 5

1. See, for instance, Kohler, Gouré and Harvey, *The Soviet Union and the October 1973 Middle East War: The Implications for Detente* (Center for International Studies, University of Miami, 1974).
2. In many interviews, including that in *Newsweek*, 28 February 1975, in which he called it 'the straw that broke the camel's back'.
3. Background briefing, San Clemente, 24 August 1970. Quoted in David Landau, *Kissinger: The Uses of Power* (London, Robson, 1974).
4. *Newsweek*, 9 April 1973.
5. See Lawrence L. Whetten, *The Arab Israeli Dispute* (I.I.S.S., Adelphi Paper 128) for a more detailed account of the way in which strategic and tactical surprise were achieved.
6. Press conference, 25 October 1973.
7. There continued to be some recrimination between the Russians and President Sadat, even as late as 1977, as to which side was misrepresenting the early events of the 1973 war. See *International Herald Tribune*, 21 February 1977.
8. Press conference, 25 October 1973. I have put Dr Kissinger's words into the form of a continuous paragraph for the sake of brevity, but they were actually responses to particular questions from the journalists present. The omission of the questions does not in any way, I think, change the meaning of the answers. The full text may be found in *Survival*, January–February 1974. In the same press conference, Dr Kissinger restated the American assumptions on detente: 'The United States and the Soviet Union are of course ideological and to some extent political adversaries. But the United States and the Soviet Union also have a very special responsibility. We possess – each of us – nuclear arsenals capable of annihilating humanity. We – both of us – have a special duty to see that confrontations are kept within bounds that do not threaten civilized life ... In the Frost interviews of May 1977 Mr Nixon revealed that the Egyptian proposal that inspired the Soviet demarche was for two divisions each of Soviet and U.S. troops to go to the Middle East.
9. See an article by Edward Luttwak and Walter Laqueur, 'Kissinger and the Yom Kippur War', *Commentary*, September 1974. The actual truth of this episode was probably more complex. See also Whetten, *The Arab Israeli Dispute*, and especially Edward R. E. Sheehan, *The Arabs, Israelis and Kissinger* (Reader's Digest Press, 1976).

10. The first Sinai disengagement to separate the Israeli and Egyptian armies was achieved early in 1974. Dr Kissinger tried for the second disengagement, to separate the parties by a demilitarized zone, in the spring of 1975, but encountered strong Israeli resistance, and was not able to achieve it until a further bout of shuttle diplomacy in September 1975. See Yair Evrom, *The Demilitarization of Sinai* (Jerusalem Papers, Hebrew University, 1975) for a general study of the strategic problems of the area.
11. During the fifteen months from the second Sinai disengagement to the end of 1976, relations between Egypt and Syria continued strained. The apparent reconciliation achieved by early 1977 appeared to be on Egyptian rather than on Syrian terms: the second Sinai disengagement, to which the Syrians had initially objected, continued in being.
12. The effect of the civil war in the Lebanon in 1976 on the relative power and standing of the Syrian and P.L.O. leaderships, and therefore on the prospects of some long-term settlement between Israel and the Arabs, is too large a question to be adequately covered here. One might say that the Palestinian involvement in the war arose in part from their feelings of frustration at the disengagement of Egypt, and to some extent Syria, from active combat with Israel, and that the effects of the war included a reduced status and ambition on the part of the Palestinian leadership, which in turn made a compromise peace with Israel appear more feasible. By early 1977 the Palestinian leadership was indicating that it might accept a 'mini-Palestine' state in Gaza and the West bank, as at least an interim substitute for its earlier objective of the destruction of the Israeli state and its replacement by a secular Palestine comprising both Arabs and Jews. Some reconciliation between the Palestinians and King Hussein of Jordan also appeared to be under way (*International Herald Tribune*, 9 March 1977).

CHAPTER 6

1. Speech at the Ecole Militaire, 3 November 1959. Quoted in Newhouse, *De Gaulle and the Anglo-Saxons* (Deutsch, 1970) p. 64. The 'tous azimuts' concept was further developed in an article by General Charles Ailleret, *Revue de Defense Nationale*, December 1967.
2. In 1973 oil supplied 72.5 per cent of fuel for France, as against 58.6 per cent for West Germany. See Louis Turner, 'Europe: the politics of the energy crisis', *International Affairs*, July 1974.
3. For the text of the 'Year of Europe' speech see United States Information Service release, 23 April 1973.
4. See, for instance, Roger Morgan, *The U.S. and West Germany* (O.U.P., 1974), Ernst Nolte, *Deutschland und der Kalte Krieg* (Piper Verlag, 1974), Roger Tilford (ed.) *The Ostpolitik and Political Change in Germany* (Lexington Books, 1975); also J. L. Richardson, *Germany and the Atlantic Alliance* (Oxford University Press, 1966) for the earlier period of German policy.
5. See, for example, an article by George Ball in *Newsweek*, 11 March 1975. The right-wing sector of American opinion, which originally denounced

any American participation in Helsinki, has more recently been vociferous in demanding that the Russians be kept to the observance of the commitments undertaken there.
6. *Conference on Security and Co-operation in Europe: Final Act* (H.M.S.O., Cmnd. 6198) p. 3.
7. *Time*, 4 August 1975.
8. The text of the Sonnenfeldt talk, along with one on the same occasion by Dr Kissinger himself, were published in *International Herald Tribune*, 12 April 1976. But such is the power of political legend that it has continued to be represented as favouring Soviet dominance in Eastern Europe.
9. Interview in *Newsweek*, 1 September 1975.
10. A name coined in 1976, because by then it had become necessary to distinguish the communist parties of Western Europe from those of the Soviet bloc, and also from the Asian, African and Latin American variants. The most influential of the Eurocommunist parties were those of Italy, France and Spain, and they held a first summit meeting in Madrid in March 1977.
11. In a speech to a United Press International Conference in October 1975.

CHAPTER 7

1. *Dept. of State Bulletin*, 8 July 1963.
2. General Van's accounts of his final victory drive in the South were first published in April 1976 in the North Vietnamese paper *Nhan Dan* and republished in various Western papers: see *International Herald Tribune*, 21–30 April 1976 and *Sunday Times*, 25 April 1976.
3. The nature of these assurances became public in April 1975 through statements by disgruntled South Vietnamese diplomats in Washington, but their general substance had been widely understood among informed circles from about March 1973.
4. There were trade and monetary matters (the latter under the charge of John Connolly rather than Dr Kissinger) that contributed at least as much to the American–Japanese frictions of this period as the opening to China, and that seem to have moved Mr Nixon to some personal resentment towards the Japanese government.
5. Lecture to the New Zealand Press Club, 7 April 1975.
6. The question of to what extent, if at all, arguments about foreign policy and in particular about the rapprochement with America contributed to or were involved in the power struggle in Peking after Mao's death, remained obscure at the time of writing. The succession appeared to have passed largely to the heirs of Chou En-lai, with the support of the army, and one of the accusations against Chiang Ching, as leader of the 'gang of four', was that she had harassed Chou on his death bed, with the implication that she had opposed his policies, including this one. But that may have been just make-weight in the general list of charges against the defeated faction, to whom all possible errors were being attributed. See *The Times* and *International Herald Tribune*, 25 March 1977, for a

reiteration of the new leadership's continued distrust of Soviet policy.
7. A first official American group revisited Hanoi in March 1977, and renewal of diplomatic relations appeared close.
8. *International Herald Tribune*, 30–31 October 1976.
9. At the time of writing, the Soviet envoy to the talks with China, Mr Leonid Ilychev, had just returned to Moscow, apparently without any progress being made in the most recent round of discussions with the new Chinese leadership, and a prominent member of the succession leadership, Mr Li Hsien-nien, had been reported as speaking of the inevitability of war with the Soviet Union (*International Herald Tribune*, 3 November 1976 and 1 March 1977).
10. The date at which the embargo on the engines was removed appears to have been late 1975 or early 1976.
11. The remaining routine problems of America's Asian policy appeared to be chiefly the renegotiation of the agreement on bases with the Philippines and the final normalization of relations with China and Vietnam. But the potentially explosive issue arose from Mr Carter's intention of phasing out the American troops in Korea and the uncertainty as to whether this could be done without risking crisis.

CHAPTER 8

1. Probably the centre of this resistance was located in British defence and foreign-policy circles. Some British opinion was still at this time hopeful of bringing to birth a Mediterranean and Middle East Defence Organization (in a later truncated form the idea was called M.E.D.O.) which would ally Greece, Turkey, Iran and some of the Arab states, especially Egypt and Iraq (then both still under British influence), in a mutual defence treaty along Nato lines to block the possible southern threat of Soviet power. It would have covered roughly the sprawl of the old Ottoman Empire and was hopefully envisaged as functioning strategically to the same effect. But obviously Greece and Turkey found it preferable to ally themselves with the strong powers of Nato rather than these weak states. The Baghdad Pact was the rather disastrous first approximation of the original idea, but reconstituted as Cento it has had quite a lengthy survival.
2. Reports that the Athens station of the C.I.A. was excessively close to the junta, to a degree that angered the American ambassador Mr Henry Tasca, were widespread before the crisis.
3. For a strongly critical account of the Washington decision-making (which appears to reflect State Department sources) see Lawrence Stern, 'Bitter Lessons: Why we failed in Cyprus', *Foreign Policy*, Summer 1975.
4. Ibid. and *Sunday Times*, 23 May 1976.
5. The official position of Brigadier Ioannides, the leader of the junta, was that of head of the military police.
6. There was a British House of Commons Select Committee enquiry into the events in Cyprus, some of whose conclusions were publicised. Britain

had formal legal obligations, along with Greece and Turkey, as one of the guarantors of the 1960 settlement. See *Sunday Times*, 23 May 1976.
7. Dr Kissinger's attention and energies were mostly absorbed during the decisive three weeks in the final act of the Watergate drama, Mr Nixon's exit and the handover to Mr Ford.
8. *Sunday Times*, 28 July 1974.
9. There were reports in early 1977 that the Archbishop had been receiving more substantial C.I.A. payments than these, but that has been strongly denied. There has, however, been evidence to sustain the report that American use of the Akrotiri base continues, and is paid for. See *International Herald Tribune*, 23 February 1977.
10. Again with substantial aid from American funds. See *International Herald Tribune*, 23 February 1977.
11. Congress, under pressure from the Greek lobby, delayed approval of the agreements during 1976, but the results of the Turkish elections of June 1977 seemed to offer prospects of change.

CHAPTER 9

1. Senator Lloyd Bentsen, for instance, wanted President Ford to cancel his attendance at the Helsinki conference because of the alleged Soviet financial aid to the Portuguese communists.
2. See, for instance, Tad Szulc's article 'Lisbon and Washington: Behind the Portuguese Revolution', *Foreign Policy*, Winter 1975–6. Though I would disagree with the conclusions of this analysis, I am indebted to it on a number of points, and it clearly reflects a good deal of State Department opinion at the time.
3. See *The Guardian*, 22 September 1976, for a summary of Soviet and Western attitudes. Also *New York Times*, 24 November 1976.
4. *The Times*, 15 August 1975.
5. *International Herald Tribune*, 27 July 1976.
6. Interview in *Time*, 27 October 1975.
7. The general line of criticism by most liberal journalistic and political comment was that Dr Kissinger's prophecies of possible communist success were unnecessarily alarmist, and might prove self-fulfilling. But this seems to have been rather the technique of the intentionally self-vitiating prophecy.
8. See John A. Marcum, 'Lessons of Angola', *Foreign Affairs*, April 1976; also Anthony Lake, *Tar Baby* (Columbia, 1976).
9. See Colin Legum in *Foreign Affairs*, July 1976; also 'The Gorschkov Strategy', *The Observer*, 20 March 1977.
10. See articles by Robert Moss in the *Sunday Telegraph*, January–February 1977, for a general history of the Angola war.
11. The text of the San Francisco speech is in *Dept. of State Bulletin*, March 1976.
12. The broadcast on 24 September 1976 by Mr Ian Smith to his Rhodesian electorate after the talk with Dr Kissinger, conceding the principle of majority rule within two years, appeared still (at the time of writing) to

be the decisive turn of events. The momentum of the movement to this end was perhaps rather lost in the abortive Geneva Conference in the succeeding weeks, and of course no further American initiative was possible in the period between the presidential election and the settling-in to office of the Carter administration. During the early weeks of that administration, the formulating of policy on southern Africa appeared to fall to Mr Andrew Young. However, Mr Smith's efforts to move towards an internal implementation of some approximation of the Kissinger plan appeared still under way in early 1977.

13. Dr Kissinger's Dallas speech is in *Dept. of State Bulletin*, April 1976.
14. This figure stems from the 'senior official' source used by Dr Kissinger. Other press reports, however, have claimed that as the Cuban troops moved out, civilian advisers moved in to replace them.
15. Mrs Thatcher's speech is in *The Times*, 1 August 1976.
16. Mr Young for instance said in a television interview that the Cubans were a 'stabilizing' influence in Angola, though he later implied that they were still heavily engaged in military operations, their own 'Vietnam' (*International Herald Tribune*, 9 March 1977).

CHAPTER 10

1. In a speech to a gathering of American businessmen in New York in August 1973, quoted in J. D. B. Miller, 'Australian Foreign Policy: Constraints and Opportunities', *International Affairs*, July 1974.
2. The American installations are related either to navigation and command systems for nuclear submarines (like the Omega base and North-West Cape) or, it is reported, to the retrieval of information from satellites, like Pine Gap or Woomera. Naturally not much information is available on their specific functions, and it may be that they are chiefly 'back-up' systems, duplicating others.
3. The project of a large naval base at Cockburn Sound is one that had been debated in Australia since the *First* World War. But there did not seem much urgency about it while the British navy still had more than ample facilities at Singapore, and the Australian navy was so very small. It was only after the winding up of the British presence 'East of Suez' in 1967 that Australians began noting that the Indian Ocean had become singularly bare of friendly naval presences, and was beginning to acquire more ambiguous ones like some vessels of the Soviet fleet, though in fact the number of its 'ship-days' there continued small, and was probably the object of quite undue alarm. A minister of Mr McMahon's government, Mr Gordon Freeth, who bravely or unwarily ventured the opinion that they ought to be regarded with more equanimity, lost his seat soon after (his constituency was in Western Australia) and this perhaps reflected local opinion, though there may have been other causes. A base at Cockburn Sound would be of particular importance to the U.S. naval forces in the Pacific if circumstances made the straits to the north of Australia (Malacca and Lombok) dangerous or seriously disadvantageous, which

could readily become the case if there were hostilities in the Indonesia–Singapore area.
4. For a partial text, see *Financial Times*, 2 July 1976. The phrases about a four-power understanding should probably not be taken very seriously.

CHAPTER 11

1. The symbolic moment of crystallization of Eurocommunism as an articulate movement was the meeting in Madrid in spring 1977. The Spanish Communist party, as it had emerged from the shadows of its long period underground by late 1976, seemed close in spirit to the Italian and French parties. The Italian party has proclaimed itself ready to acquiesce in Italian membership of Nato; the French party is more ambiguous on this point, but on the whole both should probably be seen as oriented to detente rather than armed struggle in either the national or the international conflict. The long-term influence of this change of spirit either on the European communist parties or on the parliamentary systems within which they have flourished or may flourish remained unpredictable. One might perhaps in some respects compare it to what used to be called the 'domestication' of the Indonesian Communist party before 1965, which certainly ended very disastrously for that party. But there are many differences between Indonesian and European politics. The case of Chile is said to have operated powerfully on European communist estimates of securing and maintaining power without a successful compromise with middle-class opinion. See *International Herald Tribune*, 4 March 1977, for an account of the meeting.
2. See Victor Zorza in *International Herald Tribune*, 6 March and 25 September 1975. Figures for 1976 were: U.S. exports $2,300 million, imports $221 million. *International Herald Tribune*, 18 March 1977.
3. For a strongly condemnatory article on detente, on this and other arguments, see Robert Conquest, 'A New Russia? A New World?' *Foreign Affairs*, April 1975.
4. *International Herald Tribune* and *Morning Star*, 31 January 1974.
5. The main Solzhenitsyn speech was republished in *Survey*, Summer 1975. The following quote is characteristic (p. 120 *et seq.*):

'World democracy could have defeated one regime after another, the German then the Soviet ... Instead it strengthened Soviet totalitarianism, helped to bring into existence a third totalitarian state, China ... Victorious states always dictate peace ... Instead of this, beginning at Yalta, your Western statesmen have, for some inexplicable reason, signed one capitulation after another ... Looking at this terrible tragedy in Vietnam from a distance, I can tell you a million persons will be simply exterminated while four to five million will find themselves in concentration camps ... China and the Soviet Union, both actively participating in detente, have quietly grabbed three countries in Indo-China ... This is how detente has been managed on our side ... The proposed agreement [Helsinki] is the *funeral of Eastern Europe* ... The communist leaders respect only firmness. Let us try to slow down the process of concessions and help the process of liberation!'

6. The episode was by no means the deliberate snub that it was represented as being. Mr Ford has since said that he regretted the decision, but that the reasons were mostly 'logistic'. The President was originally invited to the AFL–CIO dinner at which the attack on detente was to be made: he declined. At the time various last-minute concessions for the Helsinki meeting were being sought from the Russians. Solzhenitsyn was subsequently invited several times to various meetings at the White House or with Dr Kissinger, but refused. The Russian decision to expel Solzhenitsyn to the West rather than put him into a prison camp or a psychiatric hospital represented some mellowing of Soviet policy, whose application in other cases (it was argued) would be prejudiced if the official leadership in the West were to make unrestrained common cause with such exiles, or endorse their political use.

7. Whether the detente could and would survive Mr Carter's reversal of policy on this matter, and his open endorsement of Russian dissenters like Sakharov and others, was still an unanswerable question at the time of writing. If decision-making in international politics were purely rational, one would say that the Soviet leadership should be able to shrug off such minor pinpricks on human rights issues for the sake of the solid economic and arms-control advantages of the detente relationship with America. But politics and ideology enter these decisions, along with rational calculation, as much for the Russian leadership as for Mr Carter.

8. They did not grow as fast, apparently, after the detente with America as before. According to intelligence sources, the Chinese arms effort reached its high point in 1971, and flattened out into a plateau from that time – i.e. from the time of the first Kissinger visit. There is some logic in this: until the rapprochement with the United States was under way, the old fears of a collusive U.S.–Soviet strike perhaps continued to affect decisions.

9. Senator Jackson continued, of course, to be a powerful figure in the Senate after the advent of the Carter administration, and was prominent in the questioning of Mr Paul Warnke's appointment as President Carter's arms-control negotiator.

10. *The Times*, 11 November 1975.

CHAPTER 12

1. A previously secret National Security Council study made public in March 1977 shows that while the Soviet Union and its allies had roughly the same *number* of warships as the West, the Western *tonnage* was almost four times greater, 8.1 million tons compared to 2.8 million tons. The bulk of the Soviet ships (45%) were small coastal patrol vessels displacing 1,000 tons or less (*International Herald Tribune*, 8 March 1977).

2. One might say that there had been a determined campaign during 1976 to make the opposite case – i.e. the case that the Soviet Union was acquiring such preponderance as to make aggression an attractive or feasible

option – and that this campaign had attracted some surprising academic and journalistic support, as well as less surprising political impetus. It was of course an obvious line of attack for right-wing Republicans in the battle for the nomination, and for right-wing Democrats in the actual presidential contest.

3. The estimate was that of the Chase Manhattan Bank, published in the *International Herald Tribune*, 5–6 March 1977. The largest borrower was the Soviet Union, at $16,200 million, and the largest lenders France ($3,860 million) and West Germany ($3,200 million).

4. The assumption behind what one might call the revised detente strategy of the Carter administration (or perhaps more specifically Dr Brzezinski's theories) appeared to be that this situation of economic dependence on the part of the Soviet bloc on Western goods and credits could prove the basis of a tougher bargaining stance by the West on matters like human rights, Eastern Europe and Angola-style adventures. That is, that the Soviet Union could be successfully required to pay in political and diplomatic concessions for benefits received on the economic side of detente. At the time of writing, it remained uncertain whether this strategy could prove successful.

5. The most recently published statement of these views before Dr Brzezinski's entry into office was an interview in *Detente* (ed. G. K. Urban, London, Temple Smith, 1976). Following are extracts (p. 264 *et seq.*):

'In some ways Kissinger's idea of detente is closer to that of Brezhnev ... the Soviet leaders fear a truly *comprehensive* detente. They see in it a challenge to their legitimacy, and thus to their very existence, and I must say their fears are justified ... if detente is to become more than a transient and fundamentally unstable relationship it will have to be much more comprehensive than it is envisaged to be at present, and that means a possibly gradual but nevertheless fundamental change in Soviet positions at home and abroad ... Nixon and Kissinger prided themselves on being less ideologically motivated and more pragmatic than the Kennedys ... That is not in keeping with fundamental American traditions. It denies American foreign policy an asset which has made that policy so appealing to many people throughout the world ...

It seems to me that certain forms of behavior, none of them strictly economic, are themselves incompatible with better economic relations ...

First: ideological hostility. This contradicts the spirit of detente and is a threat to it.

Second: the secrecy surrounding Soviet strategic planning ...

Third: Indifference to global problems ...

Fourth: the Soviet disregard of human rights.

Fifth: reciprocity of treatment for our diplomats, businessmen, journalists and scholars. These then are some of the areas of strain in American–Soviet relations, and it is here we could use our economic leverage to best advantage ... My hope would be that, over a period of time, the adjustments gained would have a cumulative impact on the nature of the Soviet system.'

6. Though considerable friction crept into the Washington–Bonn relation-

ship in the early weeks of the Carter administration on matters like nuclear exports, human rights and economic policy.
7. Actually, one would say it was rather the case that the German orientation towards detente was the one that 'authenticated' it for Europe, since detente could hardly survive, for instance, a renewed West German drive for reunification. There was, however, no sign of such a development in German politics in 1977. On the contrary, the government of Chancellor Schmidt appeared apprehensive of an American disregard of the necessities of detente.
8. The actual situation of Eastern Europe in early 1977, after more than eight years of detente, appeared to support the view that this had proved a successful strategy. The ability of the Polish people to make their government rescind its decision on food prices, for instance, or the ability of Czech dissidents to maintain their demand for 'Charter 77', suggested a lively ferment of political feeling, rather than a successful process of repression or even the growth of acquiescence.
9. Angola would be the chief case study there, but the peak of that wave of feeling seemed to have passed in 1975–6. Mr Carter appeared ready early in 1977 to defend the need for some degree of ability to keep government secrets, and to want to retain some capacity for covert operations.
10. *International Herald Tribune*, 14 March 1977.
11. *A World Restored* (Universal Library, 1964) p. 6.

Bibliography

Bell, Coral, *Negotiation from Strength: A study in the politics of power* (Chatto & Windus, 1962; Knopf, 1963).
Brandon, Henry, *The Retreat of American Power* (Bodley Head, 1974).
Churchill, Winston, *Speeches*, ed. Randolph Churchill (Cassell, 1961).
Dulles and Crane (eds) *Detente* (Praeger, 1965).
Evrom, Yair, *The Demilitarization of Sinai* (Jerusalem Papers, Hebrew University, 1975).
Görgy, Lazlo, *Bonn's Eastern Policy 1964–71* (University of South Carolina, 1971).
Graubard, Stephen, *Kissinger: Portrait of a Mind* (Norton, 1973).
Heikal, Mohammed, *The Road to Ramadan* (Collins, 1976).
Holbraad, Carsten, *Super-powers and World Order* (Australian National University Press, Canberra, 1971).
Hsiao, Gene T., *Sino-American Detente and its Policy Implications* (Praeger, 1974).
Jordan, Robert, *Europe and the Super-Powers* (Allyn & Bacon, 1972).
Kalb, Marvin and Bernard, *Kissinger* (Little, Brown, 1974).
Kissinger, Henry, *Nuclear Weapons and Foreign Policy* (Harper, 1957).
— *The Necessity for Choice: Prospects of American Foreign Policy* (Harper, 1961).
— *A World Restored: Metternich, Castlereagh, and the Problems of Peace, 1812–1822* (Universal Library, 1964).
— *The Troubled Partnership: A Reappraisal of the Atlantic Alliance* (McGraw-Hill, 1965).
— (ed.) *Problems of National Strategy: A Book of Readings* (Praeger, 1965).
— *American Foreign Policy: Three Essays* (Norton, 1969 and 1974).
Kohler, Gouré and Harvey, *The Soviet Union and the October 1973 Middle East War: The Implications for Detente* (Center for International Studies, University of Miami, 1974).
Kraslow and Loory, *The Secret Search for Peace in Vietnam* (Random House, 1968).
Lake, Anthony, *Tar Baby* (Columbia, 1976).
Landau, David, *Kissinger: The Uses of Power* (Robson, 1974).
Laqueur, Walter, *The Middle East War and World Politics* (Wildwood, 1974).
Lippmann, Walter, *The Cold War* (Hamish Hamilton, 1947).
Morgan, Roger, *The U.S. and West Germany* (O.U.P., 1974).
Newhouse, John, *De Gaulle and the Anglo-Saxons* (Deutsch, 1970).
— *Cold Dawn: The Story of SALT* (Holt, Rinehart & Winston, 1973).
Nolte, Ernst, *Deutschland und der Kalte Krieg* (Piper Verlag, 1974).
Okasaki, Hisakiko, *A Japanese View of Detente* (Lexington Books, 1974).
Osgood, Robert, *The Weary and the Wary: U.S. and Japanese Security Policies in Transition* (S.A.I.S., 1972).

Tilford, Roger (ed.) *The Ostpolitik and Political Change in Germany* (Lexington Books, 1975).
Urban, G. R. (ed.) *Detente* (Temple Smith, 1976).
Westmoreland, William, *A Soldier Reports* (Doubleday, 1976).
Whetten, Lawrence, *Germany's Ostpolitik* (Oxford University Press, 1971).
— *The Canal War: Four Power Conflict in the Middle East* (M.I.T., 1975).

Index

ABM, 57, 68, 237, 258 n.23
Abrams, General, 46
Acheson, Dean, 32, 37, 45, 101, 142, 187
Adenauer, Dr, 8, 15
Adriatic, 228
Aegean, 139
Africa, 13, 161, 170–81, 209, 231, 234; East littoral, 196–7
Afrocommunism, 182, 250
Agnew, Spiro, 48, 148
Akel, 151
Akrotiri, 154
Albania, 216, 228, 234
Alexandria, 81, 83
Algeria, 105
Allende, 242
Amalrik, Andrei, 116–17, 203, 212
Amin, Idi, 172, 173
Angola, 50, 52, 63, 73, 97, 112, 156–7, 169, 170, 172, 173–7, 180, 182, 183, 208–9, 222, 223, 240, 244
Antunes, Ernesto Melo, 160, 168
Anzus Treaty, 99, 187, 191
Arab, 80, 81, 82, 83, 104–5, 106, 231, 236
Armed Forces General Assembly, 160
Armed Forces Movement, 159
ASEAN, 194
Assad, President, 85
Atlantic, 75, 104, 158, 170
Atlantic Alliance, 105
Atlanticist, 100, 106, 107, 108, 119
Attlee, Clement, 72, 191
Australia, 77, 99, 135, 170, 184–99, 211, 243, 248
Austria, 111
Austrian State Treaty, 9
Azevado, Admiral de, 160
Azores, 91, 158, 163, 165, 168

B1, 237
Bakongo tribe, 173
Balkan Alliance, 111, 140
Balkan states, 140, 143, 228
Ball, George, 142
Baltic Fleet, 77
Baltic states, 195–6
Bangladesh, 135
Barents, 77
Barre, Raymond, 65
Bavaria, 25, 178
Bay of Pigs, 46
Begin, Menachem, 248
Belbasi, 152
Belgian Congo, 173
Belgrade, 114, 140
Berbera, 77, 172, 197, 198
Beria, 9
Berlin, 15, 107, 109
Berlinguer, Enrico, 118, 241
Bessarabia, 111
Black Sea, 197
Black Sea Fleet, 77
Black Sea Straits, 140, 153
Bled, Treaty of, 140
Boer War, 185
Bosphorus, 77
Botswana, 179
Brandt, Willi, 15, 67, 91, 92, 106, 118
Brazil, 26
Brezhnev, 4, 9, 10, 58, 59, 60, 66, 67, 81, 83, 87, 88, 109, 113, 116, 165, 181, 204, 205, 209, 234, 239, 246
Brzezinski, Professor Zbigniew, 236, 252 n.15, 266 n.4, n.5
Britain, 56, 74, 77, 78, 91, 92, 100, 103, 105, 111, 136, 139–40, 141, 147, 148, 151, 152, 154, 183, 185, 186, 187, 191, 196, 197, 211, 238, 240, 248

Bukhovsky, 249
Bulgaria, 111
Burke, 23

Cabora Bassaa, 171
Caetano, 159
Cairo, 83
Callaghan, James, 166
Cambodia, 46, 50, 127, 189
Camp David, 10
Camranh Bay, 134
Canada, 71, 77
Cape Verde Islands, 169
Carlucci, Frank, 163-4
Carolingian Europe, 100, 106-7
Carter, J., 36, 40, 51-2, 53, 74, 78-9, 119, 134, 175, 181, 182, 247, 248, 249, 250, 253 n.13, 254 n.25, 255 n.10, 257 n.19, 263 n.12, 265 n.7
Carvalho, Otelo Saraiva de, 160, 161, 163-4, 167
Castlereagh, 25, 33
Castro, Fidel, 180, 209
Central Front, 15, 61, 63-4, 68, 69, 72, 79, 228, 232
Centurion tanks, 91
Chiang Ching 260 n.6
Chicom, 236
Chile, 165, 209, 242
China, 2-3, 11-13, 15-18, 57, 122-4, 129, 132-7, 172, 184, 185-6, 192-3, 202-3, 214-15, 265 n.8
Chirac, M., 65
Chou En-lai, 5, 71, 72, 133, 260 n.6
Churchill, Sir Winston, 7-8, 86, 102, 191
C.I.A., 35, 74, 143, 144, 145, 146-7, 148, 149, 162, 165, 173, 174, 175, 242, 243, 261 n.2, 262 n.9
Cockburn Sound, 198, 263 n.3
Cocom, 114, 136, 236
Cold War, 6, 7, 22, 23, 27, 35, 47, 62, 63, 75, 76, 77, 98, 99, 101, 107, 117, 120, 121, 122, 127, 128, 134, 136, 138, 139, 140, 141, 147, 148, 183, 184, 185, 186, 191, 212, 214, 236, 239, 241, 242, 243, 244-5, 246
Comintern, 204

Congo, 163, 170, 173
Congo-Brazzaville, 172
Congress, 43, 48, 49, 50, 52, 62, 66, 96, 104, 124, 125, 126, 129-30, 151, 152, 153, 174-5, 176, 219, 224
Conolly, John, 260 n.4
Conservative party, 49
Constituent Assembly, 159
Council on Foreign Relations, 44
Coutinho, Rosa, 160
Crete, 153
Cromer, Lord, 91
Cuba, 18, 39, 46, 63, 75, 144, 157, 174, 177, 180-1, 182, 183, 208, 209, 217, 231
Cultural Revolution, 234
Cunhal, Alvaro, 159, 161, 162
Cypriot, 138, 139, 141, 148, 151, 154, 155
Cyprus, 49, 50, 91, 138-55, 172, 216, 239
Czarist Empire, 57
Czechoslovakia, 57, 108, 112, 145, 212, 230

Darwin, 200
Dayan, General, 90
Dean, John, 47
Defcon Three, 87
de Gaulle, 11-12, 13, 65, 99, 100, 101, 102-3, 117
Delta, 74
Democratic party, 45, 48, 49, 50, 51, 52, 174, 180, 182, 216, 217, 219
Democratic Labor party, 188-9
Denmark, 232
d'Estaing, Giscard, 64, 65, 67, 106, 239
Diego Garcia, 198
Disraeli, 23
Djilas, Milovan, 117
Dulles, J. F., 2, 6, 8, 10, 15, 35, 37, 40, 43, 44, 51, 98, 121, 126, 127, 187, 242, 247

Eanes, Ramalho, 157, 160, 167
Ecevit, Mr, 148
Eden, Sir Anthony, 102

Index

E.E.C., 11, 98, 99, 105, 166, 195
Egypt, 77, 81, 83, 84, 141, 234, 239
Eisenhower, President, 8, 41, 46, 126
Energy Conference, 243
Enthoven, Alain, 63
Eoka B., 144, 145
Establishment, 14, 47
Estonia, 195
Eurocommunism, 118, 203, 251, 260 n.19, 264 n.1.
Europe, East, 40, 57, 58, 64, 74, 98, 100, 108, 109, 112, 114–16, 118, 119, 158, 195, 196, 205, 211–12, 215, 222, 234, 240, 246, 249, 250
Europe, southern, 99, 158
Europe, Western, 52, 66, 67, 98, 99, 100–1, 103, 106, 107–8, 112, 114, 116, 118, 119, 229
European Security Conference, 18
Evatt, Dr, 187

Famagusta, 154
Ferriera, Jose Medeiros, 167–8
Finland, 110, 111, 112, 118, 233
First World War, 11, 75, 105, 128, 186
Five Power Pact, 190
FNLA, 173, 174
Ford, President, 39–40, 42, 48, 51, 53, 95, 108, 110, 111, 119, 164, 165, 167, 175, 180, 212, 216, 217, 218, 219, 224
Forty Committee, 165
France, 8, 11–12, 18, 56, 64, 65, 67, 71, 72, 74, 77, 78, 91, 92, 100, 103, 105, 106, 107, 111, 119, 121, 127, 185, 189, 197, 203, 205, 208, 228, 239
Franco, General, 32
Fraser, Malcolm, 195–6, 198–9
Fretilin, 200
Frost interviews, 254 n.6, 258 n.8.

Galbraith, Professor G. K., 59
'Galosh' ABM, 57
Geneva, 9, 96
Germany (East, West) 8, 11, 15, 25, 55, 64, 78, 91, 100, 103, 105, 107, 108, 109, 113, 128, 162, 183, 189, 233, 238, 246

German–Polish treaty, 107
German–Soviet treaty, 107, 109
Goldwater, Barry, 217
Gomes, General Costa, 160, 164, 167
Gonçalves, General Vasco, 160, 167
Gorshkov, Admiral, 233
Grand Alliance, 100
Greece, 32, 49, 100, 111, 138–55, 238
Grivas, General, 143, 144–5
Guantanamo base, 180
Guatemala, 46
Guinea-Bissau, 169, 170
The Gulag Archipelago, 215

Haig, General A., 256 n.7, 257 n.23.
Hanoi, 13, 124
Harris, Fred, 180
Heath, E., 66, 67, 91, 92, 102, 106
Heikal, Mohammed, 71
Helsinki, 15, 52, 65, 107–18, 165–6, 167, 182, 234, 240, 241, 263 n.1.
Hilsman, Roger, 122
Hitler, 25, 56, 204
Ho Chi Minh, 126, 127
Hoffman, Stanley, 35
Hong Kong, 133
Horn of Africa, 240
House of Representatives, U.S., 175
Hua, Kuo-feng, 133
Hull, Cordell, 11
Hungary, 58, 108, 249

Iberian peninsula, 183; dictatorships, 230–1
ICBM, 61
Iceland, 77
I.M.F., 179
India, 71, 72, 77, 131, 187, 190, 191, 194, 197, 199, 248
Indian Ocean, 18, 189, 191, 193, 196–197, 198, 199
Indonesia, 135, 170, 185, 187, 190, 192, 193–4, 196, 197, 199, 200, 202, 248
Ioannides, Brigadier, 143, 145–6, 147, 149
Iran, 26, 78, 179, 197, 246, 248
Iraq, 10, 141

Islam, 50
Israel, 30, 49–50, 71, 72, 78, 80, 81, 82, 104, 111, 158, 192, 197, 248
Isvestiya, 113
Italy, 28, 100, 111, 153, 165, 166, 203, 208, 223, 227, 228, 229, 239, 240, 241
Ivory Coast, 171

Jackson, Senator, 23, 29, 51, 73, 89, 176, 203, 206, 207, 215–18, 219, 223, 252 n.9, 265 n.9.
Japan, 17, 29, 52, 72, 77, 105, 130–1, 132, 135, 185, 186–7, 190, 194, 195, 196, 197, 199, 200, 209, 231, 232, 234, 240, 242, 248
Jerusalem, 95
Jobert, M., 90, 92, 103, 105, 106
Johnson, President L. B., 19, 41, 45, 121–2, 127, 188, 224
Jordan, 10, 141

Kant, 24
Karamanlis, Mr, 147, 151
Karamursel, 152
Kaunda, Dr, 179
Kazakhstan, 215
Kennedy, Edward, 198
Kennedy, President John F., 18, 35, 45, 46, 62, 101, 120, 122, 127, 224, 248
Kenya, 197
Kerensky, 34, 164
K.G.B., 244
Khrushchev, Nikita, 8, 10, 40, 59, 60, 140, 208, 213, 233, 234
Kiev, 76
Killen, J., 199
Kissinger, Dr Henry, *passim*: and Africa policy, 170 *et seq.*; and Angola, 175 *et seq.*; and Cambodia, 45–6; and Cold War, 22 *et seq.*; and Egypt, 82 *et seq.*; and Helsinki conference, 107 *et seq.*; and Metternich, 33; and Portugal, 163 *et seq.*; and Presidents Carter, 51 *et seq.*, 247 *et seq.*, Ford, 39 *et seq.*, Johnson, 45, Kennedy, 45, Nixon, 40 *et seq.*; and Reagan, 217 *et seq.*; and SALT, 59, 218; and Sinai, 94–6; 259 n.10; and Solzhenitsyn, 33, 212–14; and Vorster, 178–9; and Vietnam, 120 *et seq.*; and 'Year of Europe', 105–6, 119
Knowland, Senator William, 217
Koestler, A., 212
Kola Peninsula, 77
Korea, 53, 58, 120, 135, 187, 188, 189, 191, 243, 248, 250, 261 n.11
Kosygin, 13
Kremlin, 7, 13, 81, 233
Kuomingtang, 17

Laird, Melvin, 48, 203, 215
Lajes, 91, 158
Laos, 127
Latin America, 203, 209, 217, 231, 242, 248
Latvia, 195
Lebanon, 10, 75, 95, 96, 141, 259 n.12
Lee Kuan Yew, 131–2, 202
Lenin, 9, 10, 21, 34, 212, 213, 224
Liberal–Country party, 188, 198
Liberia, 171
Libya, 71, 77, 81, 105
Li Hsien-nien, 261 n.9
Linkage, 30, 253 n.13
Lin Piao, 26, 220
Lippmann, Walter, 23, 47, 252 n.5
Lithuania, 195
Lockheed, 35
London, 78, 113, 118, 198
Lorenço Marques, *see* Maputo
Luanda, 174
Luce, Clare, 203

Maçao, 169–70
McCarthy, J., 47, 48, 129
Machel, Samora, 171, 183
McMahon, William, 188
MacMillan, H., 102, 189
McNamara, Mr, 55, 62, 63
Macomber, William, 148
Mahan, 233
Makarios, Archbishop, 142–9, 151, 152, 154

Malawi, 171
Malaysia, 187, 193, 199
Malenkov, 8, 9, 109, 234
Manifesto of the Nine, 160, 168
Mansfield, Senator M., 66, 69, 232, 254 n.12
Mao Tse-tung, 5, 17, 57, 132, 133, 134, 136, 161, 202, 212, 220, 226
Maputo, 171
Marjolin report, 104
Maurras, 12
MBFR, 58, 109, 239, 255 n.2
Mbundu tribe, 173
Meany, George, 206
Mediterranean, 18, 77, 140, 141, 145, 150, 151, 153, 155, 226, 228, 239
M.E.D.O., 261 n.1
Medvedev brothers, 212; Roy, 214
Menzies, Sir Robert, 185, 187
Méry, General Gui, 64-5
Metternich, 24, 33, 139, 228
Middle East, 10, 13, 28, 39, 50, 52, 67, 68, 80-97, 103-4, 106, 141, 143, 148, 158, 179, 182, 195, 197, 207, 209, 217, 223, 230, 231, 234, 244, 245
Mig, 172
Minuteman Mark 12A, 249
Mobutu, President, 173
Molotov, 110
Mongols, 57
Monroe Doctrine, 242
Morocco, 81
Morphou, 154
Moscow, 1, 3, 11, 16, 26, 41, 61, 83, 86, 109, 117, 140, 145, 176
Mount Olympus, 150
Mozambique, 156, 169, 170, 171, 172, 178, 179, 181, 183
MPLA, 173, 174, 176
Mujib, 135
Munich, 107
Muscovy, 110
M-x, 249

Nakhodka, 77
Namibia, 156, 177, 179, 181, 182
Napoleon, 25

Nasser, President, 82
National Front for the Liberation of Angola, *see* FNLA
National Union for the Total Independence of Angola, *see* UNITA
National Security Council, 45, 46, 170, 172
Nato, 12, 13, 18, 61-70, 72, 73, 74, 77, 79, 90, 91, 92, 98, 99, 103, 105, 106, 110, 114, 119, 140, 142, 143, 144, 145, 147, 148, 150, 151, 152, 153, 154, 158, 164, 165, 168, 209, 215, 216, 223, 229, 230, 232, 238-9, 240, 241, 247-8, 249
Nazi-Soviet Pact, 212, 215
Netherlands, 91, 232
New Zealand, 99, 187, 196, 248
New York, 25
New York Times, 113
Ngo Dinh Diem, 121
Nicosia, 142
Nigeria, 26
Nixon, President, 39, 40-1, 43-9, 51, 81, 101, 106, 123, 124, 125-6, 145, 146, 148, 170, 188, 217, 223, 224, 225

Nobel Peace Prize, 117
North Dakota, 61
North-South confrontation, 27
North-West Cape, 193
Northern Fleet, 77
Northern Front, 73
Northern Ireland, 248
Northern Islands, 29
Norway, 77
Nuclear Planning Group, 158, 164

O.A.U., 171, 174
Oceanic Alliance, 105
October War, 92
Opec, 195, 207, 243
Opposition to detente, 246-7
Oresund, 77
Ostpolitik, 15, 107
Ottoman Empire, 139
Ovimbundu tribe, 173

Pacific, 186, 189, 191, 196, 199

Pakistan, 18, 197
Palestine, 94, 95, 248
Palme, Olof, 181
Panama, 23, 231; Treaty, 217
Papadopoulos, Colonel, 144, 145
Papandreou, Mr, 144
Pappas, Thomas, 148
Papua–New Guinea, 190, 200
Paris, 11, 105, 107
Paris agreements, 125–6
Peking, 1, 3, 11, 26, 67, 122, 176, 188, 191, 227
Pentagon, 30, 60, 88, 147, 148, 218, 219, 247
Persian Gulf, 150, 197
Perth, 198
Petropavlovsk–Kamchatka, 77
Philippines, 135, 196, 248
Phuoc Binh, 125
Pirinclip, 152
P.L.O., 96
Poland, 57, 110–11, 113
Polaris submarine, 193
Politburo, 75, 109, 205
Pompidou, M., 67, 103, 106
Popular Front for the Liberation of Angola, *see* MPLA
Portugal, 28, 90, 156–70, 172, 173, 177, 181–2, 199, 200, 204, 223, 227, 228, 231, 238, 244
Poseidon, 74
Powell, Enoch, 102
Pravda, 113, 205
Pretoria, 179
Princeton, 45
Principe, 169
Puerto Rico, 118

Quai d'Orsay, 105
Quemoy–Matsu crisis, 10

Radio Free Europe, 114, 249
Radio Liberty, 114, 249
Radio Renascenca, 162
Rambouillet, 118
Reagan, Ronald, 23, 51, 115, 176, 203, 216, 217–18, 223, 242
Red Star, 205

Republica, 162
Republican party, 38, 40, 48, 49, 50, 51, 174, 180, 182, 216, 217–18, 219, 223, 229
Rhine, 64, 100
Rhodesia, 30, 156, 177–8, 179, 181, 182, 183, 231
Roberto, Holden, 173
Rockefeller, Nelson, 40, 41, 48
Rogers, Mr, 41, 163
Romania, 110, 111, 112
Roosevelt, F. D., 11, 44, 48, 86, 204
Russo-Jananese War, 75

Sadat, President, 81, 82–3, 84, 85, 89, 90, 91, 94, 95
Safire, William, 43
Sakharov, Andrei, 117, 212, 213, 249
Salazar, Dr, 159
Salisbury, Lord, 60
SALT, 16, 29, 42, 55, 56, 57, 59, 61, 68, 73, 90, 153, 165, 181, 207, 217, 218, 239, 247, 249, 255 n.2.
Sampson, Nicos, 142, 145, 146
Sao Tome, 169
Saudi Arabia, 248
Scandinavia, 117
Schlesinger, Dr, 40, 63, 68, 73, 134, 216, 218–19, 225, 256 n.13
Schmidt, Chancellor, 67, 106, 166, 240
Scott, Stuart, 163
Seato, 121, 130, 187, 190, 191, 192
Second World War, 11, 15, 24, 57, 73, 75, 86, 113, 200, 211, 212
Security Council, 91
Senate, U.S., 126, 175, 180; Africa Subcommittee, 180
Sharon, General, 86, 90
Shelepin, M., 205
Siberia, 10
Sinai, 81, 94, 95, 96, 259 n.10
Singapore, 199, 202
Sinop, 152
Sino-Soviet Alliance, 208
Sixth Fleet, 147, 153
Smith, Ian, 177–8, 262 n.12
Soares, Mario, 157, 161, 164, 166, 167

Solzhenitsyn, 33, 34, 156, 203, 212–214, 217, 218, 223, 249, 264 n.5, n.6
Somalia, 172
Sonnenfeldt, Helmut, 109, 115, 242, 260 n.8
South Africa, 1, 28, 30, 156, 174, 177–9, 182, 183, 190, 231, 248
Southern Africa, 52, 244, 245, 246
Soviet Union, 7–15, 16–18, 21–2, 43, 52, 57–9, 75–7, 80–7, 89–90, 94–5, 150–5, 162, 165–6, 172–5, 204–7, 212–15, 233–6
Soweto, 179
Soya Straits, 77
Spain, 32, 90–1, 158, 162, 166, 203, 223, 231, 238
Spinola, General, 159, 163, 168
Sri Lanka, 112, 197
Stalin, 6, 8, 9, 86, 202, 213, 234
State Department, 38, 47, 48, 145, 148, 163, 170–1, 198
Sudan, 185
Suez, 83, 92, 94, 96, 97, 141, 148, 197
Suharto, President, 194
Supreme Revolutionary Council, 160
Suslov, Mikhail, 204, 205
Svalbad, 77
Sweden, 181, 191
Syria, 77, 85, 88, 89, 91, 95, 96, 97, 105

Taiwan, 133–4, 135, 189, 191, 231
Talleyrand, 158
Tanzam railway, 172
Tanzania, 172, 179
Tapei, 188
Tasca, Henry, 145
Teng, Mr, 133
Thailand, 121
Thatcher, Margaret, 118, 182
Thieu, Nguyen, Van, 124–5
Third World, 12, 27, 71, 106, 158, 161, 168, 176, 190, 193, 195, 198, 202, 203, 230, 234, 243, 247
Thousand Year Reich, 56
Tibet, 215
Timofeyev, Mr, 205
Timor, East, 155, 169, 170, 200

Tito, President, 111, 118, 226, 241, 246
Tonga, 196
Triad, 74
Trident, 74, 237
Truman, President H., 45, 121, 127, 187
Tsugara Straits, 77
Tsushima Straits, 77
Turkey, 49, 50, 77, 138–55, 238–9, 246

Uganda, 172
UNITA, 173, 174
United Nations, 92, 152, 178, 179, 190, 195
United States–Japan Security Treaty, 99
Urals, 12–13

Vance, Cyrus, 142, 249
Van Tien Dung, 124–5
Vienna, 58, 69
Vietnam, 8, 13, 19, 35, 41, 44, 45, 46, 48, 50, 66, 69, 77, 83, 101, 113, 120–31, 161, 174, 175, 187–8, 189, 190, 191, 196, 224, 231, 232, 233, 243, 244, 245
Vladivostok, 50, 61, 73, 77, 165
Vorster, Mr, 171, 177–9

Wallace, George, 2, 203
Walters, General Vernon, 165
Warsaw Pact, 61, 64–8, 70, 98, 108, 111, 114 117, 118, 239, 241
Washington, 1, 3, 11, 16, 26, 36, 39, 46, 47, 70, 92, 94, 97, 104, 107, 113, 122, 136, 145, 146, 147, 148, 149, 156, 172, 174, 175, 176, 198, 246, 248
Watergate, 35, 42, 44, 46, 47, 48, 49, 72, 89, 106, 125, 126, 172, 244
Westmoreland, General, 46
White Australia Policy, 186
Whitlam, E. G., 184, 188, 189–91, 192, 193, 194, 195, 196–7, 198, 199–200
Wilson, Harold, 67–8, 102, 106, 112, 113

Wilson, Woodrow, 247
World Court, 189

Xuan Loc, 125

'Year of Europe', 105–6, 119
Young, Andrew, 182–3, 263 n.16
Yugoslavia, 58, 110, 111, 112, 116, 117, 140, 174, 216, 225, 226 228, 229, 236, 241, 246

Zambia, 172, 178, 179
Zaiire, 173
Zaradov, 205
Zumwalt, Admiral, 88, 89, 176
Zurich, 178

**WITHDRAWN
UTSA Libraries**